VISUAL FACTFINDER

OCEANS

First published by Bardfield Press in 2005
Copyright © Miles Kelly Publishing 2005

Bardfield Press is an imprint of
Miles Kelly Publishing Ltd,
Bardfield Centre, Great Bardfield, Essex, CM7 4SL

Some of this material also appears in *1000 Facts on Oceans*

2 4 6 8 10 9 7 5 3

Editorial Director: Belinda Gallagher

Art Director: Jo Brewer

Copy Editor: Stuart Cooper

Editorial Assistants: Amanda Askew, Bethanie Bourne

Picture Researcher: Liberty Newton

Production Manager: Elizabeth Brunwin

Designed and packaged by Q2A Creative

British Library Cataloguing-in-Publication Data
A catalogue record for this book is available from the British Library

ISBN 1-84236-539-8

Printed in China

www.mileskelly.net   info@mileskelly.net

VISUAL FACTFINDER

OCEANS

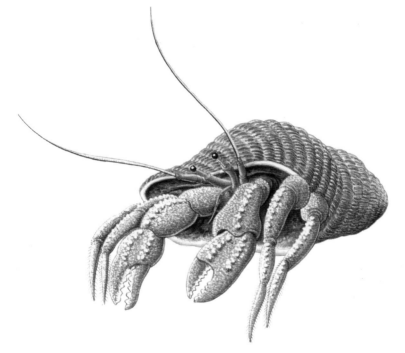

Consultant: Clint Twist

BARDFIELD
PRESS

Contents

6

OCEANS

Why do the tides rise and fall twice a day?

What is the name of the deepest ocean trench?

Which sea creature has the biggest eyes in the animal kingdom?

The answers to these and many other questions can be found in this amazing book of almost 2500 facts. Beginning with the origin of the oceans, a detailed guide to marine life is also included as well as the history of ships, sea battles and sea-faring peoples. This book also provides a quick and easy way to learn about ocean resources, famous explorers and how the oceans are threatened by pollution and overfishing.

A planet is born

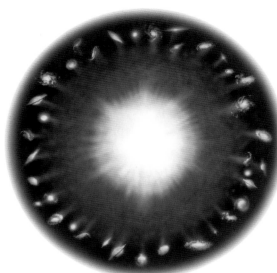

◀ The Big Bang threw cosmic matter in all directions. This theory explains why galaxies are travelling away from each other at great speeds.

- **It is believed** that about 15 billion years ago a huge explosion, called the Big Bang, led to the formation of the Universe.

- **The first galaxies**, including our own Milky Way, started to evolve about a billion years after the Big Bang. Clouds of dust and gases came together to form stars.

- **Until about 5 billion years ago**, the Solar System was a huge cloud of dust and gases drifting through the Milky Way and containing rocky and icy particles.

- **The cloud** became a swirling hot disc called a solar nebula. The gases and dust began to squeeze together until the centre became hotter and hotter and eventually exploded, creating the Sun.

- **The icy particles** near the Sun melted, but the dust particles around it started to clump together to form small rock nuggets. Over millions of years, these nuggets grew into huge boulders called planetesimals.

- **These planetesimals** began to collide into each other. They soon built up into the four rocky inner planets – Mercury, Venus, Earth and Mars.

- **Far away** from the Sun's heat, icy particles and leftover gases combined to form outer planets – Jupiter, Saturn, Uranus and Neptune. Pluto, the outermost planet, is not a gas giant, and its innermost structure is unknown.

- **Unlike the inner planets**, the atmosphere of the outer planets contains huge amounts of gases such as hydrogen, helium, ammonia, methane and carbon monoxide.

- **These outer planets** are collectively called the gas giants because they are primarily made up of gas, unlike the inner planets that are composed of rock. These planets are also bigger and colder.

- **It is widely believed** that Jupiter, the largest planet, caused the destruction of the planetesimals around it. Due to Jupiter's strong gravitational pull, these planetesimals crashed into one another, leaving behind a belt of rock fragments called asteroids.

... FASCINATING FACT ...
According to a theory, nearly 4.5 billion years ago an object as big as Mars collided with the Earth. It scattered a lot of debris in space. The debris gathered to form the Moon.

15

The blue planet

- **The Earth** is the only planet in the Solar System with enough oxygen and water to support life. However, it was not always so. At first the Earth had no oxygen or atmosphere. Only traces of hydrogen and helium were present.

- **When it first formed**, Earth was continuously being hit by rocks and other materials from space. These collisions generated immense heat, causing rocks to melt.

- **At the same time**, radioactive elements on the Earth also released a lot of heat, causing heavier elements such as iron and nickel to sink deep into the centre of the Earth to form its core. Lighter elements such as silicon floated to the surface.

- **The layer** surrounding the core is called the mantle, which is in a partially molten state. The mantle comprises the bulk of the Earth's weight and volume.

- **About 4 billion years ago** the Earth's surface cooled and solidified to form the topmost layer, called the crust. The crust was broken into several rock fragments, called tectonic plates, that floated on the mantle.

- **These plates** moved past each other, often colliding and causing friction. This collision built up pressure beneath the crust, leading to volcanic eruptions that caused cracks on the Earth's surface.

. . . FASCINATING FACT . . .
Acids in the rainwater corroded the rocks on the Earth's surface. Chemicals in these rocks were carried into the oceans. Among these chemicals were certain salts that made the ocean water salty.

- **Gases**, such as hydrogen and nitrogen, and water vapour burst through the cracks in the crust. These constant eruptions slowly led to the formation of the atmosphere.

- **Water vapour** condensed to form clouds that enveloped the Earth and eventually brought rain. However, the Earth's surface was so hot that the rainwater evaporated immediately.

- **As the rains** continued the Earth started to cool and the volcanic activity decreased. Water poured down for thousands of years to fill up huge pits and form oceans.

- **The rain** also formed smaller bodies of water such as rivers and lakes. At high altitudes, the water froze and fell as snow. The snow melted and flowed down mountains as streams and rivers.

▶ *Volcanoes continuously erupted, covering the surface of the primeval Earth with oceans of lava, making it unfit for life.*

17

Ocean floor

- **The Earth's surface** is covered by the oceans and seven huge land masses, called continents. Oceans cover about 71 percent of our planet's surface.

- **At certain places** the land rises above the water to form continents and islands. The surface under the oceans is called the ocean floor.

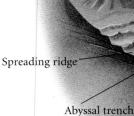

Continental slope

- **The ocean floor** is broadly divided into the continental shelf, the continental slope and deep ocean floor.

- **The continental shelf** is an underwater extension of the coast. The rim of islands and continents gently slopes into the surrounding water to form the continental shelf.

- **The average width** of the continental shelf is about 65 km but some, such as the Siberian Shelf in the Arctic Ocean, can extend up to 1500 km.

- **The continental shelf** is commercially very important. It contains large deposits of petroleum, natural gas and minerals. This area also receives the most sunlight and marine life thrives here.

Spreading ridge

- **The continental slope** is the point where the shelf starts to plunge steeply towards the ocean floor. Here the ocean floor is marked by deep canyons.

Abyssal trench

- **Below continental slopes** sediments often collect to form gentle slopes called continental rise. The continental shelf, slope and rise are together known as continental margin.

- **In many places** the ocean floor forms vast expanses that are flat and covered with sediment. These regions are called the abyssal plains.

- **The abyssal plain** is broken by mid-ocean ridges, such as the Mid-Atlantic and the East Pacific rise, and trenches such as the Mariana Trench in the Pacific Ocean.

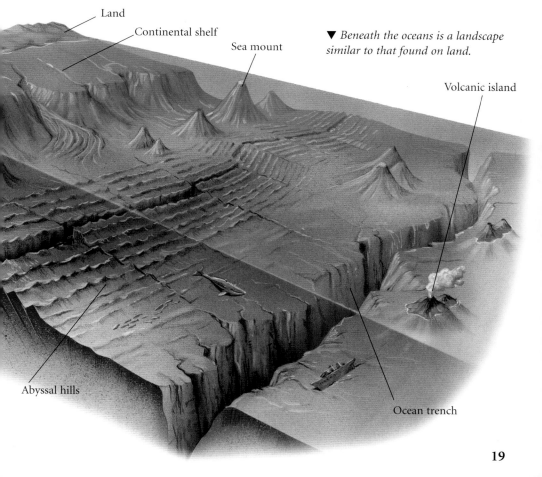

Land

Continental shelf

Sea mount

▼ *Beneath the oceans is a landscape similar to that found on land.*

Volcanic island

Abyssal hills

Ocean trench

19

Trenches and ridges

- **The ocean floor**, like land, has high mountains, deep valleys, canyons and vast plains.

- **The most dramatic** of the ocean floor structures are the trenches, or deep valleys, and ridges, or mountain chains.

- **The Earth's crust** is made up of several huge, flat rock segments called tectonic plates. These plates slide and move against each other.

- **The movement** of these plates is responsible for the formation of ridges and trenches.

- **Ridges are formed** when two plates drift apart. Hot lava oozes out through the cracks and cools to form a ridge. A trench is formed when the heavier plate plunges beneath the lighter one.

- **Mariana Trench** is one of the deepest trenches. It is located in the Pacific Ocean, to the east of the Philippines.

- **The Challenger Deep**, in the Mariana Trench, is the deepest point in the Earth. At 11,033 m its depth is more than the height of Mount Everest.

- **The mid-ocean ridge** is the longest mountain chain on Earth. It is over 50,000 km long. The crests of these mountains lie nearly 2500 m below the ocean surface.

- **At some places** the mid-ocean ridge is exposed above the sea level. Iceland is located on top of one such crest of the mid-Atlantic ocean ridge.

- **Seamounts are** underwater volcanoes. A flat-topped seamount is known as a guyot, while those with peaks are known as seapeaks.

▲ *On January 23, 1960, US Navy Leiutenant Don Walsh and Jacques Piccard, a Swiss scientist, set a record by descending to the bottom of the Challenger Deep, in the US Navy submersible,* Trieste.

Causing waves

- **Oceans** are never completely at rest. They are rocked by several kinds of movements, such as waves, currents and tides.

- **Most movements** in the oceans, such as waves and surface currents, are caused by wind. Waves are created by winds blowing over the surface of the oceans. The stronger the wind, the larger the waves.

- **The water in a wave moves** in circles and not forward as it may appear. As a wave nears land it slows down because of the shallower seabed. The top part of the wave carries on and crashes on the shore as a breaker.

- **The shape and size** of waves differ. A steep, choppy wave is one that has just been formed near the coast, while the slow, steady ones are those that originated far out in the ocean.

- **The regular rise and fall** of the oceans are called tides. They are caused by the gravitational pull of the Sun and the Moon. Since the Moon is closer to the Earth, its effect is felt more.

- **The period** of high water level is known as high tide and the period of low water level is known as low tide.

- **An ocean current** is a mass of water moving continuously in one direction. Surface currents are caused by winds and rotation of the Earth, while differences in temperature and salt content are responsible for underwater currents.

- **Most ocean currents** flow in large loops called gyres, which spin clockwise in the Northern Hemisphere and anti-clockwise in the Southern Hemisphere. This is due to the Earth's rotation and is called the Coriolis Effect.

- **When the Sun, Moon and Earth** are in a straight line their combined gravities cause unusually high tides, called spring tides. This alignment of the three happens during full Moon and new Moon. Smaller tides, called neap tides, occur at other times when the Moon is at a right angle to the Sun and the Earth.

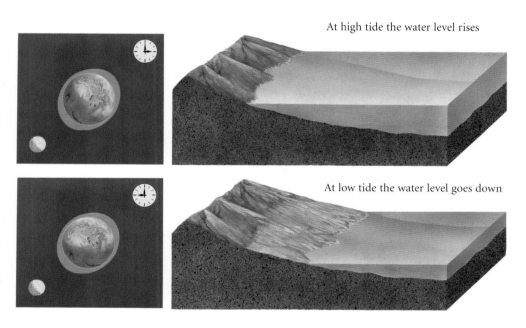

At high tide the water level rises

At low tide the water level goes down

▲ *High tide happens on those parts of the Earth that are closest to and farthest away from the Moon. As the Earth turns, approximately six hours later, the water subsides. This is called the low tide.*

Coastlines

- **A coast** is a continuous stretch of land that borders an ocean. It is made up of sand, mud and gravel. The outline of the coast is called a coastline.

- **The features** of a coast depend on the wind, rocks and currents in that area. Strong winds whip up equally strong waves that pound the rocks on the coastlines and erode them.

- **Hard rocks** are able to withstand the pounding of waves and erode slowly, forming headlands.

- **Wave power** is also responsible for the formation of structures such as cliffs, headlands, sea caves, sea arches, sea stacks and beach heads.

- **A cliff** is formed by the constant pounding of waves on weak spots on the rock face. At first, a tiny gap is created. This gap enlarges as the rock continues to erode, eventually causing its roof to collapse.

- **When softer rocks** at the base of a cliff erode first, they collapse on to the shore. They break into minute fragments, eventually forming wide beaches between the existing cliff and the ocean. This saves the cliff from further erosion.

- **Continuous erosion** leads to the creation of hollows, called sea caves, in the headlands. Sometimes waves pound the headland from either side, causing caves to form on both sides of the headland.

> ...FASCINATING FACT...
> Long Beach is the world's longest beach. It is located along the southwest coast of Washington, the capital of the United States. This beach stretches for a record 45 km.

- **When two back-to-back caves** meet, a sea arch is formed. The top portion of the arch links the headland to the mainland like a bridge.

- **After years of erosion**, the sea arches cave in. This leaves only a column of rock standing independently in the sea. This is known as a sea stack.

- **The best-known** natural structure formed by the action of waves is the beach. Waves lose much of their power in shallow waters and instead of eroding they start depositing sand and shingle, carried into the oceans by rivers, on the coast. These deposits eventually become the beach.

▼ *Waves can create amazing shapes such as pillars called sea stacks.*

Sea stack

Arch

Sea caves

- **Sea caves** are formed when the force of the waves wears away rocks situated at the base of cliffs.

- **These rocks** are usually weak due to a fault or fracture in them. Even vein-like cracks are enough to cause rocks to crumble under continuous pounding by huge waves.

- **Waves penetrate** cracks in a rock and exert high pressure, forcing the rocks to crumble from within, forming small hollows.

- **These hollows** expand further when sand, gravel and rocks brought by the waves start eroding the inner walls of the rocks.

- **Some sea caves** are submerged in water during high tide, and can be seen only when the water recedes.

- **Sea caves** are a great attraction for adventurers and tourists. They can be explored in small boats or on foot when the water level is low.

- **Sea caves** are common on the Pacific coasts of the United States and in the Greek islands. The Blue Grotto of Capri in Italy is famous for the bluish glow of its waters. This glow is caused by sunlight pouring through an underwater hole. The light shines on the water to create a brilliant blue glow.

- **One of the largest known sea caves** is the Painted Cave on Santa Cruz Island off California. It is nearly 375 m long. The cave gets its name from the colourful patterns on the rocks.

- **Sea caves are full of** marine life. Sea anemones, sponges and starfish are found in the bigger caves.

▲ *Sea caves on the island of Cyprus. Caves can be of various sizes. Some may extend hundreds of metres into the rock and have more than one tunnel.*

Oceans of the world

- **Oceans cover** almost 362 million sq km of the Earth's surface. Although there is only one ocean that covers the world, it has been divided into four major ocean basins. A fifth ocean, the Antarctic Ocean, also called the Southern Ocean, was recently added to this list.

- **The four basins** are the Pacific, Atlantic, Indian and Arctic oceans. The Arctic Ocean surrounds the North Pole and is largely frozen.

- **The Antarctic Ocean** is actually formed by the southern extensions of the Pacific, Atlantic and Indian oceans. Hence this ocean was, for a long time, not considered as a separate entity.

- **The international dispute** regarding the status of the Antarctic Ocean continued until the year 2000. The International Hydrographic Organization has since recognized the waters surrounding Antarctica as the fifth ocean and named it the Southern Ocean.

- **The Pacific Ocean** is the largest of all oceans. At 166 million sq km, it is twice the size of the Atlantic Ocean. The Pacific Ocean's average depth is more than 4000 m, making it the world's deepest ocean.

- **This ocean** gets its name from the Spanish word *pacifico*, which means peaceful. During his voyage around the world, Portuguese explorer Ferdinand Magellan found the Pacific to be calm and hence gave the ocean its name.

- **The Atlantic Ocean**, at 82 million sq km, is the second largest ocean. It is also the stormiest. The most interesting feature of this ocean is the mid-ocean ridge that runs through its entire length.

- **This ocean** contains some of the most important seas and other features. These include the Baltic Sea, Black Sea, Caribbean Sea, Mediterranean Sea, Gulf of Mexico, Labrador Sea, Denmark Strait and Norwegian Sea.

- **The Indian Ocean** has a total area of over 73 million sq km. It is bounded by the three continents of Asia, Africa and Oceania. Some of the earliest known civilizations, such as the Mesopotamian, Egyptian and Indus Valley civilizations, developed near this ocean.

- **The Arctic Ocean**, at 14 million sq km, is the smallest among the world's oceans. It is also the shallowest. The deepest point in the Arctic Ocean is only 5450 m – not even half as deep as the deepest point of the Pacific Ocean.

▼ *The Pacific Ocean is deep enough to engulf the whole of Mount Everest without trace.*

Volcanic oceans

- **Almost 90 percent** of the world's volcanic activity takes place under the ocean. Most undersea volcanoes are along the mid-ocean ridge.

- **The Pacific Ocean** contains more than 80 percent of the world's active volcanoes. These volcanoes encircle the ocean along the continent margins to form the 'Ring of Fire'.

- **Volcanoes** are formed when two tectonic plates drift apart and hot molten rock called magma oozes out. They are also formed if one plate crashes into another.

- **When the lava** oozing out of an underwater volcano comes into contact with water, it solidifies quickly. This lava often forms round lumps called pillow lava. Several tiny marine organisms thrive on these lumps of lava.

- **Underwater volcanic mountains** are known as seamounts. Some seamounts, called guyots, are extinct volcanoes with flat tops. Some guyots could also have been volcanic islands that were eroded with time.

- **Hot springs,** or hydrothermal vents, are also found on the sea floor along the mid-ocean ridge. They are formed when water seeps into the crust as two plates pull apart. This water is heated by the magma and shoots up through cracks in the ocean floor.

- **The temperature** of water in and around a vent can go up to 400°C. This water is rich in minerals and the gas hydrogen sulphide.

...FASCINATING FACT...
Mauna Kea and Mauna Loa in Hawaii are the tallest volcanic mountains on Earth. Measured from its base on the ocean floor, Mauna Kea at 9800 m is taller than even Mount Everest.

▲ *Hydrothermal vents are home to rat tail fish and sea spiders as well as giant tube worms.*

● **The scalding water** mixes with the surrounding cold water to create chimney-like jets of warm water. These jets are often black because of the mineral content in the water. Hence hydrothermal vents are also called black smokers.

● **Hydrothermal vents** were first discovered in 1977 near the Galapagos Islands along the eastern Pacific Ocean basin. Scientists travelling in the submersible *ALVIN* observed these vents about 2500 m below the ocean's surface.

● **The water** at the deep-ocean floor is too cold for creatures to survive, but hydrothermal vents are like underwater oases. Long tubeworms and other life forms that are not found anywhere else in the world thrive near these vents.

Volcanic islands

- **Undersea volcanoes** often lead to the formation of volcanic islands. Some of these islands are formed around one or two volcanic vents, while others can be made up of a series of vents.

- **Volcanic activity** usually occurs at the point where two tectonic plates meet or break away. Sometimes, volcanoes are formed away from the plate boundaries near areas called hot spots, which are fixed points of volcanic activity located beneath the tectonic plates.

- **Molten magma** from deep within the mantle forces its way through fissures in the plate and flow out to form seamounts.

- **Over millions of years** magma keeps oozing out of these seamounts, which gradually rise above the ocean surface as islands. These islands are called oceanic high islands.

- **The constant movement** of tectonic plates eventually carries an island away from the hot spot and volcanic activity ceases in that island. Meanwhile, another island is created near the hot spot. This continues until a chain of islands, such as the Hawaiian Islands, is created.

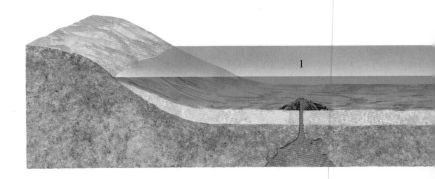

- **The hot spot** in the Pacific Ocean is currently under the Big Island, which is the largest among the Hawaiian Islands.

- **The Big Island** has five volcanoes. They are Kilauea, Mauna Loa, Mauna Kea, Hualalai and Kohala. Kilauea is the most active volcano in the region.

- **Iceland was formed** by volcano activity near the ocean ridge. It is the only part of the mid-oceanic ridge that emerges from the surface.

- **Some volcanic islands** are formed in the shape of arcs, such as Marianas and the Aleutian Islands in the Pacific Ocean.

- **Island arcs** form when one plate slides below the other. The magma oozes out, forming volcanoes on the edge of the plate above. These volcanoes eventually emerge from the ocean surface as islands in the shape of an arc.

▼ *When volcanoes erupt under the sea, new islands may appear.*
(1) Molten rock breaks through Earth's crust . (2) As more lava is deposited on the seabed, a cone shape builds up. (3) When this breaks the water's surface, a new island appears. The volcano may go on erupting.

Amazing corals

▲ *Coral reefs, which support a wide variety of marine life, are the largest ecosystems on our planet.*

- **An atoll** is a low-lying coral island consisting of a coral reef surrounding a lagoon. There are several stages in the formation of an atoll and it could take millions of years for the island to emerge.

- **The first stage** of atoll formation includes the creation of a coral reef around a volcanic island. Strong winds and waves slowly erode the island and it begins to sink. But the reef continues to grow upwards to form a barrier reef separated from the sinking island by a lagoon. At this stage these islands are called barrier reef islands.

- **The barrier reef islands** continue to sink until the land is completely submerged. However, the reef around the island continues to grow upwards to form a ring surrounding a lagoon. This is called a coral atoll.

- **Coral atolls** are formed mostly in warm and shallow waters of the Indian and Pacific oceans. Marshall, Tuamotu and Kiribati islands are atoll chains in the Pacific Ocean.

- **Sometimes, waves and wind** deposit small pieces of coral and sand on top of reefs. Over thousands of years, this debris piles up to form low-lying islands called cays.

- **Coral cays** are known to support a variety of plant and animal life. Some cays eventually become small islands that people live on. However, other cays move across the reef and even disappear with time.

- **Kiritimati**, or Christmas Island, is the largest coral atoll in the world. It is one of the Line Islands, a group of islands belonging to the Republic of Kiribati, which comprises 32 low-lying atolls and one raised island.

- **Three of the four atolls** in the Caribbean Sea can be found off the coast of Belize, near Mexico. They are the Turneffe Atoll, Glover's Reef and Lighthouse Reef.

- **The Belize atolls** are unique. Unlike other atolls, these did not grow around volcanic islands. Instead, they developed on non-volcanic ridges.

- **The Coral Sea Islands**, off the east coast of Australia, is one of the smallest countries in the world. It comprises numerous small uninhabited coral reefs and cays spread over a sea area of about 780,000 sq km.

- **The colourful reefs** that surround coral islands are home to beautiful and exotic marine creatures. These reefs have become popular destinations for undersea diving.

The angry oceans

- **The oceans**, which are a source of invaluable resources, can also wreak havoc in the form of tsunamis, whirlpools and hurricanes.

- **There are times when** a series of massive waves are generated in the oceans by certain natural disturbances. These waves, called tsunamis, lash against the shore with such great force that they cause a lot of damage.

- **Tsunamis** are most often created by earthquakes. They can also be generated by landslides and undersea volcanic eruptions, and are often incorrectly referred to as tidal waves.

- **Most tsunamis** originate along a volcanic and earthquake-prone zone known as the Ring of Fire, around the Pacific Ocean. Tsunami is a Japanese word meaning 'harbour wave'.

- **Hurricanes** are violent tropical cyclones arising in the tropical or sub-tropical waters. Hurricanes of the northwest Pacific Ocean are called typhoons.

- **The strongest and most dangerous hurricanes** are classified as Category 5. These hurricanes are rare, and the wind speed exceeds 250 km/h.

. . . FASCINATING FACT . . .
El Niño was first observed by fishermen in South America, who noticed that this phenomenon usually occurred near the time of Christmas. Hence, they named it El Niño, meaning 'the infant' in Spanish.

▶ *Hurricanes form over the Atlantic Ocean and move westward through the Caribbean and across the southern United States. These storms can cause devastation if they reach the coast.*

● **A whirlpool is** created when opposing currents or tides meet in the ocean. The uneven ocean floor makes the water swirl in with great force. Most whirlpools are not dangerous. However, some are powerful enough to destroy small boats.

● **Mokstraumen** off the coast of Norway and Old Sow near Deer Island in Canada are two of the world's most powerful whirlpools.

● **El Niño** is another interesting oceanic phenomenon that has a considerable effect on the global weather. It is the warming of surface waters in the eastern Pacific Ocean, near the Equator.

● **El Niño** causes an increase in rainfall across the southern states of the United States and in parts of South America. This usually leads to destructive floods in these regions. It is also believed to be responsible for drought in Africa and Australia.

Ocean's treasure chest

- **The oceans** are treasure-troves of precious gems and metals. Apart from diamonds, salt and other minerals, the oceans also contain vast reserves of oil.

- **A pearl** is perhaps the first precious object that comes to mind when we think of the oceans.

- **A pearl** is formed when a foreign object lodges itself inside the shell of an oyster, clam or mussel. These creatures coat the object with a substance called nacre, which lines the inside of the shell.

- **Nacre** is deposited in thin layers around the object, forming a pearl. Pearls are largely white or pale yellow in colour. However, some can be black, grey, red, green or blue.

- **Most pearls** are smooth and round, but some turn out to be uneven in shape and might not be as valuable. These pearls are called baroque pearls and are increasingly being used to make jewellery.

- **The seabed** is also a source of diamonds. These precious gems are found in the form of gravel on the seabed, especially in African and Indonesian waters.

- **Offshore diamonds** are often of superior quality when compared to some onshore varieties. The ocean diamond mining industry is growing rapidly.

- **The lure of gold** has also led man into the seas. Ocean water contains a large quantity of dissolved gold. However, the metal is difficult to extract since it is spread over a vast area.

- **It is believed that** over 10 billion tons of gold can be found in dissolved form in the oceans. However, it is present in such low concentrations that it is not possible to recover it.

- **Sand, gravel and oyster shells** found on the ocean floor are widely used to make cement for construction purposes.

▲ *Nacre, the shiny substance that lines the insides of oyster shells, is also called 'mother of pearl', since it is the main constituent of pearls.*

Mineral rich

▶ Limestone deposits often contain fossils of prehistoric marine creatures.

- **The oceans** contain an abundant supply of useful minerals. However, their vastness and inaccessibility make it difficult to extract most of these resources.

- **Sodium chloride**, better known as common salt, is one of the major minerals that are obtained from the oceans. It accounts for 3 percent of the weight of the ocean water.

40

- **Salt deposits** are formed when ocean water evaporates. Some lakes and rivers also contain salt deposits and crusts.

- **Other major minerals** obtained from the oceans are magnesium and bromine. Magnesium and its compounds are used in the agricultural, construction and chemical industries, while bromine is used in photography, and disinfectants.

- **Sedimentary rocks** such as limestone, sandstone and gypsum are also found in oceans. These are formed by erosion due to the action of water on shells and the remains of marine creatures. These are used in building materials.

- **Certain phosphorous minerals**, such as phosphorite, are also found on the seabed. These have potential uses as agricultural fertilizers.

- **Huge deposits** of manganese nodules have been recently discovered in the seabed, particularly in the Pacific Ocean. These nodules primarily consist of manganese and iron. Traces of copper, cobalt and nickel can also be found in them.

- **The oceans** are full of sulphur. Hydrothermal vents spout hot sulphur-rich water that also has a high concentration of other metals and minerals. Sulphur is used in fertilizers, food preservatives, bleaching agents and disinfectants.

- **Mining the oceans** is expensive and not very easy. There is an international dispute regarding the ownership of the oceans' mineral wealth.

- **An international maritime law** clearly defines the rules of sharing mineral wealth of the oceans. However, the debate continues on whether a particular spot in an ocean belongs to the nearest countries or to the global community.

Fossil fuels

- **Fossil fuels**, such as petroleum, coal and natural gas, are extracted from the fossilized remains of animals and plants that have been buried under layers of sediment, rocks and soil for millions of years.

- **Crude oil**, which is refined to make petroleum, is formed from microscopic plants and organisms such as bacteria that lived in the ancient oceans.

- **These micro-organisms** died and mixed with the silt in the ocean floor to form organic mud. Layers of sediment settled on this organic ooze, transforming it into crude oil.

- **Natural gas** is primarily formed by the decomposition or decaying of dead plankton that have accumulated on the ocean floor.

- **Both crude oil** and natural gas fill porous rocks nearby. These rocks containing reserves of fuel are called reservoir rocks. Since reservoir rocks are normally filled with water, the fuel, which is lighter than water, travels upwards until it reaches a layer of nonporous rocks.

- **The nonporous rocks** trap crude oil and natural gas to create a reservoir of fuel. Since natural gas is lighter than crude oil, it is found in a layer above the oil. Crude oil forms the middle layer with water as the bottom layer.

- **Coal** is a solid fossil fuel and is formed from decomposed plants that have hardened over the years. Coal is often found under the seabed, but offshore coal mining is not as widespread as that of oil and gas.

- **Scientists** have also found immense deposits of other hydrocarbon products, such as gas hydrates and oil shale, in the ocean floor.

- **Gas hydrates** are crystals of methane, while oil shale is a rock containing a waxy compound called kerogen.

- **Like crude oil**, oil shale is also formed from dead microscopic organisms. Over the years, these organisms are transformed into kerogen. However, the temperature and pressure in the ocean floor are sometimes not high enough to convert kerogen into crude oil.

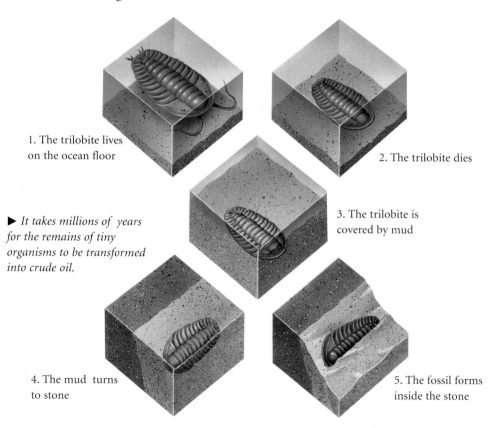

1. The trilobite lives on the ocean floor

2. The trilobite dies

▶ *It takes millions of years for the remains of tiny organisms to be transformed into crude oil.*

3. The trilobite is covered by mud

4. The mud turns to stone

5. The fossil forms inside the stone

43

Drilling for oil

- **With dwindling land resources**, the search for oil in the oceans is increasing. Natural resources found in the seabed are extracted and refined to produce fuel.

- **Oil companies** usually build offshore drilling rigs to extract resources from the seabed. Rigs are platforms set up in the sea at a distance from the shore.

- **Oil rigs** are tough structures made of steel or concrete that can withstand huge waves and storms. Alaskan oil rigs also have to withstand icy waters and ice floes.

▶ The oil platform's welded-steel legs rest on the seabed. They support the platform around 15 m above the surface of the water.

- **These rigs** are equipped with massive, tubular drills that dig several hundred metres into the ocean floor. The samples brought up by these pipes are then tested for signs of crude oil.

- **Once the existence** of crude oil is confirmed, it is extracted and sent to refineries where it is refined into petroleum and petroleum products, such as kerosene.

- **Some oil rigs are huge platforms**, which drop an anchor and float on the water. These platforms have air-filled supports, and are called semi-submersible rigs.

- **Permanent oil rigs** are built in places where production is high and multiple oil wells can be drilled. Some of these rigs, measuring over 130 m in diameter and almost 245 m high, are held in place by concrete or steel legs.

- **Sometimes pressure** builds up in the underground wells, causing blow-outs. When a blow-out occurs the drilling hole explodes, spilling oil into the surrounding waters.

- **Mud, pipes and rocks** are also thrown into the air during a blow-out. Oil spills are harmful to the environment. Apart from polluting the water they also destroy marine life.

- **Blow-out preventers** control pressure in underwater wells while drilling.

...FASCINATING FACT...
Permanent oil rigs sometimes support an ecosystem.
Their underwater structures form artificial reefs, with plenty
of marine creatures living on them. Some offshore platforms
are popular spots for rig diving.

Underwater wonders

◀ *A diver exploring the Yonaguni underwater pyramid off the coast of Japan. The structure is about 183 m wide and 27 m tall.*

- **Our fascination** with life underwater and the growing need for better transport linkages has led to the construction of undersea structures such as aquaria and submerged tunnels.

- **The Channel Tunnel**, or Chunnel, is a rail link that runs under the English Channel, connecting France and England. This unique rail service was launched in 1994.

- **The 50-km long tunnel** is an engineering marvel. It consists of two main tunnels and a service tunnel that gives maintenance workers access to the main tunnels. The Chunnel has been dug through a layer of chalk under the sea floor.

- **The Chunnel** is about 45 m under the seabed. It took 15,000 workers about seven years to complete.

- **Oceanariums** are artificially constructed undersea aquaria. Underwater World in Singapore has a submerged tunnel called the travelator, which takes visitors past marine creatures.

- **Ancient structures** such as underwater pyramids (e.g., Yonaguni) have also been discovered on the ocean floor. They may be the remains of ancient constructions that might have been swept under the sea.

- **The Yonaguni** pyramid was discovered in 1985, around 25 m below the ocean's surface off the island of the same name, near Okinawa, Japan. It looks like a series of massive stone terraces, ramps and steps.

- **There is a debate** about whether the Yonaguni is a natural or artificial structure. According to some scientists it was built or carved by humans at a time when the area was above sea level.

- **Explorations have revealed** a face-like sculpture among these formations, leading to belief that the Yonaguni structures were made by humans.

- **Another school of thought** says that the Yonaguni structures are the remains of a lost continent that existed around 12,000 years ago.

- **Stone structures** have also been discovered on the ocean floor off Cuba. These are laid out like an urban area. There are also reports of huge stone walls and a pyramid off the Bahamas.

> **. . .FASCINATING FACT. . .**
> The Seikan tunnel in Japan is, at present, the world's longest railway tunnel. This 53.9 km long tunnel connects the Japanese islands of Honshu and Hokkaido.

Living at sea

- **Developers** are always thinking of new ways to make money from the popularity of islands and seas. Underwater hotels and artificial islands, such as the Jules' Undersea Lodge and the Palm Islands, are now capturing the imagination of people around the world.

- **The Jules' Undersea Lodge** in Florida, USA, is the world's first underwater hotel. Named after the French science-fiction writer Jules Verne, it was a research laboratory that was converted into a hotel for divers.

- **Visitors** have to dive over 6m below the sea to enter the hotel through a "moon pool" entrance in the floor of the hotel.

- **The Jules' Undersea Lodge** was first designed to be an underwater research laboratory called La Chalupa. Built in a mangrove lagoon, it was used to explore life in the continental shelf off the coast of Puerto Rico.

- **The world's first** underwater luxury hotel is being built off the coast of Dubai, in the United Arab Emirates. The Hydropolis Hotel will be built on the floor of the Persian Gulf, 20 m below the surface.

- **The hotel** will have three divisions. A land station will function as the reception, while a connecting tunnel will transport guests from the land station into the depths of the ocean. A submarine complex will be the main hotel.

... FASCINATING FACT ...

The Jules' Undersea Lodge is filled with compressed air.
This prevents the water from rising through the moon pool
entrance and flooding the rooms.

▶ *Round glass windows that resemble huge portholes provide a wonderful view of the marine life at the Jules' Verne Undersea Lodge.*

- **The Hydropolis** will also have two transparent domes that will hold an auditorium and a ballroom. The ballroom will be built above water, with a retractable roof.

- **The hotel** will be built of concrete, steel and clear Plexiglas that can withstand high underwater pressures.

- **The Palm Islands** in Dubai, popularly referred to as The Palm, are another oceanic wonder. They consist of two artificial islands in the shape of date palm trees.

- **Each palm island comprises** a trunk, a crown with 17 fronds and a crescent-shaped island forming an arch around them. The palm islands will accommodate luxury hotels, villas, apartments, restaurants and spas. The structures will increase Dubai's shoreline by 120 km.

Studying the oceans

- **The study** of the chemical and physical properties of oceans and their ecosystems is called oceanography, oceanology or marine science.
- **Oceanography** comprises marine geology, physical oceanography, chemical oceanography, marine biology and meteorological oceanography.

▲ *A satellite photograph of a hurricane forming over the Earth. Meteorological oceanography deals with the influence of oceans on weather patterns across the world.*

- **Marine geology** deals with the study of tectonic plates in the Earth's crust. These plates are responsible for natural phenomena such as volcanoes, earthquakes, mountains and valleys.

- **Apart from studying** the Earth's crust and other related phenomena, marine geologists involved in offshore oil exploration and drilling also study how sediments and minerals are formed.

- **Physical oceanography** is the study of the physical processes that take place in the oceans. These include ocean currents, temperature, salt content in ocean water and the causes of tides.

- **Chemical oceanography** is the study of chemicals in the oceans. The seas contain most of the elements found in the Earth, including fossil fuels and minerals.

- **Oceanography** also includes allied sciences such as the study of caves, or speleology. This subject deals with the origin, physical structure and development of caves. It also studies the flora and fauna of caves.

- **Hydrography** is another important branch of oceanography. It is the oldest science that deals with the sea and is defined as the study of water depth and quality, and of material found on the ocean floor, with specific reference to their impact on navigation.

- **Oceanography** gained importance with the age of discovery in AD1400–1500. New lands were being discovered and oceans were mapped out during this time by explorers from great maritime nations such as Portugal and Spain.

- **Meteorological oceanography** deals with the interaction between the oceans and the atmosphere. It is the study of atmospheric reactions above the oceans and the influence of the oceans on global weather.

Marine biology

- **Marine biology** is the study of life in the oceans and other related environments, such as estuaries and lagoons.

- **Biological oceanography** and marine biology are often confused with each other. Both study marine creatures. However, biological oceanography studies the effects of a changing ocean environment on marine life.

- **Marine biology** includes several other sub-fields, such as aquaculture, environmental marine biology, deep-sea ecology, ichthyology, marine mammology and marine ethology.

- **Environmental marine biology** is the study of the health of oceans and the effect of coastal development on the marine environment. It also looks at the impact of pollutants, such as oil spills and other chemical hazards, on the surrounding marine life.

- **Deep-sea ecology** takes a closer look at how water creatures in the deep adapt to the dark and cold environment.

- **Ichthyology** is the study of fish – both marine and freshwater.

- **Marine mammology** is a relatively new subject that deals exclusively with the study of marine mammals such as whales, dolphins and seals.

...FASCINATING FACT...

Greek philosopher Aristotle was the first person to record detailed descriptions of marine life. He identified various species including molluscs, fish and crustaceans. He also classified whales and dolphins as mammals. Because of his contribution, Aristotle is often referred to as the father of marine biology.

▲ *Ichthyologists deal with various aspects of fish, such as their classification, behaviour, evolution and habitats.*

- **Marine ethology** helps us understand the behaviour of marine animals in their natural environment. It also focuses on ways to save endangered species whose habitats are threatened by human activity or changes in the environment.

- **Marine biologists** use various advanced methods to collect data for their research. Several new tools, such as plankton nets, remotely operated vehicles and fibre optics have made studying the oceans much easier.

- **Artificial underwater habitats** are built about 20 m below the water's surface to accommodate scientists who work underwater for longer periods.

Reconstructing history

- **Underwater archaeology**, also called marine archaeology, involves not only the discovery and study of sunken ships and planes, but also the unearthing of remains of ancient cities and ports that lie buried underwater.

- **It is one of the most interesting** branches of undersea science. High-profile wreck discoveries, such as the *Titanic* and *Bismarck*, have only increased the popularity of this growing field.

- **The discovery of cargo from shipwrecks** has provided a wealth of information regarding ancient trade and ways of life.

- **Wrecks also** give an insight into the shipbuilding techniques of the past. The hull tells us how the ship was designed and built, while the sail and ropes reveal how the vessel was operated.

- **A wreck's cargo** can provide information on whether the ship was a merchant ship, passenger liner or warship.

- **One of the best known wrecks** to be discovered is the Tudor warship *Mary Rose*, which sank in 1545. The pride of King Henry VIII, it was raised from the depths of the ocean and renovated lavishly for public viewing.

- **The Mary Rose** was raised in 1982, and the material from the ship offered a glimpse of domestic and military life during the Tudor reign.

... FASCINATING FACT ...
One story that has intrigued underwater archaeologists for years is that of Atlantis – the flourishing island that was believed to have sunk after a devastating earthquake. However, so far the search for Atlantis has been fruitless.

◀ *A diver exploring a wreck. Modern technology helps us to build a clear picture of how ships and boats were built and why they may have sank.*

- **The discovery of a Bronze Age ship** in the late 1900s lent some credibility to stories about treasures in shipwrecks. This ship, which was discovered off Turkey, was found to have carried a tremendous amount of copper and tin ingots, indicating that it probably was a merchant ship.

- **Underwater archaeology** involves more than merely diving into the depths of the ocean and hunting for wrecks. Archaeologists spend an immense amount of time poring over history books and diaries of explorers to learn about various ships and where they sank.

- **Searching for lost cities** is another important aspect of marine archaeology. A thrilling discovery was the massive stone structures off Yonaguni Island in Japan, which may point to a civilization that existed 12,000 years ago but was drowned beneath the waves.

Raising the wreck

◀ One of the most well-known wrecks is that of the Titanic. The ship's wreck now rests at a depth of over 3800 m on the floor of the Atlantic Ocean.

- **Raising a shipwreck** is challenging and involves a lot of risk. Wreck divers have to cope with low visibility, as well as the discomforts of staying underwater for long periods.

- **A common risk** that divers face is getting trapped under hanging wreckage that gets dislodged.

- **Wreck diving** has developed over the years. Advances in the design of diving equipment and other inventions such as submersibles and remotely operated vehicles have made wreck diving safer than before.

- **A remotely operated vehicle**, or ROV, is an underwater robot equipped with cameras that is operated by people aboard a ship. The ROV is connected to the ship by cables that carry signals back and forth.

- **The extreme conditions** that prevail in the ocean depths have prevented researchers from conducting deeper explorations. However, with submersibles it is now possible to reach these depths.

- **The reflection** of underwater sound waves is used to detect objects in the sea. This method is known as sound navigation and ranging, abbreviated to sonar, and is one of the most important tools in undersea exploration.

- **Early wreck explorers** used diving bells and compressed air to go down into the water. But the pressure restricted their movements and research activity on the ocean floor.

- **The revolution in wreck exploration** took place with the discovery of the *Titanic* in 1985. This was the first time that high-tech equipment was used to locate parts of the wreck.

- **Robert Ballard**, the explorer who discovered the wreck of the *Titanic*, used a sled, called *Argo*, to explore the depths of the ocean. *Argo* was equipped with night-vision cameras and other technology that supplied data through fibre optic wires to the research vessel.

- **After discovering** the *Titanic* in 1985, Ballard returned to the site a year later. This time he went underwater in a manned submersible named *ALVIN*. A remotely operated vehicle, *Jason Junior*, accompanied *ALVIN* to take pictures of the wreck.

... **FASCINATING FACT** ...
In 1989, Robert Ballard came up with an innovative method, termed telepresence, which allowed students in far-off places to accompany scientists on their underwater expeditions. This method was named the JASON Project. It used advanced communication technology to transmit video images of wrecks across the world.

Underwater fashion

- **Diving suits** have seen many trends over the years. The earliest example is believed to have been made around the fifteenth century. The diver was restricted in how far down he could dive by his air tube, which went up to the surface of the water.

- **It was only in the eighteenth century** that suits giving freedom of movement were first made. Klingert's diving suit, made around 1797, was one such suit. It was the first to be called a diving suit and comprised a coat and trousers made of waterproof leather.

- **In 1819,** German inventor August Siebe made a heavy-footed diving suit using canvas and leather. The unique feature of this invention was a copper helmet that was supplied with air by a surface pump.

- **Modern diving suits** can be broadly divided into soft and hard types. Soft diving suits are primarily used for scuba diving and other styles of diving. These suits protect the diver from low temperature but not high pressure.

- **Hard diving suits** are more appropriate for deep-sea diving. They are armour-like suits that have pressure joints to protect the diver from the high pressure underwater.

- **Soft diving suits** are of two kinds – wet and dry. Wet suits keep the body warm. They trap small amounts of water, which is then warmed by body heat. The warm layer of water in turn keeps the diver warm.

- **Divers entering colder waters**, such as the polar seas, wear dry suits. These are made of a waterproof material that keeps the diver completely dry. Divers wear special underclothes or use built-in electrical heating to keep warm.

- **Some suits** have a weight belt to help divers stay at the bottom. Head gear is equipped with visors and is made of the same material as the suit.

- **Another invention** that revolutionized diving is the rebreather. Invented by Henry Fleuss, an English marine officer, in 1879, this portable air supply system in the form of tanks freed divers from the constant dependence on air supplied from the surface. This was the first self-contained underwater breathing apparatus, abbreviated to scuba.

- **The invention** of the aqualung by French divers Jacques Cousteau and Emile Gagnan in 1942 further popularized diving. A high-pressure cylinder, worn on the diver's back, is connected to the mouth with a hose that has a valve.

▲ *Divers control their breathing to make their oxygen supply last as long as possible.*

Diving through time

- **The fascination** that humans have for the mysteries of the oceans is not recent. History is full of stories regarding early attempts by ancient adventurers to become great underwater explorers.

- **It is believed** that around the fifth century BC, a man named Scyllias, from the Greek city of Scione, saved the Greeks from Persian attack by diving beneath the sea and cutting off the anchors of the Persian ships.

- **The history of diving** goes back to the time of Alexander the Great. Greek philosopher Aristotle records in his writings that a diving bell was used during Alexander's reign.

- **The diving bell** was the most widely used piece of diving equipment in the early days. Its origins can be traced back to ancient times, when divers placed inverted buckets and cauldrons over their heads before going underwater.

- **These inverted objects** trapped air inside them, allowing the diver to breathe. These devices gradually gave way to a more sophisticated bell-shaped wooden barrel that was placed over the diver's head.

> **. . . FASCINATING FACT . . .**
> In his account of the Peloponnesian Wars, the Greek historian, Thucydides, recounts an incident during the Athenian attack on Syracuse, an ally of Sparta. According to Thucydides, the soldiers of Syracuse fixed wooden poles underwater to block entry into the harbour. These unseen poles caused immense damage to Athenian ships. However, Athenian diving warriors removed the poles to clear the way for their ships.

- **Air was passed** into the bell through tubes that went all the way up to the surface. Over the years the bell was made larger to allow for more air.

- **A more advanced version** of the diving bell is still used today. The modern bells are made of steel and can withstand tremendous amounts of pressure.

- **Divers in ancient Rome** were called *urinatores*, derived from the Latin word *urus*, meaning 'leather bag'. They got their name from the leather bag they carried while diving. These divers recovered treasures from sunken ships. They used heavy stones to help them dive under water to depths of about 30 m.

- **It is said** that around the first century BC *urinatores* salvaged a cargo of amphorae, or ancient wine jars, from the ancient Roman merchant ship, *Madrague de Giens*.

- **Divers** were also a major force in naval battles. According to historical accounts, Alexander the Great had to contend with *kalimboi*, or diving warriors, during the siege of Tyre in 332BC.

▲ *In ancient times, air was passed to the divers through long tubes that went all the way up to the surface.*

61

Early marine life

- **It is believed** that life on Earth originated in the oceans around 3.8 billion years ago.

- **According to some scientists**, repeated lightning strikes triggered a reaction among certain compounds and gases in the Earth's atmosphere. This reaction might have led to the formation of proteins and enzymes which are the building blocks of life.

- **The proteins and enzymes** rained down on the oceans and developed into primitive single-celled organisms.

- **Around 620 million years ago**, complex and soft-bodied multi-cellular life-forms appeared for the first time.

- **Some of the earliest creatures** looked like modern jellyfish. They were very small and had a variety of shapes.

- **These early animals** soon evolved into more complex life-forms that are recognized today. Some of these early creatures included sponges, jellyfish, corals, flatworms and molluscs.

- **The earliest fish** appeared around 480 million years ago. These were the jawless fish. The modern hagfish and lamprey are the only surviving members of this group.

- **Around 450 million years ago**, sharks and bony fish began to evolve. The first bony fish were small and had armoured plates for defence.

- **The early bony fish** were either ray-finned or lobe-finned. The coelacanth and the modern lungfish are the only lobe-finned fish that survive today.

● **Most scientists** believe that lobe-finned fish used their fins to come out of the water for very short periods. This led to the evolution of amphibians, which themselves eventually evolved into other land creatures.

▼ *Coelacanths are referred to as 'living fossils' because they have changed very little over millions of years.*

Modern marine life

- **The first modern fish** appeared around 250 million years ago. The ancient ray-finned fish gave rise to the neopterygians, which are considered to be the ancestors of the modern fish.

▼ *Oceans are home to nearly 300,000 different living species, ranging from huge whales to tiny fish.*

- **The oceans** of the modern world are no different from the primitive oceans in terms of the number of creatures that live there. Today, the oceans are home to several species of mammals and reptiles, numerous small creatures and more than 20,000 species of fish.

- **Oceans** are divided into two regions – the benthic zone, or the ocean floor, and the pelagic zone, which is the vast expanse of water.

- **The pelagic zone** is further divided into three zones. The topmost zone, called the epipelagic zone, supports around 90 percent of marine life.

- **The epipelagic zone** is the only ocean zone that gets sunlight. Apart from plants, many species of fish, reptiles and mammals dwell in the epipelagic zone. Sharks, rays, whales, dolphins, seals and turtles are just some of them.

- **The twilight zone** is just below the epipelagic zone. Very little sunlight reaches this zone, making it impossible for plants to survive here. However, animals such as octopus, squid, hatchet fish, viperfish and other deep sea fish are found in this zone.

- **Some animals** that live in the twilight zone are bioluminescent. Special organs, called photophores, in the bodies of these animals give off a greenish light.

- **The midnight zone** is the lowest zone and is completely dark and extremely cold. Very few creatures live in this zone and most of them do not have eyes.

- **Oceans** are among the most advanced ecosystems. Tiny plants and animals that float on the surface, called plankton, form the base of the oceanic food chain.

- **Many land creatures** depend on oceans for survival. These include seabirds, and animals such as polar bears. They feed on fish that swim close to the surface.

Coral reefs

- **Coral reefs** are formed by colonies of coral polyps. A coral polyp is a tiny animal that uses minerals in the sea to produce a protective outer skeleton. These skeletons form hard and branching structures called coral reefs.

- **Coral polyps** eat algae. They also use their tentacles to capture tiny creatures called zooplankton.

- **Corals** are ancient animals that have been around for 250 millions years.

- **Coral reefs** are home to numerous sea animals. Starfish, reef sharks, sponges, jellyfish, crabs, lobsters, anemones, eels and a huge variety of fish add to the colour of coral reefs.

- **Coral reefs are found** in warm and shallow waters, usually within 30 degrees north and south of the Equator.

- **There are three kinds** of coral reefs. These are fringing and barrier reefs, and coral atolls.

- **Fringing reefs** extend from the land into the sea. Barrier reefs are found further from the shore, separated from the mainland by a lagoon. Atolls are ring-shaped formations of coral islands, around a lagoon.

- **The Great Barrier Reef** in the Coral Sea off the north-eastern coast of Australia is the biggest of all coral reefs. It is over 2000 km long.

- **Coral reefs** are also found in the Indian Ocean and the Red Sea. Some of them also stretch along the Atlantic Ocean from Florida in the United States to the Caribbean Sea and Brazil.

● **Coral reefs**, especially the Great Barrier Reef, are major tourist attractions because of their fascinating structures, vibrant colours and rich marine life.

> ...FASCINATING FACT...
> The stinging hydroid coral found in the Indian and
> Pacific oceans uses special chemicals to paralyse plankton,
> which forms a major part of its diet.

▼ *A single coral reef may be home to as many as 3000 species of living things.*

Starfish

- **Starfish**, also known as sea stars, are not fish. They are spiny creatures without bones. Most starfish have five arms, but some species have seven and others have 14 arms.

- **Starfish** have developed a unique way of moving. They have hundreds of tiny, tube-like feet underneath their arms, which help them to crawl.

- **The diet of starfish** includes oysters, fish, clams and even waste deposits on the seabed.

- **The mouth** of the starfish is underneath its body. If the prey is big they push their stomach out of their mouth to grab and digest it.

- **Starfish** do not have eyes. Instead, they have a small eye-spot at the tip of each arm. The eyes-spots are linked to a network of nerves. Starfish also have good senses of touch and smell.

- **Some starfish** can regenerate lost arms. A new starfish may be regenerated from a single arm attached to a portion of the central disc.

- **To reproduce**, the female starfish releases millions of microscopic eggs. Young starfish larvae eat plankton.

- **The crown-of-thorns starfish** is covered with large, poisonous spines, which it uses to protect itself. This starfish eats coral polyps. A huge number of these starfish have been known to eat an entire coral reef!

- **Other varieties of starfish** include the mottled star and the red blood star. The deadly sunflower starfish preys on other starfish.

- **The starfish family** also includes sea lilies, feather stars, brittle stars, sea urchins and sea cucumbers.

▲ *Starfish are found in most of the oceans across the world. They live on the seabed.*

Jellyfish

- **Jellyfish** are among the most feared sea animals. Found in oceans across the world, they are shaped like a bell and have poisonous tentacles.

- **The body** of a jellyfish is soft and does not have a fixed form. Its skin is almost transparent since nearly 98 percent of its body is made up of water.

- **Jellyfish** depend on sea currents to drift about. They can swim a little, but this is limited to upward and downward movements.

- **Some species of jellyfish** can be very small, while others, such as the lion's mane, can grow to 2.5 m in diameter.

- **Jellyfish** have a central cavity in their hood that acts as stomach and intestine. They eat plankton, other jellyfish and small fish. Jellyfish use stinging tentacles to grab their prey.

- **When disturbed**, jellyfish emit a pale white light. Their senses are poorly developed, but special light sensors help them to find their way around.

- **Jellyfish** do not have gills or lungs. Oxygen is absorbed and carbon dioxide is released through their membrane-like skin.

- **Most marine creatures** do not attack jellyfish. However, they are eaten by arrow crabs, spadefish and sunfish. Some people eat them and the mushroom jellyfish is a delicacy in Japan and China.

- **Jellyfish** have a complex life cycle. They start their life as swimming larvae. The larvae attach themselves to the seabed and form a colony of polyps. Later, these polyps grow into bell-shaped structures and start drifting.

- **The tentacles** of the jellyfish are lined with hundreds of tiny stinging cells called nematocysts. These cells contain poison. The stings of some jellyfish, like the box jellyfish, can kill a full-grown man.

▲ *The stinging cells in the tentacles of a large box jellyfish contain enough venom to kill 60 people.*

Sea anemones

▲ *The tentacles of sea anemones make them look like bright underwater flowers.*

- **Sea anemones** are colourful creatures that are sometimes confused with coral polyps.

- **Unlike corals**, sea anemones do not have a skeleton to protect them. They attach themselves to solid surfaces, such as the seabed, corals or rocks.

- **Sea anemones** are most commonly found in tropical waters. They do not live in colonies like corals do.

- **Sea anemones** are mostly stationary creatures. Those which move about do so very slowly by sliding. Swimming anemones look like rolling balls of tentacles.

- **Most sea anemones** are very small, but some varieties may grow to more than 1 m in diameter. They have a cylindrical body and an opening at the top that serves as the mouth.

- **The mouth** of a sea anemone is surrounded by tentacles. These tentacles are used to grab food and for defence.

- **The tentacles** have stinging cells that paralyse the sea anemone's prey. The tentacles also carry the prey into the sea anemone's mouth. Sticky mucus on the tentacles means they can grab even the smallest of fish.

- **Sea anemones** have a symbiotic relationship with the hermit crab. Since the sea anemone cannot travel very easily, it rides piggy back on the crab. The anemone is transported, while the crab gets protection from its enemies.

- **Sea anemones** that live in shallow waters secrete mucus or dig into the wet sand to prevent their bodies from drying out.

- **Anemones** can live for 70 to 100 years. Because of their vibrant colours they are much sought after for display in aquariums.

. . . FASCINATING FACT . . .
The clownfish is quite safe living among sea anemones, despite their poisonous tentacles. The fish has a thick coating of slime that protects it against the anemone's sting and the anemone's tentacles deter predators from attacking the clownfish.

Sea urchins and sea cucumbers

- **Sea urchins** are small creatures with spherical shells. Like starfish, sea urchins also have spines on their bodies.

- **A sea urchin's spines** are movable and are used for defence and movement. They can be tiny or, in some cases, over 20 cm long.

- **Some fish**, like the triggerfish and the pufferfish, can knock off the sea urchin's spines with their hard heads.

- **Sea urchins** eat small plants and animals. Some eat sponges.

- **Some sea urchins** are venomous, and like certain jellyfish and stinging corals, they can be dangerous to divers.

- **Sea cucumbers** are relatives of sea urchins and are found on seabeds across the world. They vary from 2 cm to 2 m in length.

- **Sea cucumbers** get their name from their warty, tubular appearance. Unlike sea urchins, sea cucumbers have soft bodies. But their skin is tough and leathery.

- **The mouth** is located at one end of the body and is surrounded by tentacles that collect food. The diet of the sea cucumber consists mainly of small plants.

- **Sea cucumbers** have tube feet and move about very slowly on the seabed by contracting their body. Some deep-sea varieties can swim.

... FASCINATING FACT ...
The sea urchin's mouth is located on the bottom side of the test, or outer shell. Five teeth, moved by 60 muscles, help the urchin to scrape food off the seabed. This jaw-like apparatus is called Aristotle's lantern.

● **People are known** to hunt sea cucumbers extensively. Also known as 'trepang' in certain parts of Asia, dried sea cucumbers are used in soup.

▼ *This pencil urchin is a primitive, or cidarid sea urchin.*

Sponges

- **Sponges** might look like plants but they are, in fact, animals. While most sponges are found in the sea, some species live in freshwater.

- **They do not have eyes**, ears, a head, arms, legs or any organs. But their bodies have thousands of pores that help them filter food from the water.

- **Various shapes, sizes and colours** of sponges have evolved. They can be extremely small or as wide as 4 m in diameter.

- **Sponges cannot move about**. They attach themselves to solid objects such as shells or stones in places where food is abundant.

- **They do not have mouths**. Water containing tiny bits of food is drawn in through pores called ostia. After the nutrients are extracted, the water is released through a bigger opening, or osculum, at the top.

- **A network of canals and chambers** inside the sponges help them to pump enormous quantities of water.

- **Certain deep-sea sponges** have spiky, hook-shaped filaments. When tiny crustaceans, like shrimps, get caught in these filaments, new ones grow around the prey to digest it. It takes a whole day for new filaments to envelop the prey.

- **There are around 10,000 species of sponges**. The barrel sponge is the biggest of all. It is so big that a full-grown man could climb into it. The tube sponge is a common colourful variety, and is found mostly on reefs.

- **The red tree sponge** is extremely attractive. It is often confused with corals because of its bright, flower-like structure.

- **The skeletons** of certain sponges are made up of a soft, silky substance called *spongin*. When these sponges die, their flexible skeletons are cleaned and bleached for use as bath sponges.

▲ *The canals and chambers of sponges are home to a variety of small creatures, such as sea slugs, crabs and shrimps.*

Fish facts

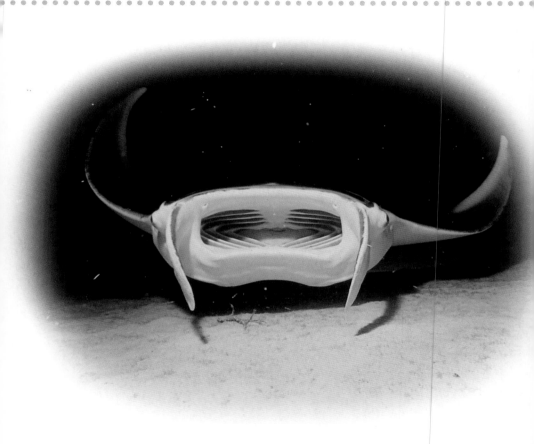

▲ *Manta rays belong to the cartilaginous group of fish. Inside a manta ray's mouth are five pairs of gill arches, which filter food from the water. The food particles get trapped in a spongy material between the gill arches, while the water passes out through the ray's gill slits.*

- **Fish are vertebrates**, and like other vertebrates, they have a backbone. They live in water, breathe through their gills and have shiny scales on their bodies.

- **There are more species** of fish than all mammals, reptiles, amphibians and birds put together. Fish are found in varied habitats – from the deepest oceans to the smallest mountain streams.

- **Most fish** live in oceans and just one in five lives in fresh water.

- **Unlike mammals**, fish are cold-blooded. Their body temperature changes with their surroundings.

- **Fish are broadly divided** into two main groups – jawed and jawless. Jawless fish, such as lamprey and hagfish, have a sucker-like mouth with horny teeth. Not many jawless fish exist today.

- **Jawed fish** can be further divided into cartilaginous and bony fish. The skeleton of cartilaginous fish is made up of a strong but flexible tissue called cartilage. Sharks, rays and chimeras are cartilaginous fish.

- **Bony fish** are the most abundant of all fish species. Their skeleton is made up of bones. Most of them have a bladder that helps them swim.

- **Most fish** have a streamlined body that helps them swim better. The sailfish and blue shark are among the fastest swimming fish.

- **Fish feed** on other creatures of the ocean. The smallest of fish feed on microscopic creatures such as zooplankton. Larger fish prey on smaller marine creatures.

- **Fish are very important** to humans as food, since they are a good source of protein. Excessive fishing has endangered some species, while others are already extinct.

Anglerfish and cod

- **Anglerfish** have a huge head and mouth. They also have numerous sharp teeth to trap their prey.

- **Some anglerfish** are only half a metre in length, while others could grow up to 2 m. These are deep-sea fish found mainly in the Atlantic Ocean.

- **Anglerfish** are normally dark brown or red in colour. Their colour gives them good camouflage.

- **The diet** of anglerfish includes small cod, sprats and dogfish.

- **Some female deep-sea anglerfish** can eat prey bigger than themselves.

- **The male deep-sea anglerfish** is much smaller than the female. It attaches itself to the female with its teeth and extracts food from her bloodstream.

- **Cod** is the common name for the genus of fish known as Gadus. Sometimes the term 'cod' is used to refer to a wide variety of fish that are not in this genus.

- **Cod** are mostly found in cold or temperate waters. They prefer to live in the depths of the ocean, close to the seabed, and feed on other fish.

- **There are three main species of cod**. They are the Atlantic, the Pacific and the Greenland cod. Some of them can grow to over 1.5 m in length.

> ...**FASCINATING FACT**...
> Anglerfish get their name from the way the female deep sea anglerfish catches its prey. It uses a long worm-like spine attached to its head to attract smaller fish, and then traps them in its mouth. The spine is luminous, with a glowing tip to attract prey.

● **Cod liver oil** is a rich source of vitamins and minerals and so cod is a very valuable food for humans.

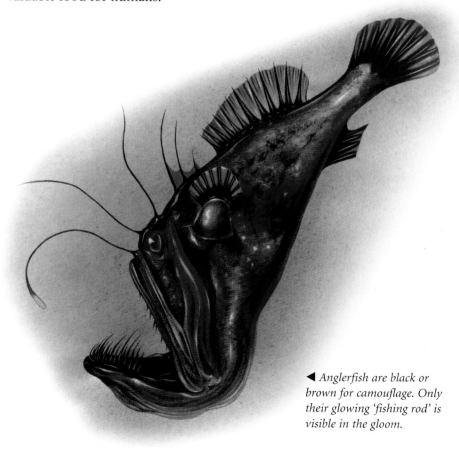

◄ *Anglerfish are black or brown for camouflage. Only their glowing 'fishing rod' is visible in the gloom.*

Salmon and viperfish

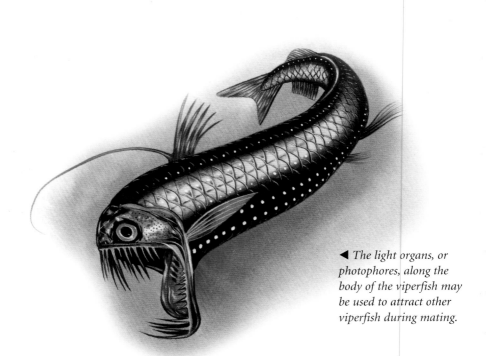

◀ *The light organs, or photophores, along the body of the viperfish may be used to attract other viperfish during mating.*

- **Salmon** have elongated bodies and are excellent swimmers. They are usually found in the cold oceans near the Northern continents.

- **The diet** of salmon consists of smaller fish and crabs. The Atlantic and Pacific salmon are the most well-known varieties of salmon.

- **Most salt water salmon** migrate to fresh waters to lay eggs. The young ones later swim into the sea and live there. These young salmon return to the place where they were born when it is their turn to lay eggs.

- **The journey** from the sea to the river, sometimes covering over 1500 km, is very tiring, especially for the Pacific salmon, which has to leap up several waterfalls on its way. By the time the fish reaches the river and lays its eggs, it is exhausted and often falls prey to eagles and bears. Most Pacific salmon die after they have spawned.

- **Unlike the Pacific salmon**, the Atlantic salmon survives its ordeal to return to the sea. They are even known to repeat their journey from sea to river two or three times in their lifetime.

- **The fierce-looking viperfish** has a very big head but a slender, snake-like body. It is usually around half a metre in length.

- **Viperfish** have long, curved teeth that look like snake's fangs. Although the mouth of viperfish is huge, it is not large enough to cover their teeth.

- **Although they are scattered** across the globe, viperfish occur mostly in tropical waters. They live near the ocean floor, at depths varying from 500–2500 m.

- **Viperfish** prefer to stay in the dark ocean depths, but at night they swim up towards the surface in search of food.

- **'Glow spots'** on the body and dorsal fin of the viperfish emit light to attract small fish and other prey.

Flounder

- **Flounder** have a unique shape - they are flat and almost round. They belong to the group of fish known as flatfish.

- **Both eyes** of the flounder are located on the same side of the body – on the upper surface.

- **Some flounder** have both eyes on the left side, so they lie on the right side. Others have both eyes on the right side, so they lie on their left side.

- **Flounder** prefer to live and swim close to the seabed. They are found in almost every ocean, but are more abundant in warm waters.

- **Flounder** undergo a dramatic transformation during their lifecycle. The young are born looking like normal fish but gradually their body becomes flatter and the eyes shift to either the left or the right side of the head.

- **The colour of flounder** varies according to their habitat. They are usually brown, mottled or sandy. The lower side of the body is often a lighter shade.

- **In addition to camouflage**, flounder have another interesting defence tactic. They cover themselves with dirt so that predators cannot spot them. Only the eyes remain visible, and these can be moved to provide a wider view.

- **When attacked**, some flounder flap their fins on the seabed to stir up a cloud of silt that blocks them from the predator's view. They can then swim away to safety.

- **Among the more common varieties** are the summer flounder, found in the Atlantic Ocean, and the winter flounder or the lemon sole, found in the south Atlantic and the Gulf of Mexico.

● **Others in the flatfish family** include halibut, plaice, dab, turbot, brill and window pane flounder. The liver oil of the halibut, one of the largest flatfish, contains more vitamins than even cod liver oil.

▼ *The flounder's flattened shape and dull colouring help to camouflage (hide) it on the seabed.*

Grouper

- **Grouper** are large fish that are found mainly in warm waters. They are abundant off the coasts of Australia and the in Caribbean Sea.

- **They are characterized** by spines, or needle-like structures, near their dorsal fin. They have a large mouth and strong jaws. Most grouper, particularly the panther grouper, are marine predators.

- **Grouper are strong swimmers**. They prefer to keep to the bottom of the sea or near coral reefs.

- **The diet** of grouper includes crabs, cuttlefish and other fish. Grouper use their strong jaws to kill prey and then swallow it whole.

- **Grouper** are capable of changing their sex. Most grouper spawn as female for one or two years and change sex to function as males after that.

- **These fish** can also change their body colour. The red grouper changes its colour according to the surroundings, while the blue-spotted grouper lightens its colour when attacked.

- **Grouper** are amongst the largest fish. Some species can grow larger than an adult human.

- **The Australian grouper** and the jewfish, or the spotted grouper, which can grow to over 3 m, are the largest species. Some grouper can be as small as 10 cm.

- **Small grouper** make fascinating aquarium fish because of their ability to change colour. However, some of them will eat their own kind.

- **Nassau grouper** are extremely popular as food and are fished extensively.

▲ *Grouper wait patiently at the bottom of the sea*
and make small, swift movements to capture their prey.

Triggerfish

- **Triggerfish** are colourful fish found in shallow, tropical waters. They grow up to 60 cm in length. They have strong jaws, sharp teeth and eyes that are located on top of their head.

- **Triggerfish** have three dorsal spines. They use one of these as a trigger to lock or open the other two, giving it the name triggerfish.

- **The triggerfish group** includes the pufferfish, the spiny porcupinefish and the ocean sunfish.

- **The ocean sunfish** is shaped like a pancake and has thin dorsal and anal fins. Its tail fin is almost nonexistent, making the ocean sunfish a bad swimmer.

- **The ocean sunfish** floats on its side on the surface of the water as if sunbathing. Hence, the name sunfish.

▲ *Despite their huge size, sunfish feed on tiny plankton.*

...FASCINATING FACT...
Ocean sunfish are among the biggest bony fish. They have a bulky, oval body and can grow up to 3 m in length.

- **Pufferfish** are mainly found in tropical waters. Most of them are poisonous. The body of a pufferfish is round and covered with spines.

- **The spines** of the pufferfish are usually not visible. But when attacked, the pufferfish swells its body, making the spines stand out. This is why they are also known as blowfish, globefish and swellfish.

- **The swelling** of the pufferfish is achieved by a sac inside its body, which it fills by gulping in air or water.

- **Predators find** it tough to bite into pufferfish once they inflate themselves and their spines become erect.

- **Pufferfish** is a popular delicacy in Japan. However, due to its poisonous nature, the fish can only be cooked by fully trained chefs. Only

▶ *Most pufferfish have fused teeth that form a beak-like structure. They use this to crush their prey.*

Snapper

- **Snapper** belong to the same group as grouper and marlin. There are over 200 species of snapper.

- **They are so called** because of their tendency to snap, or bite, swiftly at food.

- **Snapper are common** in tropical and subtropical waters of all the oceans. Certain species of snapper also foray into freshwater in search of food.

- **These fish** have a slender body and a large, prominent mouth. Some species grow as long as 90 cm.

- **Snapper** are often found travelling in large schools. They eat small fish, molluscs and other crustaceans. Some of them also eat plankton.

- **A well-known species** is the red snapper. It has a pinkish red body with a lighter belly, and is commonly found in the Atlantic Ocean, especially along the western coast. Vermilion snapper are very similar to red snapper.

- **Emperor snapper** have black and white bands on their bodies. These bands however, fade with age. They are among the larger snapper.

- **Dog snapper**, though fished for food, are sometimes toxic. They get their name from their prominent canine teeth, which make them look fierce.

- **Yellowtail snapper** have yellow spots and stripes. A prominent yellow stripe, which begins at the mouth, broadens gradually and runs to the tail. They are usually found in the Atlantic Ocean.

● **Blackfin snapper** are usually red, with yellowish fins, and have a prominent comma-shaped mark at the base of their pectoral fins.

▼ *In a large group called a school, fish like these yellow snappers have less chance of being picked off by a predator.*

Flying fish

- **Flying fish do not actually fly**. Instead, they leap into the air and glide for short distances.

- **The average length** of a flying fish is around 20–30 cm. The California flying fish, found in the Pacific Ocean, is the largest species. It can grow up to a length of 40 cm.

- **The pectoral fins** of flying fish have similar functions to a bird's wings. The two-winged flying fish have very large pectoral fins that they stretch out to soar.

- **Some flying fish** have four 'wings'. In addition to large pectoral fins, these species also have large pelvic fins.

- **When threatened**, flying fish build up speed under the water's surface by thrashing their tails and holding their fins close to the body. The fish then leap into the air and glide for about 20–30 seconds.

- **Flying fish can leap** to a height of about 180 cm and cover a distance of over 150 m. In between glides, the fish returns to the water to gain more speed.

- **They can glide** at double the speed they swim, and are known to accelerate from 36 km/h in water to 72 km/h in air.

- **The ability of flying fish** to take off from the surface of the water and glide for some time help them to escape from sea predators like tuna and mackerel. But once in the air, they become the target of sea birds.

- **Young flying fish** look very different from their parents. The young ones have whiskers on their lower jaw, which disappear when they mature.

- **Flying fish** usually swim in schools. At times, a whole school leaps into the air and glides together.

▲ *Flying fish use their gliding ability effectively to escape predators.*

Clownfish

▲ *Clownfish not only help clean the anemone but also eat its dead tentacles.*

- **Clownfish** are also called anemonefish. These fish live a sheltered life among the tentacles of sea anemones. They can grow up to 13 cm in length.

- **There are around 28 species** of clownfish. The most popular is the percula clownfish, which is bright orange in colour with white bands.

- **Clownfish** are usually found in tropical waters. Since sea anemones are abundant in coral reefs, these fish can be found in the reefs of most oceans, the Red Sea and in the Great Barrier Reef in Australia.

- **Clownfish** got their name from the fact that their colour resembles the costumes of circus clowns. Most of them are bright orange or red, with white bands.

- **Clownfish** have a unique relationship with sea anemones. The anemone protects the fish from predators, while the fish returns the favour by keeping its host's tentacles clean.

- **The bright colours** of the clownfish lure other creatures to the anemone. Once the prey comes near, the anemone stings and feeds on it. The clownfish feeds on the anemone's leftovers.

- **The close relationship** that exists between a clownfish and sea anemones is called symbiosis. In such a relationship neither animal can survive without the other.

- **Clownfish** have a protective covering of mucus that keeps them safe from the tentacles of the sea anemones. This covering also prevents infections.

- **It is believed** that a sea anemone can sense the presence of a clownfish because of certain chemical substances released by the fish. This prevents the anemone from stinging one when it comes close.

- **Their bright colours** and playful nature make clownfish popular in aquariums.

Parrotfish

- **Parrotfish** are usually found near coral reefs. They have a long body with a rather large head.

- **Parrotfish** are usually about 1 m long. Some of them, such as the Indo-Pacific surf parrotfish, are much smaller, at around 45 cm.

- **The jaw teeth** of parrotfish are joined together to form a beak-like mouth. This beak is used to scrape algae and other food from coral reefs and rocks.

- **When a parrotfish** scrapes off algae from coral reefs bits of coral are also removed. Some of the coral bits are swallowed by the fish, to be excreted later in the form of silvery coral sand.

- **Parrotfish** also have grinding plates in their throat, with which they reduce food to fine powder. They are among the few herbivorous fish, eating only marine plants.

- **Parrotfish** are active during the day. At night, they sleep at the bottom of the reef. Some species even bury themselves in sand on the seabed and stay there until morning.

- **Sometimes parrotfish** surround themselves with a cocoon of mucus, or slime. Predators cannot detect the smell of the fish because of this mucus sac.

- **Parrotfish** rarely wander away from their coral home. But during the mating season, they establish a breeding territory in the deeper waters surrounding the reefs.

- **Most parrotfish** are born as females. But as they become older, these fish transform into males. Some even change colour when they change sex.

- **In Hawaii**, parrotfish are often eaten raw. However, they are more popular as ornamental fish.

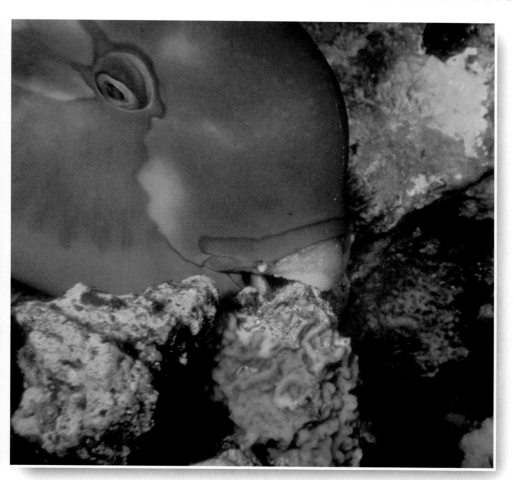

▲ *A parrotfish snaps off pieces of coral with its beak-like front teeth and then crunches the coral with its back teeth.*

Tuna and mackerel

- **Tuna and mackerel** belong to the *Scombridae* family. Both of them are fast swimmers. Their torpedo-shaped bodies coupled with crescent tails give these fish enough power to thrust through the water at great speeds.

- **Mackerel** have a sleek and shiny body with a large mouth. The head does not have any scales.

- **Huge schools of mackerel** can usually be found in cool waters, off the coasts of the northeast United States, Canada, Great Britain and Norway.

▼ *Unlike other ocean fish, tuna have pink flesh. This is because their blood can carry more oxygen. A mackerel's back shows a greeny-blue sheen, while its underside is pale, allowing it to camouflage itself and surprise its prey.*

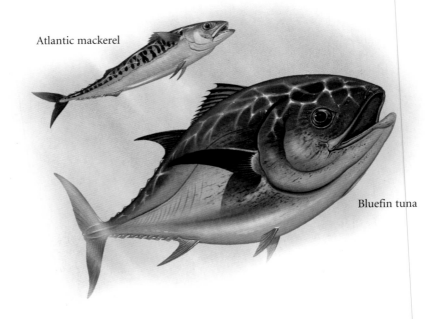

Atlantic mackerel

Bluefin tuna

- **Mackerel** remain close to the water surface and eat small crabs and fish.

- **The Atlantic mackerel** is the most common variety. It is blue and silver in colour and can grow up to half a metre long. Another equally well-known variety is the chub mackerel, found in the Pacific Ocean.

- **Tuna are found** in most parts of the world. They have a rounded structure and are sleeker than mackerel.

- **Tuna** require a lot of oxygen. These fish swim with their mouth open, shooting jets of water over their gills. The oxygen is extracted from this water. Because of this system of breathing, tuna can never remain still.

- **Unlike most fish**, tuna are not cold-blooded. They are able to maintain a body temperature that is a few degrees warmer than the surrounding water.

- **Tuna** swim in schools and can travel long distances. They come to coastal areas to lay eggs. The eggs usually hatch within 24 hours.

- **Bluefin tuna** are large marine fish. Adults weigh over 680 kg and can swim at a speed of about 90 km/h.

. . .FASCINATING FACT. . .
Tuna was sold as a canned product for the first time in 1914. Most consumers at the time thought that the meat tasted like chicken. Hence, the company that marketed canned tuna named their product 'Chicken of the Sea'.

Marlin

- **Marlin** are large sea fish, closely related to swordfish, sailfish and spearfish. Marlin and sailfish are also called billfish.

- **Sailfish** get their name from their sail-like dorsal fin. Able to swim at a speed of over 100 km/h, they are considered to be the fastest fish.

- **The dorsal fins** of marlin are smaller than those of the sailfish. But like sailfish and swordfish, marlin have snouts that are used for defence and attack.

- **The upper jaw** of marlin extends to form a long, rounded spear-like snout. Marlin use this snout to capture food.

- **The diet** of marlin consists of squid, herring, mackerel and crabs.

- **Marlin** are most abundant in the warm waters of the Atlantic and Pacific oceans.

- **Like sailfish,** marlin are fast swimmers and remain close to the ocean surface.

- **The blue marlin,** one of the largest species in the family, grows to a length of over 4.5 m. It is found mainly in the Gulf Stream, in the northern Atlantic Ocean.

- **The striped marlin** of the Pacific Ocean and the white marlin of the Atlantic are smaller varieties.

● **When caught**, marlin, particularly black marlin, leap into the air and fight vigorously to free themselves. This characteristic has made them popular game fish.

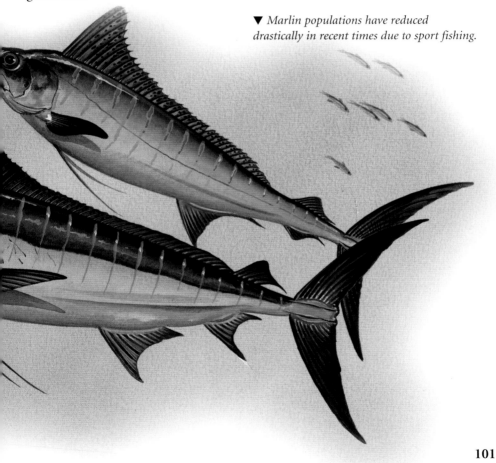

▼ *Marlin populations have reduced drastically in recent times due to sport fishing.*

Swordfish

- **Swordfish** are found in tropical and temperate waters. They are mostly dark in colour, but have a lighter coloured belly.

- **Swordfish** get their name from their upper jaw, which extends to form a long sword-like snout with a sharp point. This jaw does not have teeth.

- **The snout** is used for both defence and attack. It is believed that swordfish dash into schools of fish to injure or spear prey with the snout.

- **Like marlin and sailfish**, swordfish are good swimmers. They can swim very long distances in pursuit of prey.

- **Swordfish** have a crescent-shaped tail that is characteristic of fast swimmers belonging to the same family. However, unlike marlin, swordfish do not have pelvic fins.

- **Swordfish swim** near the surface of the water. Some species have been known to swim in schools, but most prefer to be alone.

- **Swordfish feed** on mackerel, herring and other small fish that swim in schools. Sometimes they dive deep into the ocean in search of sardine.

- **Swordfish** can grow over 4 m in length. Their 'sword' accounts for almost one third of their length. The jaws of a young swordfish are equal in length. The upper jaw grows longer with age.

▼ *Swordfish prefer to swim in water where ocean currents meet.*

- **When attacked**, swordfish can become very violent. It is believed that they can punch holes into small wooden boats. When they are wounded, they thrash about and can cause serious injury.

- **Swordfish** is a popular seafood. The swordfish population has decreased significantly because of overfishing.

103

Barracuda

- **Barracuda** are powerful predators. In some coastal regions, they are more feared than sharks.

- **Barracuda** are fierce-looking with an elongated head and a long, slender body. Their length varies from 40 cm to almost 2 m.

- **These powerful swimmers** are found in the tropical waters of the Pacific, Atlantic and Indian oceans.

- **The mouth of the barracuda** contains a number of fang-like teeth. These predators have a forked tail, and their dorsal fins are widely separated.

- **The great barracuda**, found in the Pacific and Atlantic oceans, grows to a length of 1.8 m and can be as heavy as 41 kg. Also called the 'tiger of the sea', this aggressive predator is known to attack divers and swimmers.

- **The diet of barracuda** includes sardine, anchovies and squid.

- **Smaller barracuda**, especially those found in the Pacific Ocean, swim and hunt in schools. The larger ones lead a solitary life and hunt alone.

- **Barracuda** are often compared with sharks because of their aggressive nature. But unlike sharks, barracuda do not attack their prey repeatedly.

...FASCINATING FACT...
Smaller barracudas are eaten by humans. The flesh of species, however, is poisonous because they feed on certain algae-eating smaller fish that are also poisonous. The barracuda are themselves immune to this poison.

- **Barracuda** are guided by their sense of sight rather than smell. Divers avoid wearing bright costumes that can attract these aggressive fish.

- **Their strength** and vigour have made barracuda extremely popular with anglers. Barracuda usually succeed in escaping from the fish hook, making the sport of game fishing more challenging.

▲ *Barracuda are fearsome predators, which seize, maim and tear up other fish with their fang-like teeth.*

Oarfish

- **Oarfish** are so called because of their elongated, oar-shaped body. They are also known as ribbon fish.

- **Oarfish** are deep-sea creatures and can be found in most oceans. They never come up to the surface of the sea.

- **Live oarfish** have rarely been sighted by humans. People usually see them after they die and are washed ashore.

- **Oarfish** have a bright red crest on the top of their head. This is the beginning of dorsal fin, which stretches like a ribbon along the entire length of their silvery body.

- **It is believed** that oarfish can raise and lower the crest on their head at will.

- **Oarfish** are considered to be the longest bony fish in the world. They usually grow to around 6 m in length, but some have been reported to reach over 16 m.

- **Common varieties** of oarfish include the king-of-the-herring and the streamer fish.

- **Oarfish** have a protruding mouth that is small compared to the rest of their body. They feed on smaller fish found near the bottom of the ocean.

- **It is believed** that the legend of the sea serpent originated from sightings of oarfish.

- **The long body** of the oarfish helps it move. The fish swims by swaying its body in a snake-like manner.

▲ *People once thought oarfish swam horizontally through the water. Now they know they swim upright.*

Eels

- **Eels are long**, slender, snake-like fish that live in shallow coastal waters around the world. Most eels live in the sea. However, a few are also found in freshwater.

- **Eels are normally** found among coral reefs and on the ocean floor. There are about 690 species of eels. The most common types include, the conger, moray and gulper eels.

- **Most species** of eel are around 1 m long. However, the conger eel can grow up to 3 m in length.

- **Eels do not have a tail fin**. Their dorsal fin, which runs along the top of the body, makes up for it and provides them with the power to swim.

- **Most eels** do not have scales on their body. Some species, however, have tiny scales. The body of most eels is covered with a slippery layer of mucus.

- **Some moray eels** can grow quite large. A species found in the Pacific Ocean has been known to grow over 3.5 m in length. There are about 100 different species of moray eels.

- **Eels are graceful swimmers** but are not very fast. Some species, like the American eel, can breathe through their skin and can survive for some time out of water.

- **Gulper eels** live at a depth of almost 1000 m. Since light does not reach these parts of the ocean, they have very small eyes or none at all. These eels swim with their mouths open, ready to gulp down any creature that comes their way.

- **Freshwater eels** travel to the sea to lay eggs. The adults dive deep into the sea to breed and then die.

- **The eggs of freshwater eels** hatch into leaf-shaped larvae that drift about for almost four years. Once they mature, the young eels, called elvers, swim back to the rivers, where they live until it is time for them to breed.

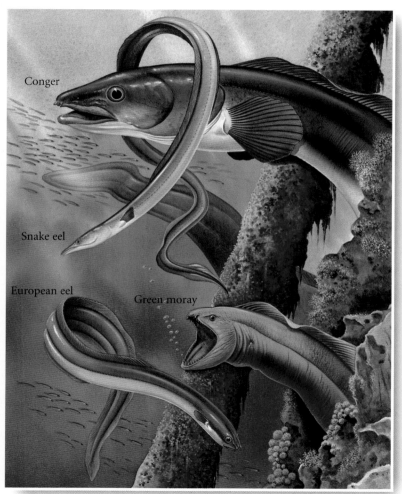

Conger

Snake eel

European eel

Green moray

◀ *There are more than 600 species of eels that are broadly divided into 19 families. Of these, 18 live in the oceans, while one spends part of its life in fresh water.*

Herring

- **Herring** are a family of small, silvery marine fish that swim in large schools. They are often found in the temperate, shallow waters of the North Atlantic and the North Pacific.

- **Herring** feed on small fish and plankton. They are, in turn, an important part of the diet of larger creatures such as sharks, seals, whales and seabirds.

- **There are over 360 species** in the herring family, which includes fish such as sardines, anchovies, shad, menhaden and sprats.

- **Sardines** get their name from an island in the Mediterranean, called Sardinia. The fish was once abundant near the coast of this island.

- **The name sardine** refers to various small fish canned with oil or sauce. In the United States, it is another name for herring. However, the true sardine is the young of the pilchard, found off the Mediterranean and Atlantic coasts.

- **The body of herring** is streamlined, making them excellent swimmers. Most herring, sardines and anchovies are less than 90 cm in length.

- **The Atlantic herring** is the best-known variety. The term 'herring' is often applied to this particular variety. The Atlantic herring is believed to be the most abundant species of fish in the world.

> **...FASCINATING FACT...**
> The term 'red herring' in detective novels is derived from the smoked and salted processed version of the fish, which takes on reddish hues. Since it gives off a very strong smell, it used to be drawn across hunting trails to confuse dogs. 'Red herring' refers to something that distracts.

- **Atlantic herring** are bluish green in colour, with a silvery underside. The Pacific herring is quite similar to the Atlantic herring.

- **The wolf herring** is the largest of the herring family. It is a fierce hunter and can grow to a length of 3 m.

- **Herring are processed** and sold in several forms. They can be smoked, dried, salted or pickled. Processed herring are sold as kippers, bloaters and red herring.

▶ *It is believed that herring swim in huge schools to increase their chances of survival.*

Seahorses

- **Seahorses** are tiny creatures that are very different from other fish in appearance. They get their name from their horse-shaped heads.

- **The size** of a seahorse ranges from less than a centimetre to about 13 cm. The common seahorse, found in the northern Atlantic Ocean, is the largest species.

- **Seahorses** have a long, snout-like mouth with tubular jaws and an elongated tail. Their only similarity to fish is the dorsal fin.

- **Seahorses** use their curly tails to attach themselves to coral branches and seaweeds. They swim very slowly by flapping their dorsal fin.

- **Seahorses** live close to seashores across the world. They eat small fish and plankton by swallowing them whole.

- **Instead of scales**, seahorses have a series of large rectangular bony plates. These plates protect them from predators, such as crabs.

- **The pencil-shaped pipefish** belongs to the same family as the seahorse. Like the seahorse, the pipefish too has a long snout with no teeth. It can grow up to a length of about 50 cm.

- **The seahorse family** consists of over 270 species. Others in this family include seadragons, shrimpfish, sea moths and trumpetfish.

- **A female lays** eggs in a pouch on the male's body. The male carries the eggs while they hatch and until the young seahorses are able to swim out through an opening in the pouch.

- **The Chinese** use seahorses to make traditional medicines. Seahorses are also valued as aquarium pets because of their unique shape and colours.

▲ *Seahorses exhibit beautiful, vibrant colours and are usually found swimming among coral reefs.*

Rays

- **Rays are cartilaginous fish**. Unlike bony fish, their skeletons are not made up of bones. Instead they are made of a tough, elastic tissue called cartilage.

- **Sharks and chimaeras**, or ratfish, belong to the same group of fish as rays.

- **Rays are found** in oceans across the world. Most rays live near the seabed. When in danger, they bury themselves in the sand.

▲ *The spotted eagle ray is identified by the distinct spots on its back, which can be white, yellow or green in colour.*

- **These fish** have broad, flat bodies. Their eyes are located on the upper surface of the body, while the mouth and gills are on the lower side.

- **Rays are usually brown** or black in colour, but their underside is lighter. Certain species change their colour to match the surroundings, which makes them hard to spot.

- **Some species** are less than 10 cm in width, while others measure over 6 m across. Manta rays are the biggest of all rays.

- **The pectoral fins** of rays are located just behind their heads. These huge, wing-like fins stretch from both sides of the head to the tail. The ray uses its 'wings' to swim through the water.

- **Rays' tails** vary in size and structure. While most rays have a long tail, some have a short, broad one. Rays use their tail as a rudder while swimming and also to defend themselves.

- **Different species** of rays have different forms of defence. The long, whip-like tail of the stingray has one or more sharp spines that inject poison into prey.

- **Most species** of rays feed on crustaceans, such as crabs, krill and shrimps. The manta ray, however, prefers to eat plankton.

. . . FASCINATING FACT . . .
The electric ray, also called the 'torpedo', has a pair of large electric organs between its head and pectoral fins. These organs can give powerful shocks, measuring up to 200 volts. These shocks can stun or even kill prey.

Sharks

- **Sharks** belong to the cartilaginous group of fish. There are over 350 species of sharks.

- **Sharks** are found in oceans across the world. Some sharks, like the bull shark, can also survive in fresh water.

- **Most sharks** have torpedo-shaped bodies, which make them very good swimmers. They also have large tail fins that give them extra power for swimming.

- **A shark's skin** is not covered with smooth scales like bony fish. Instead, its skin is covered with tiny, tooth-like structures called dermal denticles that give the skin a sandpaper-like quality.

- **Sharks** are the primary predators, or hunters, of the ocean. They have special abilities to locate prey. The great white shark, the most feared predator of all, can smell a drop of blood in 100 litres of water.

- **The whale shark** is the largest fish. It can grow up to 14 m in length. However, some species, like the spined pygmy shark, are no more than 20 cm long.

- **There are different shapes of shark**. Hammerheads have a T-shaped head, which helps them make sharp turns. Reef-dwelling sharks have a flat body.

- **The diet** of sharks includes seals, squids, fish and other marine creatures. Some sharks, like the whale shark and the basking shark, eat plankton and small fish.

- **Depending upon their diet**, sharks have different kinds of teeth. Some, like the great white and tiger sharks, have sharp pointed teeth that help them tear into their prey.

- **Certain species**, like the reef sharks, have flat plate-like teeth that can crush the hard shells of the animals they eat.

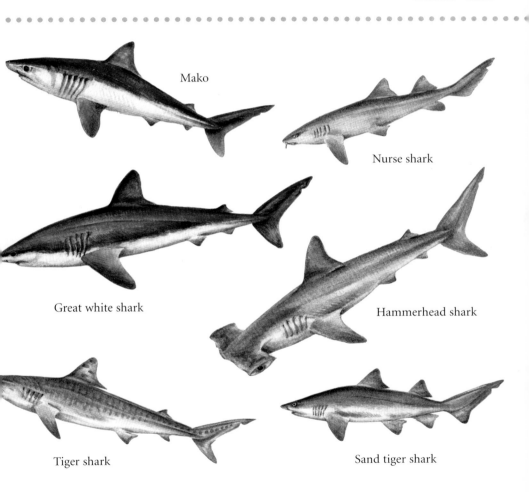

Mako

Nurse shark

Great white shark

Hammerhead shark

Tiger shark

Sand tiger shark

▲ *Six of the most dangerous sharks. All of these sharks have been known to attack people.*

Incredible hunters

▲ *When great white sharks feel threatened, they open their mouths wide to show off sharp teeth.*

- **Sharks** are considered the best hunters in the ocean. These creatures have strong senses that help them hunt and travel great distances.

- **The most powerful weapon** of a shark is its teeth. A shark can have as many as 3000 teeth set in three rows. The fish relies on the first row of teeth to strike the first blow. This first charge often injures or kills the prey.

- **Most sharks** have a very good sense of smell. It is believed that almost one-third of the brain is devoted to detecting smell.

- **Some bottom-dwelling sharks** have thick whisker-like projections on their snouts called nasal barbels. These organs help the shark to feel around for prey.

- **Sharks** also have good eyesight. Most of them hunt at night and, like cats, have enhanced night vision. In clear water, sharks can spot their prey from a distance of 15 m.

- **Sharks** do not have external ear flaps. Instead, their ears are inside their head, on either side of the brain case. Each ear leads to a small sensory pore on the shark's head.

- **It is believed** that sharks can hear over a distance of 250 m. They can detect sounds in the frequency of 25–100 Hz.

- **A pair of fluid-filled canals** runs down either side of the shark's body, from its head to its tail. This is the lateral line and helps the fish sense minute vibrations in the water.

- **The lateral line canals** are lined with tiny hair-like projections. These projections are triggered by even the slightest movement, which in turn alert the shark's brain.

- **Most sharks** can detect weak electric currents released by other creatures. They do this with tiny pores located on their snout, which lead to jelly-filled sacs called ampullae of Lorenzini.

...FASCINATING FACT...
Sharks, such as the great white and the blue shark, have a special membrane in their eyes called nictitating membrane. The shark can draw this membrane across its eyes at will. It protects the shark's eyes from being injured by thrashing prey during feeding.

Great white shark

- **The great white shark** is the largest predatory shark. It has a pointed snout and a large tail fin. Great whites are commonly found in temperate to warm waters.

- **The great white shark** is actually grey or bluish grey in colour, with a white underbelly. The great white is also known as 'white pointer' and 'white death'.

- **One of the biggest of all sharks**, the great white, is normally about 4.5 m in length. However, it is believed that some can grow as long as 6 m.

- **Great white sharks** have around 3000 sharp teeth with serrated, or saw-like, edges. The shark's teeth can grow up to 7.5 cm long.

- **The diet** of this shark includes sea lions, seals and sea turtles. Young great whites eat fish, rays and other smaller sharks.

- **Great white sharks** do not chew their food. They use their sharp teeth to rip the prey into small pieces that are then swallowed whole.

- **The shark usually** approaches prey, such as seals, from below. Sometimes, while chasing seals, the shark leaps out of water. This is called breaching.

- **Unlike other sharks**, great whites do not have a gas-filled swim bladder to keep them afloat. Therefore, they have to keep swimming to stay afloat.

- **The great white shark** does not lay eggs like other fish. The eggs remain inside the female's body until they hatch. The shark then gives birth to live young.

> ...FASCINATING FACT...
> The great white shark is feared because of its reputation as a man-eater. Although the reports of great white attacks are true, the shark has been responsible for only 58 deaths since 1876!

● **A surfer**, when viewed from below, looks very similar to a seal – the favourite food of the great white. Most biologists believe that this is the reason for great white attacks on surfers.

▲ *The massive great white shark has been reported to have attacked boats, even sinking one near Nova Scotia, Canada.*

Tiger shark

▲ *The tiger shark is big and powerful. It could swallow this monk seal in one gulp.*

- **Tiger sharks** are dark grey in colour, with an off-white belly. They get their name from the dark stripes on their back, which become lighter as the sharks grow older.

- **The tiger shark** has a large, pointed tail fin. This provides it with the extra power that it needs to chase prey. The tiger shark also has a thick body and a blunt snout.

- **Tiger sharks** are found in both tropical and temperate waters. They are most common in the Indian and Pacific oceans and the Caribbean Sea. After great whites, tiger sharks are the second most feared sharks in the world.

- **The average length** of a tiger shark is about 3 m. Some can grow as long as 6 m. They are rarely attacked by other sharks because of their size.

- **The mouth** of the tiger shark is large, with powerful jaws. The shark has three rows of curved, triangular teeth with saw-like edges.

- **Old or broken teeth** are immediately replaced with new ones. It is believed that an average tiger shark can produce over 20,000 teeth in just ten years!

- **Tiger sharks** are largely nocturnal and usually hunt at night. These sharks have a good sense of smell and keen eyesight that aids them in hunting.

- **These sharks** have excellent electro-receptors that can detect even the slightest movements in water. This helps them to locate prey even in dark, murky waters.

- **Tiger sharks** eat almost anything – from fish and turtles to seals, seabirds and other sharks. People have found tins cans, deer antlers and even shoes in the stomach of dead tiger sharks.

- **A slit-like opening** behind each eye, called the spiracle, helps the tiger shark breathe. The spiracle passes oxygen directly to the eyes and brain, improving the shark's reflexes.

▶ *Tiger sharks leave their newborn pups to fend for themselves.*

123

Whale shark

▲ *The whale shark has patterns of light spots and stripes on a dark body. These help the shark to blend into its surroundings.*

- **Whale sharks** are the largest fish in the world. They are not aggressive and pose no threat to humans.

- **Whale sharks** prefer to live in warm tropical waters and are found in many areas across the world. They are rarely found in temperate waters.

- **The average length** of a whale shark is about 14 m. However, some have been known to grow to over 18 m in length.

- **These gentle giants** are also very heavy. An average adult whale shark weighs about 15 tonnes. Owing to their size, these sharks cannot move fast. They swim by moving their enormous bodies from side to side.

- **Whale sharks** are dark-grey or brown in colour and their underside is off-white. They have white dots and lines on their backs.

- **The mouth** of the whale shark is extremely large and can be as wide as 1.4 m. They have around 300 rows of tiny, hook-like teeth in each jaw.

- **These sharks** move about with their mouths open and suck in vast quantities of water, rich in plankton. Special bristles attached to the gills filter the tiny prey, while the water is thrown out through the gill slits.

- **Whale sharks** have a huge appetite. They feed mainly on plankton, sardines, krill and anchovies.

- **These sharks** also love to eat fish eggs. They are known to wait for hours at breeding grounds to capture freshly laid eggs. They are even known to return to the same mating grounds year after year during the breeding season.

- **Sometimes**, whale sharks can be seen swimming in schools. However, they usually travel alone.

Basking and megamouth shark

- **Basking sharks** are similar to whale sharks but slightly smaller. Their average length is around 10 m, but some species grow up to 13 m.

- **Like whale sharks**, basking sharks have filters on their gills, which trap prey while they draw in water. These sharks also feed on plankton and small fish.

- **Basking sharks** are greyish-brown or black with an off-white belly. Found in temperate coastal waters around the world, these sharks get their name from the fact that they spend most of their time at the surface of the water, appearing to 'bask' in the Sun.

- **Unlike whale sharks** that swim alone, basking sharks have been known to swim in schools of up to 100 fish.

- **Basking sharks** have more teeth than most sharks. Their gaping mouths can accommodate as many as 1500 teeth!

- **The megamouth shark** gets its name from the fact that it has a large head and a huge mouth. This deepwater shark can be found in the Indian and Pacific oceans.

- **Thought to be less active**, megamouth sharks are even slower than the basking shark. It is believed that a flabby body and soft fins are responsible for its poor mobility.

- **The megamouth shark** was first discovered in 1976 and only 18 sightings of the shark have been reported since then.

  - **Like basking sharks**, megamouth sharks are also filter feeders. Both these species are related to the great white shark.

    - **The megamouth** is so rare that not much is known about its habits. However, like the basking shark, this species is harmless to humans.

▼ *The megamouth shark is so different from other sharks that is was classified under its own, unique name* – Megachasmidae.

Sharks of the seabed

- **Carpet sharks** are bottom-dwelling sharks. They have beautiful patterns on their skin that help them blend in with their surroundings. Most of these sharks are found near coral reefs.

- **Wobbegong sharks**, nurse sharks, zebra sharks, bamboo sharks and collared carpet sharks belong to this group.

- **The whale shark** is another carpet shark. However, unlike its relatives, it is not a bottom-dweller.

- **Some species**, such as bamboo sharks and collared carpet sharks, use their wide fins to 'walk' on the seabed.

- **The wobbegong** has a flat body and is very sluggish. It has fringes and tassels on its body that that make it look like rocks covered with seaweed. This shark waits motionless until the prey comes close and then grabs it.

- **Like wobbegongs**, angel sharks are found near the seabed. Their large and wing-like pectoral fins make angel sharks look very similar to rays.

- **Angel sharks** are found in warm waters where food is abundant. Their size varies from 1.5 to 2 m.

- **Like wobbegongs**, angel sharks are also camouflage specialists. These sharks bury themselves in the sand. Only their eyes and a part of their head can be seen. When prey approaches, the shark lunges at it.

- **Angel sharks** like to eat fish, crabs, lobsters and squid. They are harmless to humans but can deliver a painful bite with their sharp teeth if disturbed.

- **The eggs** of the angel shark are contained in a purse-like casing that is commonly known as a mermaid's purse. The colour of the eggs matches that of the surroundings.

▼ *The wobbegong has green, yellow, or brown skin. This helps it hide among the rocks and seaweed on the seabed. It can grab any passing fish to eat.*

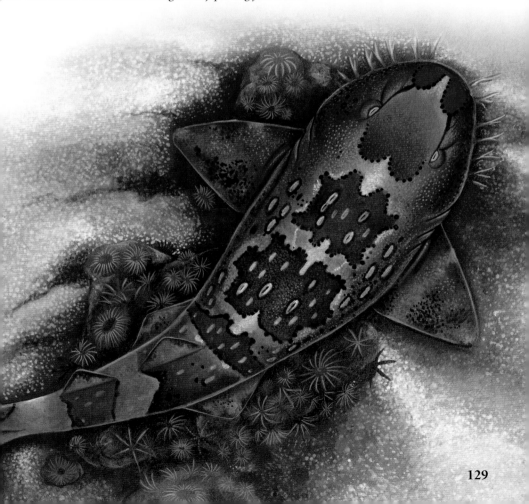

Hammerhead shark

▲ *A scalloped hammerhead shark cruises across a coral reef – an underwater structure built by tiny creatures called coral polyps.*

- **Hammerhead sharks** have a thick, wide hammer-shaped head. Their eyes are located on either side of this T-shaped head.

- **The head contains** tiny receptors that detect the prey. Its unusual shape also helps the shark to take sharp turns.

- **The hammerhead** is common in tropical and temperate waters. It is grey or brown in colour, with an off-white belly. This shark migrates towards warmer waters near the Equator in winter.

- **The first dorsal fin** of the hammerhead, which is located on its back, is large and pointed. Like most sharks, it can be seen cutting through the water surface, as the hammerhead cruises along.

- **The great hammerhead** is the largest in the hammerhead family. It can measure up to 4 m in length. Bonnethead sharks are smaller and have a shovel-like head.

- **Hammerhead sharks** normally feed on fish, smaller sharks, squid and octopuses. Stingrays, however, are their favourite food.

- **The great hammerhead** is an excellent hunter. It uses its highly developed senses of smell and direction to track prey.

- **Large teeth** enable the great hammerhead to bite big chunks off its prey.

- **Other varieties of hammerhead** sharks include the scalloped and the smooth hammerhead. Both types are found in moderately temperate waters.

- **Most hammerheads** are harmless, but the great hammerhead is one of the few dangerous species. It is known to have attacked humans.

Lemon shark

- **Lemon sharks** are often confused with bull sharks because of their short snout. Like bull sharks, they are stocky and have big eyes.

- **These sharks** are found in the Atlantic and Pacific oceans and prefer to live in sub-tropical waters. They are found in abundance in the Caribbean Sea.

- **Lemon sharks** get their name from their colour. The upper part of the body is deep yellow or yellowish-brown. The belly is either off-white or cream.

- **Most lemon sharks** are found near the shore. Sometimes they are known to even venture into river mouths, bays and slightly salty or brackish waters, such as mangrove systems.

- **The average length** of a lemon shark is 2–2.5 m. It can grow up to a maximum length of 3 m.

- **Lemon sharks** feed on small sharks, crabs, shrimps, stingrays and eagle rays. They have also been known to prey on seabirds.

- **These sharks** are bottom-dwelling creatures and can keep still near the seabed waiting for prey.

- **Their long**, thin and sharp teeth allow the lemon shark to easily bite into the flesh of slippery prey, such as squid.

- **Young lemon sharks** lose an entire set of teeth, one at a time, every seven to eight days. The lost teeth are replaced quickly.

- **Some people**, especially in China and Japan, eat lemon shark. The fins are used to make sharp fin soup – a delicacy in China.

▲ *Lemon sharks really are lemon in colour. This helps to distinguish them from bull sharks, which are their close relatives.*

Blue shark

▲ *Blue sharks make the longe.*
migrations and can cover a
distance of more than 6000 km
in one year.

...FASCINATING FACT...
When swimming at great speeds, the body temperature
of blue sharks can rise almost 10° C above the
temperature of the surrounding water.

- **The blue shark** is sleek with a long, pointed snout and large eyes. Its body is deep blue in colour with pale blue sides and a white belly.

- **This shark** is also called the blue whaler because of its tendency to be present at the scenes of whale kills, to scavenge on the remains of dead whales.

- **The blue shark** is one of the most abundant of all shark species. It prefers to live in the open sea and swim close to the surface. Blue sharks are found in tropical, sub-tropical, and temperate waters.

- **The average length** of a blue shark is nearly 3 m. The largest ones can grow to 3.8 m.

- **Its streamlined body** makes the blue shark the most graceful swimmer in the shark world. It has a long, pointed tail fin that gives it more power while swimming.

- **The blue shark** can swim as fast as 37 km/h, making it one of the fastest marine creatures. In fact, it is second only to the mako in terms of speed.

- **The diet** of the blue shark includes small fish and squid. These sharks have long saw-edged teeth, which help them grip the squid and other slippery animals.

- **The blue shark** is one of the larger ocean predators. However, it is hunted by other sharks, such as the great white and shortfin mako.

- **Blue sharks** are not very aggressive. They are not considered harmful to humans, but they have been known to attack injured victims of air or sea disasters.

- **Blue sharks migrate** the longest distance of any shark, travelling across the Atlantic Ocean each year.

Nurse shark

- **Nurse sharks** belong to the carpet shark group. They are bottom-dwellers and hunt mainly at night.

- **There are several theories** regarding the origins of the nurse shark's name. According to one, it was derived from the word 'nusse', a name that was used to describe cat sharks. Originally, the nurse shark was thought to belong to this group.

- **Nurse sharks** have cat-like whiskers on their jaws, which is why they were initially categorized in the cat shark group. In the Caribbean region, the shark is still called *tiburon gato*, meaning cat shark.

- **The cat-like whiskers** of the nurse shark are called nasal barbels. These barbels are used for locating prey in the sand.

- **Nurse sharks** can be found in tropical and the sub-tropical waters in the Atlantic Ocean and eastern Pacific Ocean. They live mostly in coastal areas.

- **The nurse shark** has a large, stout body, which is dark brown or grey in colour. Its average length is 2.2–2.7 m. Some can grow up to 4 m.

- **Nurse sharks** have small openings behind each eye. These openings, called spiracles, help the shark to breathe while eating or resting on the seabed.

> **. . . FASCINATING FACT . . .**
> The nurse shark used to be hunted extensively at one time.
> Its liver oil was often used as fuel. The oil was also used by sponge
> fishers to locate sponges on the ocean floor. It was believed that the
> oil could calm the water surface, thus helping the fishermen to see
> clearly through it to the bottom.

- **During the day**, nurse sharks rest on the sandy seabed or in caves. They are known to live in the same shelter during their lifetime.

- **The nurse shark has a unique** way of feeding. It sucks its prey in at high speed.

- **The diet of the nurse shark** comprises fish and crustaceans, such as shrimps and crabs. The shark has sharp teeth that are capable of crushing hard shells.

▲ *A diver creeps close to a nurse shark to get a closer look. The shark is hiding in a gap in a coral reef, a favourite habit of nurse sharks.*

Bull shark

▲ *This bull shark is accompanied by a remora fish, which attaches itself to the shark. In return for ridding the shark's skin of parasites, the remora gets protection and scraps of food from its host.*

...FASCINATING FACT...
Most bull sharks are not migratory, but the South American bull shark travels thousands of miles from the Amazon River to the Atlantic Ocean.

- **Bull sharks** are among the most feared fish in coastal regions. They get their name from their stocky build. They are heavy-bodied and have wide, blunt snouts.

- **These sharks are** very aggressive and live in relatively shallow coastal waters. They have two dorsal fins and, as in all sharks, the first one is more pointed.

- **These are the only sharks** that can be found in rivers and freshwater lakes. They have been reported to travel a great distance upstream in warm rivers, such as the Mississippi and the Amazon.

- **Bull sharks** are known by various names around the world. Some of these names are Ganges shark, Nicaragua shark, freshwater and Swan River whaler, Zambezi shark and Van Rooyen's shark.

- **On average**, bull sharks measure up to 2 m in length. The females are much larger than the males.

- **Bull sharks** are also responsible for attacks on humans, after great whites and tiger sharks.

- **The diet** of these sharks includes a wide variety of creatures. They eat rays, turtles, crabs, dolphins, seabirds, other sharks and even dogs.

- **Bull sharks** are not fast swimmers because of their bulk. However, they are capable of touching speeds of more than 19 km/h in short bursts.

- **Adult bull sharks** do not have natural enemies. But the young fall prey to larger sharks, including other bull sharks.

- **These sharks** are rarely hunted for their meat. However, the hide is used to make leather products, while the fins are used to make shark fin soup.

Sawshark

- **Sawsharks** have flat bodies and long, saw-like snouts, lined with small, sharp teeth. The snout can measure up to one third of the shark's body.

- **These sharks** live in warm and temperate waters around the world. They are abundant in the Gulf of Mexico and the coastal waters of the Indian Ocean.

- **Sawsharks** normally keep close to the coastline and can even be found in lagoons, river mouths and bays. They are bottom-dwellers.

- **The average length** of a sawshark is less than 2 m. Its body is blue or grey in colour, with an off-white belly.

- **Sawsharks** use their snout to injure their prey. It is believed that these sharks move their heads from side to side, swiping at the prey.

- **The sawshark's snout** is also used to dislodge hidden prey from the seabed. This shark eats small fish, squid, shrimps, crabs and other crustaceans.

- **Unlike the nurse shark**, the nasal barbels of the sawshark are located towards the tip of the snout instead of near the mouth. These barbels help the shark to detect hidden prey.

- **The saw-like snout** of a sawshark pup lacks sharp teeth and is covered with a protective membrane. This ensures that the mother is not injured during birth.

- **Sawsharks** are harmless and normally do not attack humans. However, divers have been injured accidentally by the snout.

- **In Japan**, the meat of the sawshark is used to make *kamaboko*, a traditional Japanese fishcake. The saw-like snout is often sold to collectors.

▼ *A sawshark may lose and re-grow as many as 30,000 teeth during its lifetime.*

Thresher shark

▲ *A thresher flicks its tail like an underwater whip, bashing small fish to stun or wound them. Then the thresher snaps them up in its mouth.*

- **The thresher shark** is easily identified by its long, whip-like tail fin, which often exceeds the length of its body.

- **Thresher sharks** can be found in tropical and cold-temperate waters around the world, but are most common in temperate waters. The common thresher is the most abundant species of them all.

- **These sharks** are very shy and usually stay far away from the shore, but at times they swim close to the surface of coastal waters in search of food.

- **The average length** of a thresher shark is 5–5.5 m, but some species can grow up to 7 m. It is dark blue or grey in colour with an off-white belly.

- **Thresher sharks** are very good swimmers. Like all fast swimmers, they can maintain a higher body temperature than their surroundings.

- **The thresher's** favourite food includes fish that swim in schools, such as herring, mackerel, bluefish and butterfish. They also eat squid.

- **This shark** gets its name from the way it hunts. Since its teeth are smaller than those of other sharks, the thresher cannot use them to bite into its prey. So it uses its tail to kill prey.

- **The shark** first encircles schools of fish. It then stuns the prey by hitting it with its tail. Thresher sharks are also known to have attacked seabirds with their long tails.

- **Thresher sharks** hunt in groups or in pairs. They are nocturnal creatures, hunting at night.

- **These sharks** are extremely shy and are considered harmless to humans. However, they have been known to attack boats. Apart from their meat and fins, thresher sharks are also fished for their hide and liver oil.

Port Jackson shark

- **The Port Jackson** shark belongs to the family of horn sharks. All sharks in this family have horn-like spines on their dorsal fins, hence the name.

- **Other species** in the horn shark family include Galapagos horn sharks, crested horn sharks, Californian horn sharks and zebra horn sharks. Of the eight species of horn shark, Port Jackson sharks are the best known.

- **Port Jackson sharks** are most commonly found off the coast of Australia. They are usually grey in colour with brown or green tints. The upper part of the body has dark brown or black bands on it.

- **These horn sharks** were named after Sydney Harbour, which was originally known as Port Jackson. The shark was first discovered in this area.

- **Port Jackson sharks** are not very large and can grow to a length of 1.7 m. They have a small, blunt snout.

- **These sharks are bottom-dwelling** creatures and prefer to live near coral reefs or seaweed, where food is abundant.

- **Port Jackson sharks** hunt at night. During the day, they rest in large numbers in sheltered areas like caves and reefs.

- *Heterodontus*, the scientific name of the Port Jackson shark, means 'different tooth'. This shark, like all the others in the family, has spiky front teeth, which it uses to hunt and hold its prey.

- **Port Jackson sharks** eat reef-dwelling creatures such as crabs, oysters and sea snails. Flat teeth-plates at the rear of their jaws help them to crush hard shells.

- **These sharks** are also known as pigfish because of their blunt snout. In some parts of the world they are called oyster-crushers as they can crush hard oyster shells.

▲ *The female Port Jackson shark lays about 10–16 corkscrew-shaped eggs, which she then wedges into crevices of rocks so that they are not washed away.*

Reef shark

- **Reef sharks**, as their name suggests, live close to coral reefs. They are most common in the shallow tropical waters of the Indian and Pacific oceans.

- **There are three main species** of reef sharks. These are the black-tip, the white-tip and the grey reef sharks.

- **The black-tip reef shark** lives in shallow waters. The tips of the fins are marked black and a white streak runs along their body. They have a blunt snout.

- **These sharks feed** on squid, octopuses and reef fish, such as sturgeon and millet. Black-tip reef sharks are often seen in groups.

- **The average length** of a black-tip reef shark is 1.5–2 m. Although they are not very large, they can become aggressive when disturbed.

- **White-tip reef sharks** have a body structure similar to that of black-tips. However, unlike black-tips, they have a white-tipped dorsal fin.

- **White-tips** have sharp teeth and feed on reef fish such as parrotfish, triggerfish and eels.

- **White-tip reef sharks** spend most of their time resting at the bottom of the ocean. They are not as aggressive as other reef sharks.

- **Grey reef sharks** are larger and more aggressive than the other two reef sharks. They can grow up to 2.5 m in length. These sharks dwell in deeper waters.

● **The diet** of a grey reef shark includes squid, octopuses, shrimps and lobsters. Grey reef sharks are night hunters. During the day they spend hours resting near the seabed.

▼ *White-tip reef sharks sleep by day in caves ou under rocks. At night, they go their separate ways and swim off to hunt.*

Squid and cuttlefish

- **Squid** are soft-bodied animals. Like cuttlefish and octopuses, squid belong to a group of molluscs called cephalopods. All of them are fierce predators.

- **All squid** have ten tentacles, or arms, two of which are long and slender. All the tentacles have suckers at the ends. They are used to grab prey.

- **These creatures** can swim very fast. They move by releasing jets of water through a fleshy tube called a siphon, located near the head.

- **When in danger**, the squid shoots out a cloud of dark, ink-like liquid. This hinders the attacker's vision, allowing the squid to escape.

- **The diet of a squid** includes fish, crabs, shrimps as well as smaller squid. Predators of squid include whales, sharks and big fish. Squidis also a popular food for humans.

- **The giant squid** is not only the biggest of all squid, it is also the largest animal without a backbone. Its eyes, which measure more than 40 cm across, are also the largest among all animals.

- **The cuttlefish** looks like a small, flattened squid. It has a fin that runs around the entire length of its body.

- **Like squid**, a cuttlefish also have ten tentacles, eight of which are small. Cuttlefish move in the same way as squid, releasing jets of water for short bursts of speed.

> **...FASCINATING FACT...**
> Giant squid can measure around 18 m in length.
> They live in the deep seas. A live giant squid is a rare sight.
> Their main enemy is the sperm whale.

● **The skin** of the cuttlefish has tiny spots of various colours. Using special muscles, the cuttlefish can control the size of these spots.

● **Cuttlefish** have a bone called the cuttlebone, which is rich in calcium. It is sold in pet shops as bird food. In some parts of the world, people eat cuttlefish.

▶ *Cuttlefish are also known as 'chameleons of the sea', due to their ability to change colour according to their surroundings.*

Octopuses

- **Octopuses belong** to the *Cephalopoda* group that includes squid and cuttlefish. They have soft, sack-like bodies and large eyes that can distinguish colours.

- **These marine creatures** vary in size. Most octopuses are, on an average, one metre long. The giant octopus, however, grows over 7 m in length.

- **The most striking feature** of the octopus is its eight arms, or tentacles. Each tentacle has two rows of suckers, which help the octopus not only to hold its prey, but also climb rocks.

- **Octopuses** use their arms to seize prey and pull it towards their mouth. They secrete poisonous saliva to paralyse the prey and chew it using their jaws.

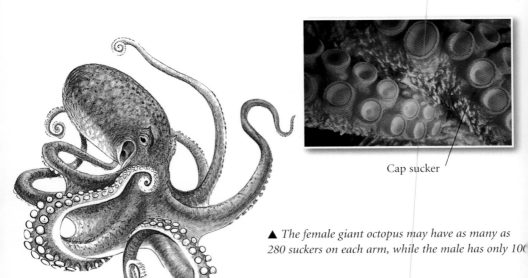

Cap sucker

▲ *The female giant octopus may have as many as 280 suckers on each arm, while the male has only 100*

- **The main diet** of the octopus consists of crabs and lobsters. Some species feed on small shellfish and plankton. They are, in turn, eaten by moray eels and sharks among other creatures.

- **Octopuses are considered** to be the most intelligent animals without a backbone, or invertebrates. They can recognize various shapes and are known to have a good memory. They can even work out how to open a jar.

- **These creatures** are largely bottom-dwellers and live in small coves. They create a pile of debris in front of their hiding nook to protect themselves. The Atlantic pygmy octopus lives in clam shells.

- **The octopus can change** colour quickly to camouflage itself. Some species produce fake eye-spots when alarmed, while others use colours and lights to lure prey.

- **Like squid**, some octopuses produce a dark ink-like fluid when in danger. Apart from clouding the predator's vision, the fluid is also believed to paralyse it.

- **The blue-ringed octopus**, found in the Indian and Pacific oceans, has a very poisonous bite. When threatened, the blue rings on its body glow brightly to warn the predator.

> **...FASCINATING FACT...**
> Octopuses have a well-developed brain and the most advanced nervous system amongst invertebrates. Their nerve fibres are about 50 times thicker than human nerve fibres.

Sea snails and sea slugs

▲ *Snails belong to the class* Gastropoda, *which means 'belly-footed animals'.*

- **Sea snails** are small, soft-bodied animals. They live inside coiled shells and move very slowly.

- **There are over 50,000 kinds** of sea snails. These include whelks, limpets, top shells, winkles, cowries and cone shells.

- **Some sea snails** live along the coast, in rock pools and shallow water, while others live on the deep ocean floor. Unlike land snails, sea snails are very colourful.

- **Sea snails swim** or float along with the ocean currents. They use their muscular foot, or lower part of the body, for crawling over the seabed.

- **Most sea snails** have four tentacles on their heads. One pair helps them to feel their way around, while the other often has eyes at the tip. Some species do not have eyes at all.

- **These creatures** have a tongue-like organ called the radula that consists of numerous tiny teeth. Some sea snails use the radula to pierce the shells of small animals.

- **Like sea snails**, sea slugs also have a soft and slimy body. However, their body is not enclosed in a hard shell.
- **Most sea slugs** have tentacles to sense prey. They eat algae, small snails and sea anemones. Some of them also feed off corals.
- **They are very colourful creatures**. Because they do not have a shell, sea slugs have developed various forms of defence. Some feed on poisonous sponges and develop toxins of their own.
- **Some sea slugs** have long, hair-like tentacles on their backs. These tentacles often carry stings or fluids that taste foul. Certain species feed on corals to acquire their colour patterns. This helps them blend in with their surroundings.

▶ *The yellow-spotted sea slug is one of the rarest species of sea slugs. Its brilliant red body covered with bright yellow spots is hard to miss.*

Mussels

- **Several species** of freshwater and marine mussels are found around the world. They are usually wedge-shaped or pear-shaped and are 5–15 cm long.

- **Mussels** are known as bivalves because they have two shells enclosing their soft and delicate body. Others in this group include oysters, clams, scallops and cockles.

- **Mussels** breathe with the help of their gills. The gills have hair-like filaments, called cilia, over which water passes. The cilia are also used to capture food.

- **Mussels** are filter feeders that feed on planktonic plants and animals. In some areas mussels are so plentiful that this filtering action actually clears the normally turbid water..

- **Most mussels** have a strong and muscular tongue-shaped foot that extends from their body and sometimes remains outside their shells. They use this foot to dig.

- **Towards the end** of the foot lies the byssus gland, or pit, which produces a tough thread. The mussel uses this thread to attach itself to various surfaces such as rocks.

- **Mussels** are known to defend themselves by tying down predators, such as snails, with their byssus threads.

- **Some mussels** also use their hard shells to dig. They can drill holes into the wooden planks of ships.

- **Mussels** often attach themselves to one another and form colonies or beds. Such formations are very common in the Wadden Sea, off the coast of Denmark.

- **Pearls** are obtained from certain species of mussels. Those obtained from the pinctada pearl oysters are considered among the most valuable.

▲ *Concentric rings can be seen on the shells of mussels. These creatures have strong muscles to help them open and close their shells.*

155

Clams

▲ *A giant clam may grow over 1.5 m in length and weigh as much as 227 kg.*

- **Clams** are soft-bodied animals. They belong to the same group as mussels, the bivalves, and are found across the world.

- **Like other bivalves**, clams have two shells covering their body. Some clams can close their shells tightly when in danger.

- **Clams** have a single muscular foot that helps in digging. They use this foot to burrow into the sand.

- **Most clams** are small in size, but the giant clam can be over 1.5 m long. Giant clams are common in the depths of the Pacific Ocean, especially among coral reefs.

- **The largest pearl** in the world was found in a giant clam shell. It was about 12 cm in diameter.

- **Geoducks** are another variety of clams. They can be over 20 cm in length. They burrow deep into the sand and can extend a long siphon to collect food.

- **Unlike geoducks,** hard-shell clams do not burrow very deep. They are also called northern quahogs and found to the north of the Atlantic Ocean. Southern quahogs have bigger shells than their northern counterparts.

- **Razor clams** have thin and elongated shells that resemble a razor. They are found near sandy beaches, and are very fast diggers.

- **Soft-shell clams** are also known as steamer clams. They have long, brittle shells that do not cover their entire body. Their neck hangs out from the shell.

- **Clams** are eaten across the world and are, therefore, fished extensively. Clam farms have been set up in several countries, and these help to protect the natural populations.

Barnacles

- **Barnacles** are tiny crustaceans found in oceans, seas and lakes across the world.

- **The body** of a barnacle is covered with a hard shell made up of plate-like structures. The number of these plates varies from species to species.

- **Most barnacles** are around 1.5–2 cm across. However, the diadem whale barnacle grows to 6.5 cm. This species attaches itself to whales.

- **Their long feather-like limbs,** or cirri, help barnacles to trap tiny food particles. They mainly feed on plankton.

- **Apart from rocks,** seaweeds, reefs, driftwood and ships, barnacles also attach themselves to the bodies of whales, turtles and other marine animals.

- **Some barnacles** are tiny, parasitic organisms. They attach themselves to creatures such as crabs and feed off them.

- **Acorn barnacles** use their plates to hold on to a surface. They are commonly seen on rocks along the seashore and in shallow water.

- **In addition** to their shell-like plates, goose barnacles have muscular, stalk-like structures. These help the creatures to attach themselves to floating objects, such as driftwood.

- **Whelks are the most common** predators of barnacles. They can drill a hole through the barnacle's shell and eat the flesh inside. Mussels also feed on barnacles.

- **Barnacles** are a great nuisance to mariners. These crustaceans often attach themselves to the bottoms of ships and boats, thus increasing fuel consumption. A lot of time and money is spent removing them from the hulls.

▲ *Barnacles attach themselves to hard surfaces underwater, such as rocks and other marine creatures, and are commonly found on the hulls of ships and boats.*

159

Crabs

- **The oceans** of the world are home to a group of joint-limbed creatures, or arthropods, called crustaceans. This group includes crabs, lobsters, shrimps and barnacles.

- **Crabs** are the most well-known of all crustaceans. They have a flat body covered by a hard shell. There are over 5000 species of crabs.

- **Most crabs** live in the sea, but a few species can be found in fresh water. The common shore crab can live in both salty and fresh water. It can even stay out of water for a few hours.

- **Crabs have five pairs of limbs**. One pair of large, claw-like limbs, called pincers, is used for grabbing prey. The rest of the limbs are used to move around. The rear part of the crab, or the abdomen, is very small and can be tucked under its shell.

- **A crab** also uses its pincers to defend itself. It digs a hole with the pincers and buries itself under the sand to hide from predators.

- **Crabs** have highly specialized gills that do not clog even when they stay in muddy waters.

- **Unlike other crustaceans**, crabs can move sideways. Due to their peculiar body shape, it is easier for crabs to escape into their burrows this way.

> ...FASCINATING FACT...
> The Japanese giant spider crab is the largest of all crabs.
> It can measure over 3.5 m across its outstretched limbs. It is
> commonly found in the northern Pacific Ocean.

- **Large fish**, otters and octopuses are the crab's main enemies. These predators are able to break the shell easily. Certain seabirds also feed on crabs.

- **Some crabs** enlist the help of other creatures to protect themselves. The porcelain crab lives amongst the poisonous tentacles of sea anemones. This tiny crab also feeds on the anemone's leftovers.

- **Certain crabs**, such as boxer crabs, grab hold of sea anemones with their pincers and wave them about like torch flames to scare away their enemies.

▲ *The ghost crab is so-called because it is white or light grey in colour.*

161

Hermit crabs

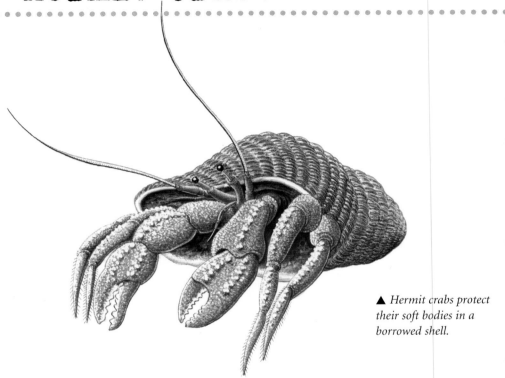

▲ *Hermit crabs protect their soft bodies in a borrowed shell.*

- **The hermit crab** is very different from other crabs. It has a long, twisted abdomen, which lacks a protective shell.

- **The abdomen** of a hermit crab contains most of its important organs, such as the liver. The crab protects its soft abdomen by pushing it into the abandoned shells of certain sea snails, such as whelks.

- **The hermit crab** carries its shell around. It holds it from the inside with two pairs of small rear legs. When in danger, the crab withdraws deep into this shell.

- **Normally** the hermit crab only has one large pincer because the shell cannot accommodate two. While hiding from its enemies, the crab uses this pincer to guard the entrance of the shell.

- **As they grow in size**, hermit crabs start searching for bigger shells. They often fight among themselves to occupy a shell that suits their size.

- **Sometimes the hermit crab** carries sponges and sea anemones on its shell to keep enemies away. When the crab moves into a new shell it takes its protectors along with it.

- **Hermit crabs** have highly developed antennae. These are much longer than those of other crabs and hence more effective in finding food.

- **Robber crabs** belong to the same family as hermit crabs but are slightly different. Only young robber crabs use snail shells to protect their abdomen. Adults have hardened abdomens that do not require protection.

- **The robber crab** lives on land and cannot swim. However, it has modified gills that need to be kept moist. The crab does this by dipping its legs in water and stroking them over the spongy tissues near the gills.

- **Robber crabs** dig into the sand and hide during the day. They are excellent tree climbers. They are also known as coconut crabs, because they can break open coconuts with their powerful pincers.

> **. . . FASCINATING FACT . . .**
> Robber crabs get their name from the fact that they are
> easily attracted to shiny materials. They have been known to steal
> pots and pans from houses and tents.

Lobsters

- **Lobsters** belong to the same group as crabs. Unlike crabs, these crustaceans have elongated bodies. They are often confused with crayfish, which are smaller.

- **Lobsters** have big heads and their bodies are covered by a shell. They have five pairs of legs, one or more pairs of which are modified into pincers.

- **In some species**, such as the American lobster, the pincers are enlarged and claw-like. One pincer is usually heavier and is used to crush, while the smaller one is used to cut and tear.

- **American lobsters** are found near the west coast of the Atlantic Ocean, from Canada to North Carolina. They are extremely common near Maine and hence are more popularly known as Maine lobsters.

- **Lobsters** have two pairs of antennae on their heads. The larger pair can be longer than the lobster's body. The lobster uses its antennae to feel its way around and to find food.

- **The stomach** of the lobster contains tooth-like grinding surfaces. The food is actually chewed within the stomach, which is located very close to the lobster's mouth.

- **A fan-shaped tail** helps the lobster swim. It is believed that this tail also allows it to swim backwards at high speed.

- **When grabbed** by a predator, lobsters can discard their limbs and antennae to escape. Later, these lost parts grow back.

- **Spiny lobsters** do not possess huge claws. Instead their shells are covered with spines. This species can live for as long as 50 years.

- **Most lobsters** live on the ocean floor, where they can hide by slipping into the spaces between rocks. They mostly feed on the remains of dead creatures. Lobsters also eat clams, snails, worms and sea urchins.

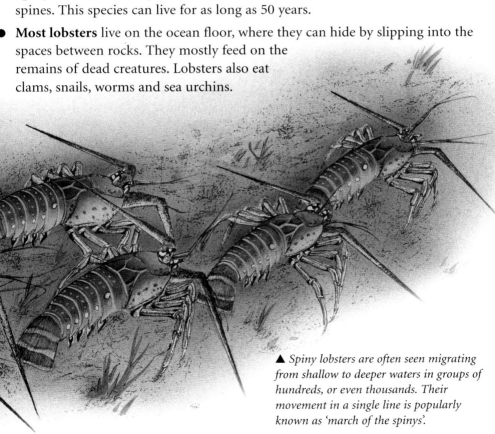

▲ *Spiny lobsters are often seen migrating from shallow to deeper waters in groups of hundreds, or even thousands. Their movement in a single line is popularly known as 'march of the spinys'.*

165

Shrimps and prawns

- **Shrimps and prawns** are very similar in appearance. Both look like miniature lobsters. A hardened shell also covers their bodies, but this shell is not as thick or hard as that of lobsters.

- **Shrimps** have bodies that are flattened from top to bottom, while the body of a prawn is flattened from either side.

- **Shrimps** crawl around the seabed, while prawns swim using five pairs of paddle-like limbs located on their abdomen.

- **Most shrimps and prawns** are almost transparent. This helps them hide from enemies. They turn pink only when cooked.

- **Shrimps** need to shed their hard outer covering during their growth. At such times, most shrimps go into hiding.

- **Shrimps**, like prawns, are scavengers. They feed on almost anything, including dead marine animals. They use their small pincers to search through the sand and mud.

- **Certain species**, such as scarlet and skunk cleaner shrimps, live on coral reefs.

- **These brightly coloured** shrimps clean larger fish by picking tiny parasites off their bodies. The bigger predators therefore, rarely harm cleaner shrimps. These shrimps even enter the mouths of the larger fish without being eaten.

- **Krill** are small, shrimp-like creatures that are found in cool oceans. They are the favourite food of some whales and sharks.

- **Millions of krill** swim together in swarms that can be several kilometres long.

▼ *The spotted cleaner shrimp not only cleans the tentacles of the sea anemone, but it also attracts other marine creatures close enough for the anemone to prey on them.*

Sea turtles

- **There are only seven species** of marine turtles. They are found in tropical and sub-tropical waters around the world.

- **The leatherback turtle** is the largest sea turtle. The other species are loggerhead, hawksbill, olive ridley, Kemp's ridley, flatback and green sea turtles.

- **A hard shell** covers and protects the sea turtle's body. Compared to the freshwater turtle, the sea turtle has a flatter, less domed shell, which helps it to swim faster.

- **The front limbs** of the sea turtle are larger than the back limbs. These flipper-like limbs help the turtle to 'fly' through the water, although moving on land is quite awkward.

Loggerhead turtle

Hawksbill turtle

Green turtle

Leatherback turtle

▲ Turtles only come ashore to lay their eggs. Although they are born on land, turtles head for the sea the minute they hatch.

- **The shell** of the leatherback sea turtle is made of a thick, rubbery substance that is strengthened by small bones. These turtles are named after this unusual shell.

- **Sea snakes and sea turtles** are the only reptiles that spend most of their lives in the ocean. The females swim ashore for a few hours each year to lay eggs.

- **Sea turtles** prefer to lay their eggs at night. The female digs a pit in the sand with her flippers. She then lays about 50–150 eggs, and covers the nest with sand.

- **Once the eggs hatch** the young turtles struggle out of their sandpit and make their way to the sea. On the way, many babies fall prey to seabirds, crabs, otters and other predators.

- **The diet of sea turtles** differs from species to species. Leatherbacks prefer jellyfish, while olive ridleys and loggerheads eat hard-shelled creatures such as crabs. Sponges are a favourite of hawksbills.

- **Most turtle species** are under threat because they are hunted for their eggs, meat and shells. The trade in turtles has been declared illegal in most countries, but people continue to kill them.

...FASCINATING FACT...
It is believed that sea turtles have been on our planet for over 100 million years. They have survived, while other prehistoric animals, such as dinosaurs, have become extinct.

Leatherback turtle

- **Leatherback turtles** are the biggest sea turtles, with an average length of about 2 m. In some cases, a leatherback may grow to almost 3 m. These turtles can weigh over 500 kg.

- **The largest leatherback** ever recorded was an adult male that was found stranded on the West Coast of Wales in 1988. It weighed over 900 kg.

- **The body temperature** of the leatherback is usually higher than the surrounding water. This is the reason leatherbacks can survive even in extremely cold places, such as Greenland and Iceland.

- **The turtle's rubbery shell** has prominent ridges that run along its length. The ridges make the shell look like a boat's hull. Leatherbacks floating on the surface of the water are, therefore, often mistaken for upturned boats.

- **The outer shell**, or carapace, of the leatherback is either dark grey or black, with white spots. Newborn turtles have white blotches on their carapace.

- **These turtles** have delicate, scissor-like jaws that are easily damaged. These animals, therefore, eat only soft-bodied creatures.

- **Leatherbacks** feed almost exclusively on jellyfish, although some have been known to eat sea urchins and squid.

- **The food pipe**, or oesophagus, contains long spines that point backwards. This allows the turtle to swallow jellyfish and other slippery food.

- **Many leatherbacks** have reportedly died by eating floating plastic bags, which they mistake for jellyfish.

- **In 1982**, an estimated 115,000 adult female leatherbacks existed worldwide. These numbers have drastically declined in recent years, largely due to pollution and overfishing. Leatherbacks are often bycatches, caught accidentally in fishing nets.

▲ Swimming to depths of over 1000 m, leatherback turtles dive deeper than any other sea turtle. They also migrate the furthest, travelling up to thousands of kilometres at a stretch.

171

Loggerhead turtles

- **Loggerhead turtles** get their name for their unusually large heads. Compared to other sea turtles, their head is bigger than their body. The Scottish word logger means 'block of wood', while loggerhead means 'stupid' or 'clumsy'.

- **The upper shell** of loggerhead turtles averages over one metre in length. Adult loggerheads weigh more than 100 kg.

- **Most loggerheads** prefer temperate and sub-tropical waters. Some species inhabit muddy waters, while most others live in clear seas.

- **Like other sea turtles**, female loggerheads come ashore to build their nests and lay their eggs. These nesting activities take place during the night.

- **The heart-shaped shell**, or carapace, is bony and lacks any ridges. The front flippers of the turtle are short and thick with two claws. The rear flippers might have two or three claws.

- **The loggerhead's shell** is reddish-brown in colour. The scales on top of the head and flippers are the same colour, but with yellow borders. Loggerheads' shells have a paler, yellowish underside.

- **Young loggerheads** are mostly light brown in colour with a dark brown shell. They are about 4.5 cm long and weigh nearly 20 g.

- **Loggerheads** are carnivorous and have powerful jaws that can crush hard shells. They feed mainly on crabs, mussels, sea snails, lobsters and clams. They are also known to eat jellyfish.

- **Like leatherback turtles**, loggerheads often mistake plastic bags for jellyfish and eat them. This often proves to be fatal.

- **Loggerheads** are an endangered species. A large number get caught and killed in fishing nets. Overcrowding on beaches has also led to a decline in nesting activities.

▼ *Masirah Island, off the coast of Oman, supports the largest single nesting population of loggerhead turtles. It is home to as many as 30,000 nesting females each year. These young loggerheads have just hatched. Not all of them make it to the sea. As they race down the beach, some are picked off by hungry gulls or crabs.*

Hawksbill turtle

▲ *The hawksbill turtle has been listed as endangered since 1970.*

- **Hawksbill turtles** get their name from their narrow, curved upper jaw that looks like a hawk's beak.

- **These turtles** are not very large. On average, their upper shell is less than one metre in length. They have an elongated head and body and claws on their flippers.

- **Hawksbill turtles** are black, grey or brown in colour. Their underside is light yellow or white, while their shell is orange, brown or yellow.

- **Newly hatched turtles** are about 4 cm in length and weigh about 13–20 g.

- **These sea turtles** prefer tropical waters. They are commonly found among coral reefs in the tropical Atlantic, Pacific and Indian oceans.

- **The shell** of a young hawksbill is heart-shaped. However, this becomes more elongated as the turtle grows older.

- **The turtle's narrow head** and beak-like jaws allow it to pick food from small openings in coral reefs. Although sponges form their main diet, hawksbills also feed on shrimps, squid, and anemones.

- **Like other sea turtles**, female hawksbills lay their eggs in sandpits. However, these turtles have very specific nesting areas, to which they return year after year.

- **In Japan** the hawksbill's ornate shell was widely used to make richly crafted jewellery, such as brooches, necklaces, combs, hairpins and other accessories. These turtles are, therefore, also called tortoiseshell turtles.

- **As with most sea turtles**, the population of the hawksbill is threatened. Apart from being killed for their shells, a large number of them die each year by getting caught in fishing nets.

Olive ridley turtles

◀ *Olive ridley turtles are also called Pacific ridley turtles. They are larger than their Atlantic counterparts, Kemp's ridley turtles.*

- **Olive ridley turtles** are one of the smallest sea turtles. They are named after the colour of the olive green shell. Some believe it was named 'ridley' after H.N. Ridley, a botanist who reportedly sighted the species first.

- **The average length** of the olive ridley's shell is less than 70 cm. Although the shell is wide, it is not as wide as that of the closely related Kemp's ridley turtle.

- **The front and rear flippers** of olive ridleys have one or two claws, but an extra claw is often seen on the front limbs. Like loggerheads, they have strong jaws.

- **These turtles** are found in the warm waters of the Indian, Pacific and Atlantic oceans. Most of them prefer shallow waters.

- **Olive ridleys** are also called Pacific ridleys. They are distinguished from Kemp ridleys by their colour and size.

- **When the water gets too cold**, olive ridleys are known to bask in the sun in large groups. This helps them to maintain their body temperature.

- **During the nesting season** a large number of females, sometimes thousands, come together on the same beach to lay eggs. These nesting groups are called *arribadas* or *arribazones* and are characteristic of olive ridleys.

- **An olive ridley turtle** can nest more than once in a season, with an interval of 14 days in between.

- **Olive ridleys** like to eat jellyfish, crabs, shrimps, sea urchins and other small marine creatures. They also feed on algae.

- **These turtles** are an endangered species, said to be near extinction. They build their nests on a select few beaches. Human activities on these beaches have led to destruction of their nests.

> **...FASCINATING FACT...**
> *Arribadas* can be found on isolated beaches in the Bay of Bengal in India, and in Costa Rica and Mexico. These nesting groups, however, are unpredictable and could be caused by climatic conditions, such as strong off-shore winds, or by certain moon or tide phases.

Green sea turtle

- **Green sea turtles** get their name from the green colour of the fat under their shell. These turtles have a small head that cannot be retracted into the shell.

- **The shell** is black-brown or greenish-yellow in colour, with black markings. It is smooth to the touch. The underside is paler in colour.

- **The shell** can be up to 1.5 m in length and is fairly smooth. It has big plates on either side. Atlantic green turtles tend to be larger than their Hawaiian relatives.

- **Newly hatched green sea turtles** are about 5 cm long and weigh almost 25 g. They are black in colour with white undersides.

- **Green sea turtles** prefer the warm waters of the tropical and temperate seas. They are found in oceans across the world, and are often seen in shallow coastal waters.

- **Hawaiian green sea turtles** love to come ashore and lie motionless in the sun for hours. It is believed that they do this to rest and warm up.

- **Adult green sea turtles** feed mainly on marine plants. However, the young also eat shrimps, jellyfish and insects.

- **People kill these turtles** for their eggs, shells and meat. At one time the green sea turtle was extensively hunted for its calipee, which is a vital ingredient in turtle soup.

- **Calipee is the cartilage** found under the bottom shell, or plastron, of the turtle. Poachers used to cut the calipee out and leave the turtle to bleed to death.

● **The biggest threat** to the survival of green sea turtles is a condition called fibropapillomatosis. Almost half the green sea turtle population is affected by this disease in which a tumour, or cancerous growth, blocks the turtle's ability to breathe, see and even feed, eventually resulting in its death.

▼ *Female green sea turtles travel up to 3000 km to their breeding grounds to lay eggs.*

Sea snakes

- **Sea snakes** are mainly found in the warm waters of the Indian and Pacific oceans. They can be ten times more venomous than most land snakes.

- **They feed on small fish**, eels and fish eggs. Sea snakes use their strong venom to kill their prey, and then swallow it whole.

▼ *Sea snakes use venom (poison) to stun prey. The venom of sea snakes is more powerful than that of any land snake.*

Banded sea snake

Yellow-bellied
sea snake

- **The scales** on a sea snake are small. This reduces friction, and helps the animal to swim faster. The sea snake also has a flat, paddle-like tail that aids in swimming.

- **Being reptiles**, sea snakes do not have gills. They have to come up to the surface of the water to breathe. However, they are able to absorb some oxygen from the water that they swallow. This helps them stay underwater for longer periods.

- **The sea snake** has a special gland under its tongue that gets rid of excess salt from sea water. It also has highly developed nostril valves that can be closed while diving into the depths of the ocean.

- **There are two kinds of sea snakes**. Aquatic sea snakes never leave the water, not even to breed, while amphibious sea snakes, or sea kraits, slither on to land to lay their eggs.

- **Aquatic sea snakes,** or 'true' sea snakes, are viviparous. This means that the female does not lay eggs, but gives birth to live young.

- **The yellow-bellied sea snake** is the most easily recognized 'true' sea snake. It is named after its bright yellow belly. Although this snake is extremely poisonous, it attacks only when disturbed.

- **This sea snake** can also swim backwards and is the fastest swimmer amongst sea snakes, reaching a speed of 3.6 km/h. It is also capable of staying underwater for three hours before coming up to the surface to breathe.

- **Sea kraits** have coloured bands on their body. Unlike 'true' sea snakes, sea kraits have wide scales on their bellies that help them to move on land.

Whales

- **Whales** are among the largest and heaviest animals on the planet. Their size can range from 2–3 m to over 30 m.

- **Being mammals**, whales breathe with their lungs. They do not have gills. The nostrils of whales, called blowholes, are located on top of the head.

- **When underwater**, whales need to hold their breath. They come up to the surface and open their blowholes to breathe. After taking in the required amount of air, these animals dive into the water again. The blowholes remain closed underwater.

- **The spout, or blow** that can be seen rising from the blowhole is not water. It is actually stale air that condenses and vaporizes the moment it is released into the atmosphere. This spout can sometimes reach a height of 10 m.

- **Whales** are divided into two main groups: toothed whales and baleen whales. Together, these groups consist of 81 known species.

- **Toothed whales** have small teeth in their jaws, which are used to kill prey like fish and squid. This group includes dolphins, killer whales, sperm whales, beluga whales and porpoises.

- **Toothed whales** emit sound waves that are bounced off an object, revealing its size, shape and location. This is known as echolocation. Toothed whales can even use this technique to distinguish between prey and non-prey objects.

- **Baleen whales**, on the other hand, are toothless. They trap their prey in sieve-like structures that hang from their upper jaws.

● **Baleen whales** are also known as great whales. This group includes grey, humpback, right and the mighty blue whale.

...FASCINATING FACT...

Whales use a series of moans and clicks to communicate amongst themselves. Most of these are either too low or too high for humans to hear. Blue and fin whales are believed to produce the loudest sounds of any animal.

▲ *The tails of these marine mammals have wide flukes, instead of fins. These flukes move up and down to power the animal through water.*

183

Baleen and blubber

- **Baleen whales** have a huge mouth that contains rows of baleen plates. These plates have fringed edges like a comb that filter plankton from the water.

- **Whales** of this group swim with their mouths open and take in thousands of litres of water containing krill and other small marine creatures. These creatures get trapped in the fringed edges of the baleen. The whale licks the food off the baleen and swallows it.

▲ *Humpback whales, like all baleen whales, are filter feeders.*

- **Baleen**, also called whalebone, was once valued for its plastic-like attributes. Great whales were widely hunted for their baleen. However, with the wide availability of good-quality plastic, the demand for baleen has diminished.

- **Heat loss is greater** in water than it is on land at the same temperature. Whales have a thick layer of fat, called blubber, between the skin and the flesh that preserves body heat.

- **Blubber also helps** to keep the animals afloat and is a source of stored energy. Until recently, it was extensively used in the manufacture of cosmetics and ointments.

- **Toothed whales** have smaller mouths than great whales. However, unlike meat-eating animals of the land, the teeth of these whales are uniform in size and shape.

- **Most whales swim** and feed in groups called pods. Many whales are known to migrate long distances between their feeding places and breeding grounds.

- **Whales** sometimes pop their head above the surface and float motionless. This is known as 'logging'.

- **Some whales**, like humpback whales, are very acrobatic and can leap out of the water. This is known as 'breaching'. They also indulge in 'lob-tailing' – sticking out their tail and then splashing it in the water.

- **Some whales** also lift their head vertically out of the water before slipping back below. This is known as 'spyhopping'. It is believed that they do this to obtain a view above the surface.

Blue whale

- **Blue whales** are the largest creatures to have ever lived on this planet. They are even larger than the mighty dinosaurs that lived millions of years ago.

- **Their average length** is 25 m but some can grow to more than 30 m. *Brachiosaurus*, the largest dinosaur, was only 20–25 m long.

- **These whales** are blue-grey in colour with light patches on the back. Sometimes, the underside of this animal can be yellowish in colour. This is caused by a kind of algae and has given the blue whale the nickname 'sulphurbottom'.

- **The body** is streamlined with a large tail fin. The dorsal fin is small, while the tail is thick and large. Blue whales have splashguards in front of their two blowholes.

- **Blue whales** are migratory animals. They live near the tropics during winter and migrate towards icy waters in summer.

- **The diet** of a blue whale consists of small fish, plankton and krill in enormous quantities. They can eat over 4 tons of krill every day.

- **These whales** have been known to gather in groups of 60 or more. However, they are largely solitary animals.

- **The spout** of a blue whale is vertical and can be 10–12 m high.

- **Blue whales** are relatively slow swimmers. However, when threatened, these animals can swim at a speed of over 30 km/h.

● **Merciless hunting** over several decades has caused the blue whale population to decline drastically. It is currently an endangered species, and only 5000 are thought to exist worldwide.

▲ *Blue whales have 300–400 pairs of baleen plates that they use to strain food from the water. The calves feed on their mother's rich milk until they are around eight months old.*

187

Killer whale

- **Killer whales,** also known as orcas, are the largest dolphins. Despite their name, killer whales have more in common with dolphins than with great whales. Hence they are considered a part of the dolphin family.

- **They have a black body** with white patches on their underside and behind each eye.

- **These animals** are found in oceans across the world, but prefer to live in colder temperate waters. They do not migrate in summer like great whales but can swim for long distances.

- **Killer whales** prefer to live close to the coast. Their average length is 8–10 m. They have sharp, hooked teeth, which they use to rip their prey apart.

- *Dephinus orca* was the earliest scientific name for the killer whale. It meant 'demon dolphin'.

- **It is believed** that the name 'killer whale' might itself have been derived from the name 'whale killer'. This name was given to these animals by 18th century whalers who saw them feeding on other whales and dolphins.

- **The diet of orcas** is varied. However, they largely prey on fish, squid, sharks and warm-blooded animals such as seals, seabirds and larger whales, including blue whales.

- **Orcas are known** as the 'wolves of the sea'. Like wolves, they hunt in groups and hence are able to tackle prey of all shapes and sizes.

- **The pods of killer whales** are divided into resident and transient pods. Resident pods can consist of 5–50 members who communicate frequently using whistles and high-pitched screams.

- **Transient pods** are smaller, with a maximum of seven members who feed mainly on marine mammals. Members of transient pods do not communicate frequently with each other.

▲ *Killer whales live in groups called pods. The older females are in charge. Their offspring may stay together for 10 to 20 years.*

Right whale

- **Right whales** got their name from the fact that whalers thought that they were the 'right' whales to hunt, since they were easy to approach, floated when they died and provided large quantities of oil and whalebone.

- **These great whales** have a large head and a bow-shaped lower jaw. They are easily recognized because of the presence of light-coloured wart-like growths called callosities. These are usually located on the head, near the blowhole and around the eyes and jaws.

- **The average length** of right whales is 15–18 m. They are dark grey, black or light brown in colour, with white patches on the underside.

- **These whales** can be found in cool, temperate waters in both hemispheres. They migrate to warmer waters when they breed.

- **Based on certain minor differences**, especially in the shape of their skulls and habitat, right whales are broadly divided into two species. Northern right whales are found in the northern hemisphere, while southern right whales live in southern waters.

- **There are two other species** in the right whale family. They are the bowhead whale and the pygmy right whale.

- **Bowhead whales** live in cold waters in the north. Like all Arctic whales, they do not have a dorsal fin.

- **Pygmy right whales** are rare and are found mostly in temperate waters in the southern hemisphere. They are small and are not known to grow more than 5 m in length.

- **These great whales** prefer to live close to the surface and are filter feeders. They swim just below the surface and feed on krill, shrimps and small fish.

● **Right whales**, despite their size, are very acrobatic. They often flap their fins on the surface, and can be seen breaching. But they particularly love to 'sail', when they stand on their heads and wave their tail flukes in the air for up to two minutes.

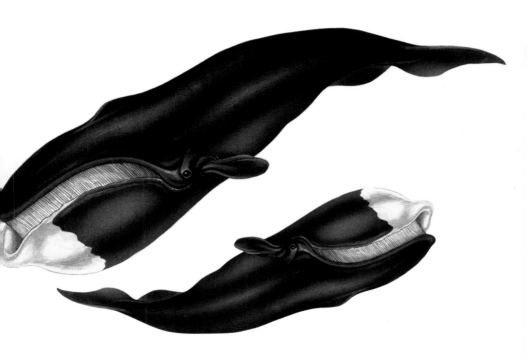

▲ *Bowhead whales have huge heads that measure nearly one-third of their total length.*

Grey whale

- **Grey whales** are grey in colour with mottled patterns in lighter shades. They have a low hump instead of a dorsal fin and their heads are covered with parasites, such as barnacles and whale lice.

- **These whales** can grow up to 15 m long. They have a layer of blubber that is nearly 25 cm thick. Their head is slightly arched and pointed.

- **They are commonly** found along the coastal regions of the North Pacific Ocean. In winter, they breed in the shallow waters off the coast of Mexico, and in summer they make their way back to the Bering Sea in the north.

- **Every year, during autumn**, grey whales embark on a migration of almost 20,000 km. This is believed to be the longest migration of all mammals.

- **Grey whales** are bottom feeders. Their diet consists of shrimps, krill, and marine worms that live on the seabed. On average, grey whales eat more than 1000 kg of food per day.

- **Grey whales** are the only species in their family. They differ from other great whales mainly in the way they feed.

- **These great whales** turn on their sides to scrape up the mud on the ocean floor, leaving huge holes in the seabed. They use their baleen to filter the creatures in the silt.

- **Grey whales** are one of the most active great whales. They often indulge in lobtailing – waving the tail fin in the air – and spyhopping – sticking their heads above the surface and turning around gently.

- **Until the 1700s,** there were three populations of grey whales in the world. Of these the north Atlantic species has been hunted to extinction.

- **Today,** there are about 24,000 grey whales in the world. This is believed to be the same number that existed before extensive hunting of these whales began in the 18th century.

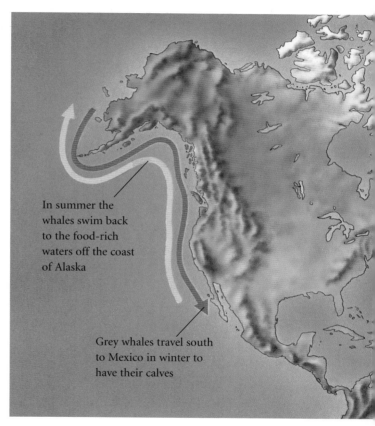

In summer the whales swim back to the food-rich waters off the coast of Alaska

Grey whales travel south to Mexico in winter to have their calves

▲ *The Californian grey whale spends almost one-third of its life migrating, from Chuchki Sea in the Arctic Ocean to the Baja Peninsula off the coast of Mexico and back.*

Pilot whale

- **Pilot whales** belong to a group of dolphins called 'blackfish'. Orcas also belong to this group.

- **These animals** have a small beak and a rounded head. They are dark brown or grey in colour and have a distinct, swept-back dorsal fin.

- **Pilot whales** have slight patches behind their eyes and dorsal fins. They are smaller than orcas and can grow as long as 7 m. They largely feed on octopus and squid.

- **There are two** species of pilot whale – the short-finned and the long-finned. Apart from their habitats, most of the characteristics of these species are similar.

- **The short-finned variety** can be found in warm tropical waters and cooler sub-tropical waters. They cannot adapt well to shallow waters.

- **Long-finned pilot whales** live in cold waters in the north, near Greenland and Norway, and in the South Atlantic Ocean.

- **Pilot whales** are known for their strong family units. They live in close-knit pods of six or more. Females never leave the pod they were born in.

- **Members of a pod** are known to stick together, even in times of danger. It is believed that when the leader of the pod becomes disoriented due to illness or loses its way in shallow water, it gets stranded. In such situations the rest of the pod follows suit. This phenomenon is common in the long-finned variety.

Female pilot whales feed their young for several years. They will also take care of the young of their sisters and daughters.

This whale, particularly the long-finned variety, was extensively hunted for its meat. Whalers in Newfoundland and the Faroe Islands used to drive large groups of pilot whales ashore and kill them.

Each pilot whale in the group makes its own special clicks and whistles, which the others recognize.

Sperm whale

- **Sperm whales** are the largest of the toothed whales. Males can grow up to 20 m long and weigh 50 tonnes. The whale in Herman Melville's novel *Moby Dick* was a sperm whale.

- **The whale** is named after the highly valued spermaceti oil, which is a waxy substance found in the sperm whale's head. This substance is believed to help the whale during deep dives.

- **Spermaceti oil** is used by Arctic natives as an ointment. It is also used to make high-quality candles that burn with a clear flame.

- **The sperm whale** has an extremely large head, which is square and blunt. The head is almost one-third of its total body length. These whales have the largest brain in the animal kingdom.

◀ *Sperm whales have been known to dive to depths of up to 3000 m in search of their favourite food, the giant squid.*

● **Sperm whales** are dark brown or dark grey in colour and their skin is wrinkled. They have broad, powerful tail flukes, but their flippers are short and stubby.

● **They have only one blowhole** and the spout is angled. Large conical teeth are located on the lower jaw and fit into sockets on the upper jaw.

● **Sperm whales** are good swimmers. Capable of diving to depths of 3000 m, these whales are also the deepest divers among sea mammals. After a long dive, sperm whales need to stay on the surface for 15 minutes to replenish oxygen.

● **Sometimes** sperm whales can be spotted floating on the water with a part of their head popping out of the surface.

● **Sperm whales** can hold their breath for more than one hour, as they dive down and down. They use clicks of sound, which they hear bouncing back off nearby objects, to find their prey in the darkness.

● **Many sperm whales** bear injuries from the suckers of giant squid. Scientists have mounted cameras on sperm whales to capture giant squid on video.

. . . FASCINATING FACT . . .
Sperm whales produce a wax-like substance known as ambergris.
This is used in perfumes to make their scent last longer.

Humpback whale

- **Humpback whales** are large baleen whales. They are one of the most active whales and can often be seen leaping out of the water.

- **These whales** are found in most parts of the world. During summer they migrate to the icy waters in the north and south. In winter, they breed in warm, tropical waters.

- **They have a round**, flat head that has fleshy bumps called tubercles. The body is black or grey, with mottled white patches. The underside is off-white.

- **The humpback** can grow up to 15 m in length. At almost 5 m, its flippers are the longest among whales. The animal is named after a hump on which the whale's dorsal fin is located. This is most pronounced when the whale dives.

- **The tail fin** measures nearly 5.5 m across and has black and white patterns. Since no two humpback whales have the same pattern on their tails, scientists use it to identify and monitor them.

- **They feed** on shrimps, krill and small fish. Humpbacks have various methods of feeding. These include lunge-feeding, tail-flicking and bubble-netting.

- **In lunge-feeding**, the humpback opens its mouth wide and swims through a group of prey, often coming to the surface with food in its mouth.

- **When tail-flicking**, the whale lies with its belly just below the surface. It uses its tail to flick the prey into the air and down its mouth.

- **Bubble-netting** is the most spectacular of all feeding habits and the most commonly used by the humpback. The whale slaps its flippers around a school of fish, creating a wall of bubbles. This action forces the fish to move to the surface in large groups, making them easy prey.

● **Male humpbacks** are known for their unusual and eerie songs. The sounds vary from high-pitched squeaks to deep wails and can last for half an hour or more. These songs are usually heard during the breeding season.

▲ *Humpbacks have lots of lumps and bumps on their heads called tubercles. Hard-shelled sea creatures called barnacles also live there.*

Narwhal

▲ *Adult male narwhals often carry scars of brutal tusk fights on their head.*

- **Narwhals**, like belugas, belong to the dolphin family. Both these species are white whales. The long tusk on their snout is a distinctive feature.

- **The word** 'narwhal' means 'corpse whale' in an ancient Scandinavian language. Its mottled white colour makes it look like a corpse floating on the water.

- **Narwhals** can be found in northern Arctic seas. These rarely sighted whales can survive in the coldest temperatures.

- **These whales** have a small round head and a small beak. Their skin has white patches and a dark stripe. Like belugas, narwhals lack a dorsal fin.

- **Narwhals** have a thick layer of blubber, which accounts for over one-third of their body weight.

- **These whales** can grow up to 5 m, without the tusk. The tusk can grow to more than 3 m in length.

- **This toothed whale** has only two teeth, both in the upper jaw. The left tooth grows into the whale's unusual tusk. Sometimes both teeth grow to form double tusks. In this case, the right tusk is smaller than the left one.

- **These tusks** are seen only in males. However, females with smaller tusks can occur. The tusk has earned the narwhal the nickname, 'unicorn of the sea'.

- **Some scientists** believe that the whales use their tusks to fence with rival males during the mating season. Other scientists believe that narwhals also use their tusks to spear prey and poke holes in the ice.

- **The narwhal's tusk** is thought to possess medicinal properties. It is also used to make fine jewellery. For years, this whale has been hunted for its tusk as well as its skin and oil.

Beluga

- **Beluga whales** are fascinating creatures. Their playful nature, along with their unusual colour, makes them popular attractions in aquariums.

- **Related to dolphins**, the adult beluga whale is milky white in colour. Its name i derived from the Russian word *belukha*, meaning white.

- **The colour** of the whale matches its surroundings. This whale lives close to icebergs in the Arctic Ocean. Young belugas, however, are grey in colour.

- **Belugas** do not have a dorsal fin, which makes swimming under ice much easier.

- **They have narrower** necks compared with other whales. Unlike most other baleen and toothed whales, belugas can also nod and shake their heads from side to side.

- ***Delphinapterus leucas***, the scientific name of the beluga, means 'white dolphin without wings', referring to the absence of a dorsal fin in this species.

- **The beluga's diet** consists of crab, squid, shrimp and fish. They love salmon and often swim into the mouths of rivers to feed on them. They use their teeth to grab prey rather than to chew.

- **Belugas** are very social and tend to travel in groups consisting of 5–20 members. These groups are usually led by a single male. During migrations, the groups can exceed 10,000 members.

- **These whales** emit various sounds, from whistles to chirps and squeaks. They are the most vocal whales, earning them the nickname of sea canaries.

- **Belugas** are hunted by killer whales. The young are often killed by polar bears. It is not uncommon to find adult belugas bearing scars from polar bear attacks.

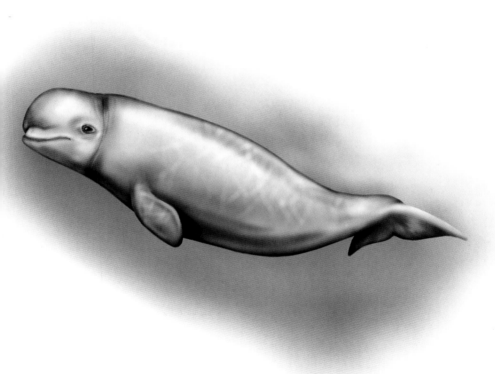

▲ *Belugas have a thick, stout body, a small beak and a prominent forehead, which is called a 'melon'.*

Dolphins

- **Dolphins** are close relatives of whales and form a large part of the toothed whales group. They have a beak-shaped snout and are extremely active and playful.

- **They are found** in all oceans, and are powerful swimmers. The shape of their body and their big flippers help in rapid movement. Dolphins are often spotted riding on waves, probably to conserve energy.

- **Dolphins** are good at diving deep into the ocean and also leaping into the air. Many of them can leap as high as 7 m. They can even turn somersaults before landing into the water with a splash.

- **Like baleen whales**, dolphins have blowholes on top of their head. They surface every two minutes to breathe, before diving under again.

- **Dolphins** use echolocation to hunt and navigate through cloudy waters. They emit a series of high-pitched sound pulses, which bounce off prey or obstacles, enabling dolphins to locate them.

- **These animals** hunt in groups. They chase their prey, surround it, and catch it with their powerful jaws. Dolphins have numerous conical teeth.

- **The smallest dolphin** is the tucuxi dolphin, which is hardly 1 m long. Bottlenose dolphins can reach a length of over 3.5 m, while common dolphins are about 2.5 m long.

...FASCINATING FACT...
Some scientists believe that dolphins have a language of their own, heard by humans in the form of whistling sounds. Some even believe that they are able to understand sign language.

- **The killer whale** is the largest member of the dolphin family. It can reach a length of almost 10 m. Like others in the family, the killer whale is very intelligent and can be trained to do tricks.

- **The playful nature** of dolphins has made them extremely popular, especially with children. They are common sights in sea life centres.

- **Dolphins used** to be hunted for their meat and oil. Until recently, thousands used to die every year by getting caught in fishing nets.

▲ *Bottlenose dolphins usually swim at speeds of 5–11 km/h, but sometimes they can exceed 32 km/h.*

Porpoises

- **Porpoises** are small, toothed whales. They are close relatives of dolphins, and are often mistaken for them.

- **They are usually smaller than dolphins**, and not as sleek and streamlined. Porpoises rarely grow to more than 2.2 m. They are usually grey, blue or black in colour.

▼ *While on the move, the harbour porpoise surfaces six to eight times within one minute. Normally, they can stay under water for about 5 minutes before surfacing again.*

The dorsal fin of a porpoise is triangular, whereas the dolphin's is curved. Porpoises do not have a beak.

There are several varieties of porpoises, including Dall's and the spectacled porpoise. The harbour porpoise, also called the common porpoise, is the best known.

Harbour porpoises are found in cold, northern waters and are known to frequent bays and estuaries. They have a small body and dorsal fin.

There are two varieties of Dall's porpoises – the *dalli* type and the *truei* type. Both are found in the northern Pacific Ocean.

Dall's porpoises are known for the splash they make in the water with their tails. This is referred to as the 'rooster-tail splash', and has earned this species the other name of 'spray porpoise'.

- **Another well-known species** is the spectacled porpoise, found in the South Atlantic. The upper part of its body is bluish black, while the lower half is white.

  - **Spectacled porpoises** have black patches around their eyes, which are surrounded by a white line. These resemble spectacles.

  - **Other varieties of porpoise** include Burmeister's porpoises, which is commonly found off the coasts of South America. It is named after the German biologist Burmeister, who gave this species the scientific name *spinipinnis,* meaning spiny fin. This was due to the blunt, thorn-like structures, called tubercles, along the edges of the porpoise's fins.

Seals

- **Seals** are marine mammals, which belong to the same group as walruses and sea lions. Together these animals are called pinnipeds, which means 'fin-footed'. All of them have limbs that look like fins.

- **There are two families of seals**: true seals and eared seals. Unlike eared seals, true seals do not have external ear flaps.

- **There are 19 species of true seals,** making them the largest group of pinnipeds. Eared seals consist of sea lions and fur seals.

- **The limbs of seals** are modified into powerful flippers that help in swimming. Their strong, torpedo-shaped body, coupled with the ability to store oxygen, make them great swimmers.

- **Eared seals** have long rear flippers that are more mobile than those of true seals. Their front flippers are also large and more powerful. Eared seals mainly use their front flippers to paddle through water.

- **Seals** spend most of their lives in water, but they have to come ashore to breed and nurse their young. Some live at sea for several months at a time, while others return to the shore every day.

- **Most species** live in cold regions. Hence they have a thick coat of fur that keeps them warm. These animals also have a layer of fat, called 'blubber', under their skin, which not only provides warmth but also serves as a storehouse of energy when food is scarce.

- **Seals** range in size from 1–4 m. Galapagos fur seals and ringed seals are the smallest species. The largest is the male southern elephant seal, which can grow to 5 m in length.

- **The diet** of seals consists mainly of fish, squid, crabs and shellfish. Leopard seals are among the most aggressive hunters. They kill other seals and penguins for food. They are also known to have injured divers.

- **Killer whales**, sharks and polar bears are the natural predators of seals. They are endangered because of excessive hunting by man for their meat, fat and fur. The Caribbean monk seal is now extinct due to excessive hunting.

▼ *Seals are clumsy on land. They slide along the shore with difficulty. However, the large flippers of ared seals are better adapted for moving on land.*

Harp seal

- **Harp seals** are found in the cold waters of the Arctic and the North Atlantic oceans. They get their name from the harp-shaped mark on their back.

- **They have a silvery** grey coat of fur and cat-like whiskers. The harp-shaped mark on the back is dark brown or black in colour, and is less distinct in females.

▲ *About five weeks after their birth, harp seal pups are left to fend for themselves. During this period the pups lose about 10 kg of their body weight. This is because they are unable to hunt on their own for at least four weeks.*

- **Newborn seals** have a white coat, hence their common name, whitecoats. Since the colour of their coat matches their surroundings, predators find it hard to spot young harp seals.

- **The pups** are born with yellowish fur, which turns white after a couple of days. This white fur starts to moult in two week-old pups to give way to a silvery grey coat with irregular dark spots.

- **Adult males** grow up to 1.7 m in length and weigh about 130 kg. Female harp seals are smaller in size. Pups are usually about 10 kg at birth.

- **These seals** are good swimmers, and are known to dive to great depths in search of food. They can also stay underwater for over 15 minutes at a stretch.

- **Harp seals** are highly social, migratory creatures. Long before the approach of winter, they gather in huge numbers and head south towards their winter breeding grounds.

- **During the breeding season**, thousands of harp seals gather on pack ice in dense breeding patches. Pups are born between February and March and are nursed for about two weeks. They are then left to fend for themselves.

- **Polar bears** are the main enemies of harp seals. Other predators include Arctic foxes, killer whales, Greenland sharks and walruses.

- **Harp seals** have been widely hunted for their meat and their coats. The pups were once killed for their white fur. Today, there are laws controlling harp seal hunting.

Weddell seal

- **Weddell seals** are large, non-migratory creatures commonly found in the southern Atlantic Ocean and around Antarctica.

- **These large seals are named** after the British explorer James Weddell, who first described them.

- **Weddell seals** can measure over 3 m in length. The females are usually bigger than the males.

- **Weddell seals** have strong, modified front teeth that point forwards. They can use them to dig holes in the ice so that they can breathe while swimming in ice-covered water.

- **Weddell seals** blow air into cracks in the ice in order to draw out small prey.

- **The diet** of the Weddell seal consists mainly of fish such as cod and Antarctic silverfish. They also feed on crab, squid and octopus.

- **Leopard seals** and killer whales are the main predators of the Weddell seal. These animals usually prey on the pups.

- **Weddell seals are** very noisy, especially underwater. They use a variety of calls to communicate among themselves. These sounds can also be heard from the surface of the water.

...FASCINATING FACT...
Weddell seals are good swimmers and excellent divers.
They are known to be the best divers of all seals, and can remain at depths of over 500 m for more than an hour.

▲ *The coats of adult weddell seals are normally spotted and bluish grey in colour. The pups have a lighter, greyish-brown coat.*

● **During the freezing winter** these seals prefer to stay underwater rather than on land, since the water under the ice is warmer.

● **Weddell seals** have very good underwater vision. This helps them to hunt for prey.

Northern fur seal

◀ *The underfur of northern fur seals is thick and waterproof, with over 46,000 hairs per sq cm.*

- **Northern fur seals** are found in the cold waters of the north Pacific, particularlyin the Bering Sea and the Okhotsk Sea.

- **These are** the only fur seals that are not found in the southern hemisphere.

- **Northern fur seals** are eared seals and have small external ears.

- **Like all other eared seals**, northern fur seals have modified flippers that help them to 'walk' on land as well as swim.

- **A thick layer of fat,** or blubber, protects the northern fur seal from the extremely cold temperatures.

- **Adult males** are over 2 m in length. The females are smaller at around 1.4 m.

- **Male and female seals** differ in colour. The males have reddish brown coats, while the females' coats are brownish grey.

- **Northern fur seals** have dense fur, arranged in two layers. The coat has a thick undercoat of soft fur, covered by longer, coarser hair. These seals keep themselves warm by trapping air in their fur.

- **The diet** of northern fur seals includes a variety of fish, but they feed mainly on squid and octopus. They also eat herring, mackerel and anchovies.

- **Killer whales**, sharks, Steller's sea lions and foxes are the main predators of northern fur seals.

- **Northern fur seals** are also hunted for their meat and fur. A number of these seals have died by accidentally getting caught in fishing nets.

Monk seal

- **Monk seals** are true seals, which means they do not have ear flaps. There are three kinds of monk seal: Mediterranean, Hawaiian and Caribbean.

- **It is believed that monk seals** got their name because their smooth brown coats resemble the robes of a Franciscan monk. They might have also been given this name because they lead a solitary life, much like monks do.

- **Monk seals** are often referred to as 'living fossils' because, according to fossil records, they have existed for about 15 million years.

- **Mediterranean monk seals** are the most endangered of all seals. It is illegal to kill these seals but they are still killed by fishermen who view them as pests that damage nets and eat up fish stocks.

- **Hawaiian monk seals** are the second most endangered seal species. They are found off the north-west coasts of the Hawaiian Islands.

- **Hawaiian monk seals** were once killed in great numbers by seal hunters, or sealers, for their meat. Shark attacks are also responsible for the decline in their population.

- **Male Hawaiian monk seals** are known to be very aggressive and often injure and kill the females and younger seals. This is known as mobbing.

> **. . .FASCINATING FACT. . .**
> History tells us that Christopher Columbus ordered his ship's crew to kill several Caribbean monk seals for food during an expedition. This marked the beginning of a cruel exploitation which eventually led to their extinction.

▲ *Monk seals can dive to depths of about 500 m in search of food. They can stay under water for 15 minutes while hunting.*

- **Today,** there are only about 1500 Hawaiian monk seals and 500 Mediterranean monk seals left in the world.

- **The Caribbean monk seal**, also known as the West Indian monk seal, is extinct.

- **This seal** was wiped out as a result of being extensively hunted by humans, for its meat and fat. It was last recorded in 1952, off Seranilla Bank between Jamaica and Honduras.

Sea lions

- **Sea lions** are eared seals. Unlike true seals, they have external ear flaps and their flippers are quite big.

- **These extremely vocal animals** make a roaring noise, which gives them their name. They are brownish in colour, with the males being darker than the females.

- **Sea lions** use their flippers to swim and paddle in water as well as walk on land. They can use their flippers as legs.

- **Being highly social creatures**, sea lions swim in large groups.

- **Steller's sea lion** is the largest type of sea lion. The males can grow up to 3 m in length. They are found in the northern waters of the Pacific Ocean, and are very common off Alaska.

- **The diet** of a sea lion includes mainly fish, crab, squid, octopus and clams. Steller's sea lion also feed on seals and small otters.

- **Steller's sea lion** and California sea lion are the best-known species. The former are tamed very easily and are popular attractions in water parks.

- **California sea lions** are found along the rocky western coast of North America. They are also found on the Galapagos Islands. The males are over 2 m in length and the females are smaller.

- **Killer whales** are the biggest enemies of sea lions. Sharks are also known to hunt California sea lions.

- **A large number** of sea lions die as a result of getting caught in fishing nets. There are now laws restricting the hunting of sea lions. Steller's sea lion has been declared as endangered.

▼ *Sea lions nurse their pups for about a year. Duing this period they leave their pups to go hunting in the sea and return after five days to continue nursing.*

Sea cows

- **Manatees and dugongs** are both types of sea cow. They are large, thick-bodied mammals. Apart from whales and dolphins, sea cows are the only other mammals that live completely in water.

▲ *A diver tagging a manatee. Florida manatees usually swim at a speed of 3–10 km/h or less. However, they can manage speeds of about 24 km/h for short bursts.*

- **Dugongs** are found in the tropical waters of the Indian and Pacific oceans, while manatees are found off the Caribbean Islands, the southeast United States and West Africa.

- **Sea cows** graze on seagrasses and other aquatic plants, hence the name 'sea cow'. There are only four living species in this group, of which three belong to the manatee family.

- **Sea cows** are also called sirenians, after the Sirens, or mermaids, of Greek mythology. It is believed that sailors probably mistook sea cows for creatures that were half human and half fish, thus giving rise to the mermaid legends.

- **Steller's sea cow**, one of the largest species, is now extinct. It was killed for its meat and skin. Since this slow-moving mammal could not defend itself the population was completely wiped out.

- **Steller's sea cow** was first discovered in the Arctic waters in 1741 by the crew of the famous Russian explorer, Captain Vitus Bering.

- **Manatees have a long**, rounded body that tapers towards the tail. Their average length is 3.5 m. They have a short, square snout, and are mostly grey in colour.

- **Dugongs and manatees** are closely related to elephants. Dugongs are very similar to manatees in both looks and habits, although some are slightly smaller.

- **Both manatees and dugongs** are slow swimmers and use their forelimbs and tails to move in the water. They do not have hind limbs.

- **Unlike the dugong**, the manatee's forelimbs are set very close to its head. The tail of the dugong is forked and pointed like a whale's, while the manatee has a round, flat, paddle-like tail.

221

Walruses

- **Walruses** are close relatives of seals and sea lions. They are, however, much bigger and they also have tusks.

- **These animals** are found in the Arctic region, at the edge of the polar ice sheet. There are two types of walrus: the Pacific and the Atlantic.

- **Pacific walruses** live in and around the Bering Sea and off Siberia, Alaska and Kamchatka in Russia. They are bigger than Atlantic walruses, which are found in the Canadian Arctic, the west Russian Arctic and off the coast of Greenland.

- **Walruses** are bulky creatures and can measure over 4 m in length. The males are bigger than the females and their tusks are longer.

- **The body** of the walrus is reddish-brown and has very little hair. Although it has a huge body, the head of the walrus is quite small in proportion.

- **The tusks** are in fact a pair of elongated upper canine teeth. The walrus uses its tusks to defend itself and also as hooks for pulling itself out of the water onto the slippery ice.

- **Like most marine mammals**, walruses have a thick layer of fat or blubber that protects them from the cold.

- **Walruses have four limbs** that are well adapted for walking on land.

...FASCINATING FACT...
Walruses are noisy, social creatures. They often gather in huge numbers and bellow together.

● **Polar bears** are the natural predators of the walrus on land. In water, killer whales are their biggest enemies. Walruses eat clams and mussels.

● **People have killed walruses** in large numbers for their tusks. Eskimos used to hunt them for their fat and meat.

▲ *Male walruses use their tusks to threaten rivals and thus establish dominance.*

Sea otters

▼ *Sea otters use pieces of rocks to crack open clams, mussels and other shellfish.*

● **Sea otters** are close relatives of weasels, skunks, ferrets, badgers and minks.

● **They are commonly** found along the coasts of the Pacific Ocean. Southern otters are found off California, northern otters near Alaska and the Asian ones off Japan and Kamchatka, Russia.

- **Sea otters** live in waters close to the shore. They prefer rocky bottoms and coasts. Some, however, are found along sandy shores.

- **Sea otters are,** on average, around 1.5 m long. These animals have an elongated, streamlined body and sharp claws on their feet.

- **The hind feet** are webbed, making sea otters fast swimmers. However, they move slowly on land. Sea otters spend most of their time in the water.

- **A dense coat** of fur protect sea otters from the cold waters of the Pacific Ocean. The coat is dark brown in colour, and much paler at the head.

- **Sea otters** spend a lot of time grooming and cleaning their fur, which they comb with their claws.

- **The animals feed** on fish, crab, squid and sea urchins. They also eat clams and abalone, a type of shellfish, by beating them against the rocks to break open the shells.

- **Sharks**, killer whales, bears, coyotes and eagles are the primary predators of sea otters.

- **Sea otters** are endangered. They have been regularly hunted for their thick fur, causing a steep decline in their numbers. Oil spills have also killed numerous sea otters.

. . . **FASCINATING FACT** . . .
The sea otter is the only marine mammal that does not have a layer of blubber to protect it from cold water. Instead, its dense fur traps warm air, keeping the animal warm.

Symbiosis

- **A unique bonding**, known as symbiosis, exists among certain animals. This refers to the dependence of two species on each other for food, protection, cleaning or transportation.

- **Symbiosis** occurs in many habitats, although it is more prevalent in the oceans.

- **Symbiosis** is divided into three main categories, based on the kind of relationship that the animals share. These are mutualism, commensalism and parasitism.

- **A relationship** in which both creatures benefit is known as mutualism. This kind of bonding helps them survive in extreme conditions.

- **A well-known example** of mutualism is the relationship between the sea anemone and the clownfish. The sea anemone's poisonous tentacles protect the clownfish, which lives among them. The fish returns the favour by keeping the tentacles clean.

- **Cleaner fish**, like gobies, wrasse and shrimps, also represent mutualism. These fish are found at the 'cleaning stations' in coral reefs, where they clean bigger fish by removing parasites, dead skin and tissue.

- **In commensalism**, one species benefits while the other is unaffected. For example, remoras attach themselves to sharks and get a free ride. They also feed on the scraps of their hosts.

- **In parasitism**, one species benefits at the expense of the other. The one that benefits is called a parasite.

- **Parasites** can be found inside or on the body of the host. External parasites are called ectoparasites, while those found inside the body are called endoparasites.

- **Lice and barnacles** that attach themselves to the body of whales and turtles are examples of ectoparasites.

A cleaner wrasse fish cleaning a giant grouper's eye.

Gulls

▶ *Larger species of gulls, such as this common gull, attain their full plumage within four years, while the smaller ones take only two years.*

- **A large number** of birds live around the oceans. Of these, gulls, or seagulls, are the most common. These birds are migratory, and there are about 43 species around the world.

- **Gulls** range in length from 28 cm to 80 cm. Most species have white and grey plumage or feathers. Some have black markings on the back, wings and head.

228

- **These birds** have a sharp, hooked bill, which helps them kill small birds and similar prey. They also have webbed feet to paddle on water surfaces. Gulls cannot dive underwater.

- **Gulls** use the wind to stay aloft without flapping their wings.

- **The colour** of the plumage changes throughout the gull's life. Some even have a different winter and summer plumage.

- **Black-headed gulls** have dark heads and red-coloured bills in summer. In winter, however, the heads of these species turn white with a dark grey spot. It is believed that this gives the bird better camouflage in the snow.

- **Many gulls** venture inland and hunt among garbage for food. They are also great scavengers and feed on dead animal matter along seashores.

- **Gulls** are able to fish in shallow waters and often prey on the eggs of other seabirds. Some of them even feed on eggs laid by their own species.

- **Gulls** make simple grass-lined nests, mostly on flat ground in isolated areas of beaches. Some nest on ledges in cliffs.

- **Commonly found** species include herring, common, black-headed and ring-billed gulls. The great black-backed gull is the largest of all.

...FASCINATING FACT...
Gulls might be popularly called seagulls but very few species actually venture into the open seas. Most prefer to keep to the shore, while some come to the coast only during the breeding season.

Pelicans

- **Pelicans** can be easily identified by their long bill and massive throat pouch. They are strong swimmers and the largest diving birds.

- **They are big birds**, with a long neck and short legs. Adult pelicans grow up to 1.8 m in length and weigh 4–7 kg. Males are larger than females. Their wing span can measure up to 3 m.

- **There are seven species** of pelicans. All are found in warmer climates. Most pelicans can also live near bodies of fresh water. The brown pelican, however, is excusively a seabird.

- **Most pelicans** are white, except for brown and Peruvian pelicans, which are dark in colour. American white pelicans have black wing tips.

- **Pelicans** breed in colonies. Nearly 40,000 birds come together on isolated shores or islands to breed.

- **In some species**, the colour of the bill and pouch changes during the mating season. The front part of the pouch turns a bright salmon pink, while the base becomes deep yellow. Parts of the bill change to bright blue and a black strip can be seen from the base to the tip.

- **The female pelican** builds a nest by digging a hole in the ground using her bill and feet. She then lines the hole with grass, leaves and feathers. Three days later, she lays about three eggs in her new nest.

- **While fishing**, this bird uses its pouch as a net to catch the prey. Once the prey is caught, the pelican draws the pouch close to its chest to empty the water out and swallow the prey. Food is also carried in the pouch and later retrieved to feed the chicks.

- **Different species** have different hunting techniques. Brown and Peruvian pelicans dive headlong into the water to catch fish.

- **Most other pelicans** swim and then pounce on their prey. Some fish in groups and drive the fish towards shallow waters where it is easier to capture them. Pelicans feed on small fish and crustaceans.

▼ *The American white pelican does not dive for its food but prefers to fish in large groups.*

Albatrosses

▶ *Albatrosses are also known as goonie or gooney birds. Once airborne, these graceful creatures can glide for hours without flapping their wings.*

- **The albatross** is the largest seabird, weighing about 12 kg. It is commonly found in oceans of the southern hemisphere, but some species also dwell in the North Pacific.

- **Most albatrosses** are white or pale grey in colour, with black wing tips. Some albatrosses have shades of brown.

- **The wandering albatross** has the largest wingspan of all birds, at about 3.7 m. It can grow up to 1.4 m in length, with females being smaller than males.

- **Albatrosses** have a sharp bill with a hooked upper jaw. They also have tubular nostrils and webbed feet. Their long, narrow wings make them powerful gliders.

- **These birds** are so heavy that they have to leap from cliffs to launch into flight.

- **Albatrosses** prey on squid, cuttlefish and small marine creatures. Unlike gulls, these large birds can drink seawater.

- **Of all seabirds** albatrosses spend the most time at sea. They even sleep while floating on the surface of the ocean. They come ashore only during the breeding season.

- **Albatrosses** nest in colonies on remote islands. Most of them have complex mating dances and may even change colour during courtship.

- **These birds** can travel thousands of kilometres. Adult albatrosses often go out into the sea in search of food for their young. Since the distances are great, the parents swallow the prey and regurgitate the food into the chick's mouth when they arrive back at the nest.

- **There is a superstition** among sailors that killing an albatross brings bad luck. This belief forms the theme of Samuel Taylor Coleridge's famous poem *The Rime of the Ancient Mariner.*

Petrels

- **Petrels** are closely related to albatrosses and are also excellent fliers. These birds spend most of their lives at sea, coming ashore only to nest.
- **There are about 100** known species of petrels. Although storm petrels and diving petrels are different from true petrels, all are closely related.
- **Most petrels** are migratory. A distinctive feature of this bird is the tubular nostrils on its bill. Storm petrels, however, have only one opening, serving both nostrils.
- **Petrels**, like albatrosses, are found mainly in southern waters.
- **Most petrels** breed in colonies on islands in the southern hemisphere. But some gadfly petrels breed farther north on islands such as the Hawaiian Islands.
- **The petrel's bill** is hooked at the end. The bill consists of several plates, which fit into grooves.
- **Common varieties of petrels** include the grey petrel, the snow petrel, the Westland petrel and the giant petrel. The giant petrel is the largest petrel and can grow up to a length of 90 cm, which is larger even than some albatrosses.
- **Storm petrels** are named so because they are often seen along the coast immediately before storms. This group of petrels includes the smallest species among seabirds. Some storm petrels are only 13 cm long, while the largest are only 25 cm long.

> ...FASCINATING FACT...
> Petrels can flutter and hover over the water, stirring up small fish and plankton that they pick up with their bill. While doing this, it looks as if they are walking on the water.

▲ *There are over 60 species of petrels in the world.*

● **Diving petrels** can be distinguished from others in the group by their nostrils, which point upwards instead of forwards. Unlike other petrels, they do not migrate.

● **Petrels** do not usually dive very deep into the water. Diving petrels, however, are excellent divers. Sometimes they can also be seen flying through the waves.

235

Murres and kittiwakes

◀ *Kittiwakes are the only species in the gull family that make nests on cliffs.*

- **Murres** look like smaller versions of penguins. These birds migrate up to 6000 km every year, covering the first 1000 km by swimming.

- **These birds** have a thin, pointed bill and a small, rounded tail. Like all seabirds, they are good swimmers and can dive to depths of 20 m in search of food.

- **Murres** come to land only to nest. They spend the rest of the year at sea, in waters that offer plenty of prey. They nest in colonies on cliffs or on rocky terrain along the coast.

- **There are two species** of murre: the common murre and the thick-billed murre. Although both species look very similar, the common murre's back is lighter in colour during summer compared to that of the thick-billed murre. In winter, a white streak is visible behind the common murre's eye.

- **Thick-billed murres** breed in large colonies on cliff ledges in and around the Arctic and sub-Arctic regions. They are 42–48 cm in length, while common murres are slightly smaller.

- **Kittiwakes** belong to the gull family. They are found in shades of white, grey and black. Their wings are mostly grey with black tips. Juvenile kittiwakes have a distinctive black 'W' band across the length of their wings.

- **It is believed** that kittiwakes were named because of their call, which sounds like 'kitti-wake'! They can also be called 'frost gulls' or 'winter gulls'.

- **Unlike other gulls**, kittiwakes do not have a hind toe and do not scavenge or prey on other birds. They feed on fish and live more at sea than other gulls.

- **Kittiwakes** are hardly seen on land except during the breeding season. They nest in large colonies on narrow cliff ledges.

- **There are two species** of kittiwakes: the black-legged kittiwake and the red-legged kittiwake. The black-legged kittiwake is the most common.

Frigate birds
and boobies

- **Frigate birds** are related to pelicans and cormorants. All five species in this family are found along tropical coasts. They are named after the battleship frigate because they attack other seabirds and steal their prey.

- **They are big** water birds, and their wings are large in proportion to the rest of their body. These birds cannot walk or swim. They take off from cliffs or trees.

- **Frigate birds** have long, pointed wings and forked tails, and they fly very fast.

- **There are two well-known species** of frigate birds: the great frigate and the magnificent frigate bird. The great frigate bird is more widely distributed and can be found along the tropical coasts of the Pacific and Indian oceans.

- **Male frigate birds** have a black, glossy body with a red patch of skin at the throat, called the 'gular sac'. During the mating season, the male fills the sac with air, causing it to inflate like a balloon. It then waggles its head and shakes its wings to attract the females.

- **Boobies** are close relatives of frigate birds. They are largely found in the tropical and sub-tropical coasts and islands.

- **They are large** water birds with webbed feet and long, pointed wings. These birds also have a long, sharp bill.

> ...FASCINATING FACT...
> It is difficult to distinguish between the males of the great frigate bird and the magnificent frigate bird. One of the most striking differences between these two species is their call. The great frigate bird makes a sound very similar to the 'gobble' of the turkey, while the magnificent frigate bird make a rattling noise.

- **Their webbed feet** help them to swim and dive. They are good divers and catch fish for food. Boobies nest in large colonies near the coast.

- **The name 'booby'** comes from the Spanish word *bobo*, which means stupid. Sailors thought these birds were silly since they allowed themselves to be caught easily.

- **Well-known booby species** include blue-footed, red-footed, Peruvian and brown boobies.

▲ *The blue-footed booby is commonly found in the Galapagos Islands.*

Terns

▲ *The common tern can be seen flying over fishing boats, waiting for discarded fish.*

- **Terns** are members of the gull family. They are found in most seas and oceans of the world, but are more common in the tropical and sub-tropical regions.

- **There are about 50 species** of terns. Of these the Arctic, Caspian, Royal and common terns are well known.

- **Terns** are lighter, smaller and more streamlined than gulls. They have a long forked tail, and because of this they are often called sea swallows.

- **These birds** are usually found in shades of black, grey and white. Some terns have black markings on their head. They have sharp, pointed bills.

- **Terns** are faster than gulls and can hover. They rarely go far without flapping their wings and usually do not alight on the water unless to catch prey.

- **The smallest** tern is the least tern, which is only 20 cm long. It has a wingspan of about 50 cm. The Caspian tern is the largest tern. It can reach over 50 cm in length and has a wingspan of over 130 cm.

- **Terns** do not swim. However, they are skilled at fishing and can dive into the water to catch their prey. Apart from fish, terns also eat other small marine creatures and insects.

- **The male tern** often performs a complex fish flight to attract females. He carries a small fish in his beak and flies low over a female sitting on the ground.

- **Most terns** nest in huge colonies on the beach. Some species also nest on trees, cliffs and rocks.

- **Royal terns** are seen in large, dense colonies on sandy beaches. Their nests, which they make on the ground, are often washed away, but they rebuild them.

Icy water

▲ *The term 'iceberg' has its origin in the German word* berg, *meaning mountain.*

- **The oceans** close to the North and South poles – the Arctic and the Antarctic – are partly frozen throughout the year.

- **These oceans** are covered with dazzling white icebergs and huge sheets of floating ice, which make it difficult for ships to navigate these waters.

- **The Antarctic Ocean** surrounds Antarctica, which is an island continent. The Arctic Ocean surrounds the North Pole.

- **In winter** the water close to the land is frozen. The ice melts in the summer and large chunks of ice, called icebergs, break off and float in the sea.

- **Massive slabs** of permanent ice, or ice shelves, break off and also float close to the shores in the Antarctic Ocean. The Ross Ice Shelf is the largest of these.

- **Unlike the South Pole**, there is no land mass around the North Pole. Most parts of the Arctic Ocean are covered by ice sheets.

- **Apart from the Arctic** and Antarctic oceans, there are other seas that freeze during winter. The Okhotsk Sea and the Bering Sea, divided by the Kamchatka Peninsula in the north-western Pacific region, remain frozen during the winter.

- **The water** in the Polar Regions might be freezing cold, but it is still home to a wide range of marine life. Whales, sharks, jellyfish, squid, seals, polar bears and seabirds can be found living in and around these oceans.

- **The harsh climate** on the Antarctic continent, however, is not conducive to life. This region is largely uninhabited. Only scientists brave the cold to conduct research. However, Inuit are known to live in the Arctic region.

Exploring Antarctica

- **Norwegian explorer** Roald Amundsen (1872–1928) was no stranger to the Polar Regions. After two successful expeditions to Antarctica and the North West Passage in the north, Amundsen made plans to go to the Arctic.

- **On September 1909**, Robert E. Peary became the first man to reach the North Pole. Upon hearing this news Amundsen immediately turned his attention to the South Pole.

- **British explorer** Robert F. Scott also began his expedition to the South Pole at the same time.

- **Amundsen**, who wanted to be the first to reach the South Pole, chose a different route when he set off in his ship *Fram*. His crew members were unaware of the change of route for a month.

- **On January 14, 1911**, Amundsen and his crew arrived at the Bay of Whales on the Ross Ice Shelf, where they set up their winter base camp. Throughout the winter Amundsen and his team prepared for their journey.

- **On October 20, 1911**, after several initial setbacks, a team of five men eventually set off for the South Pole. Each travelled on a sledge pulled by 13 dogs.

- **Meanwhile**, Scott was facing problems. He had taken ponies instead of dogs to haul sledges. The ponies soon became exhausted and were unable to go on.

...FASCINATING FACT...
In 1926, 15 years after first setting foot on the South Pole, Amundsen became the first person to fly over the North Pole, in an airship called *Norge*.

- **Scott's** winter camp was set up at McMurdo Sound, which was almost 100 km further from the South Pole than the Bay of Whales.

- **Amundsen** and his team took a mountainous route that was almost 3000 m high. He named the mountains Queen Maud's Range, after the Queen of Norway. At the summit, the party had to slaughter a few of their dogs to feed the other ones.

- **The team** persevered despite a searing blizzard. Their final obstacle was the Devil's Ballroom – a thin crust of snow covering a number of crevasses.

- **After braving** frostbite and exhaustion for almost two months Amundsen finally reached the South Pole on December 14, 1911.

▲ *Amundsen arrived at the South Pole 35 days before Scott. He left a letter addressed to Scott to show him that he had got there first.*

Antarctica – a profile

- **Antarctica** is the fifth largest continent. It lies in the southernmost point of the globe, and surrounds the South Pole.

- **It is an island** continent, surrounded by the icy Antarctic Ocean. The total area is about 14 million sq km in summer. This is almost 50 times the size of the United Kingdom.

- **Antarctica** is roughly round in shape. Two seas, Weddell Sea to the northwest and the Ross Sea to the southwest, cut into the continent.

- **Antarctica** was the last continent to be discovered. It is the remotest land mass, and by far the coldest and the windiest.

- **This continent** has the lowest temperatures on Earth. During winter, the temperature falls below –90 °C.

- **Antarctica** receives no rainfall. It is often referred to as a cold desert. The snow hardly melts or evaporates. Instead, it accumulates in icy layers year after year.

- **The thick ice cover** makes Antarctica the highest of all continents, with an average height of about 2300 m. The ice covering this continent makes up 70 percent of the Earth's freshwater.

- **The continent** has been broadly divided into Greater Antarctica and West Antarctica. Both these areas are separated by the Transantarctic Mountains. A large portion of this mountain range is buried under ice.

. . . **FASCINATING FACT** . . .
The Antarctic Treaty (1961) allows only peaceful activities such as scientific research on the continent and its ocean.

At certain places taller parts of the Transantarctic Mountains manage to peek out of the ice. These tips of rocks, called *nunatak*, are often home to birds, such as snow petrels.

▲ *Antarctica has been covered with ice for about five million years.*
It is home to large colonies of penguins.

Finding the North Pole

▲ *Robert E Peary was a civil engineer in the US Navy. He went on seven polar expeditions, the first of which was to Greenland in 1889.*

- **The North Pole** lies in the frozen waters of the Arctic Ocean. Its ice sheet shifts during very heavy snowstorms. This makes any expedition to the North Pole extremely difficult.

- **American explorer Admiral Robert E. Peary** (1856–1920) and his companion Matthew Henson understood the perils of an expedition to the North Pole. They made repeated trips to the region to assess the problems they might face.

- **Peary spent time** among the Inuit of Greenland, learning their way of life.

- **When he realized** that the North Pole was not a part of Greenland, and that it was further north, Peary chose Ellesmere Island in Canada as the starting point for the expedition.

- **Peary** and his companion had failed to reach the North Pole in two earlier attempts, but the lessons they learned during these trips proved invaluable and eventually led to their success.

- **The route** to the North Pole is especially difficult since ships cannot get close due to the ice sheets. Walking is not easy either, as the ice pack is full of pressure ridges and crevices.

- **The ship Peary used** for the expedition was called the *Roosevelt*. He designed it so that it was capable of crushing through the ice to reach as far north as possible. He took several Inuit to help with the expedition.

- **About 765 km** from the North Pole, the crew set up their winter base camp and began to prepare for the final part of the expedition.

- **A team of 24 men** and 19 sledges pulled by 130 dogs began the journey on February 28, 1908. Peary chose this time because the snow is slightly firmer during late winter. Support teams left in advance to set the trail and build igloo camps for Peary and Henson.

- **About 246 km** from the North Pole, Peary, Henson and four Inuit left the last support team to make the final dash with the best dogs and light sledges. They had good weather and the team finally reached the North Pole on April 6, 1909.

The Arctic - a profile

- **The Arctic region** is not a clearly defined area. All of the Earth that falls inside the Arctic Circle is termed as 'the Arctic'. The Arctic Circle is the imaginary circle surrounding the North Pole. Unlike Antarctica, it is not a single land mass or continent.

- **The North Pole** is in the middle of the Arctic Ocean. The ocean is surrounded by Russia, Greenland, Iceland, Canada and Alaska.

- **Contrary to popular belief**, the North Pole is not the coldest part of the Arctic region. Oymyakon in Siberia is actually the coldest, with a temperature of −68°C.

- **A large part of the land** surrounding the Arctic Ocean is extremely cold and treeless. This region is called the tundra. The word tundra is from the Finnish word *tunturia*, which means barren land.

- **The Arctic tundra** is so cold that the ground beneath the surface remains frozen throughout the year. This frozen ground is called permafrost. The topmost layer of the permafrost thaws every summer.

- **The permafrost** does not allow plants to grow deep roots. Hence, the tundra is not suitable for trees. However, a large variety of mosses, lichens, shrubs and small flowering plants can be found in this region.

> ...FASCINATING FACT...
> The Earth revolves around the Sun on a tilted axis. This means the North Pole faces the Sun during the summer and faces away from the Sun in the winter. As a result, in summer the North Pole has sunshine all day long, even at midnight, but in winter it is in total darkness all day, even at midday.

▲ *Snowmobiles have replaced dog sledges as a popular mode of transport in the Arctic region.*

- **The Arctic is home** to animals and birds such as the Arctic fox, seals, orcas, beluga whales, Greenland sharks, polar bears, and caribou. However, not all creatures live in the region throughout the year. A lot of mammals and birds are seen only during the summer.

- **Inuit**, or Eskimos, are the original inhabitants of the Arctic region. The word 'Eskimo' means 'eater of raw meat' in Algonquian, a Native American language. Today these people prefer to be called 'Inuit', which means 'the people' in the language Inuktitut.

- **Traditionally the Inuit** depended mostly on seals for their survival as the meat provided food, while the blubber was used as fuel and to make tents. During summer they travelled in boats made from animal skin, called kayaks. In winter they used dog sledges.

- **Today most Inuit live** in houses made of wood instead of igloos or tents. They wear modern clothing and travel in motorboats and snowmobiles. They also speak English, Russian or Danish apart from their native tongue.

251

Glaciers and icebergs

▲ *The process by which icebergs break away from glaciers is called 'calving'. Icebergs are said to make a fizzing sound when they calve.*

- **Glaciers** are moving masses of ice. They form on top of high mountains and in the polar regions, where temperatures are well below freezing point during winter and the summer is not warm enough to melt the snow.

- **Continuous snowfall** leads to the accumulation of snow. Each year, new layers of snow compress the previous layers, gradually forming ice.

- **Once the glacier** attains enough weight, it slowly starts sliding down a slope. Glaciers can be broadly divided into four types depending upon where they were formed. These are icecap, alpine, piedmont and continental glaciers.

- **Alpine glaciers** originate from mountains and feed mountain rivers. Piedmont glaciers are formed when alpine glaciers join at the foot of a mountain.

- **A huge blanket** of ice and snow covers most of Greenland and Antarctica. These formations are known as continental glaciers, or ice sheets.

- **Icecap glaciers** are miniature versions of continental glaciers. They usually occupy elevated regions such as plateau. Sometimes these icecaps break off at the edges and fall into the ocean.

- **Icebergs** are massive chunks of ice that break off the ends of ice sheets, glaciers and ice caps and then float into the sea.

- **The largest icebergs** are formed from ice shelves. These shelves crack at the outer ends, and icebergs drift into the sea.

- **The ice in some icebergs** contains tiny air bubbles that reflect light and give the iceberg a dazzling, white look. Ice that melts and freezes again can give the iceberg a blue tint.

- **Icebergs** are of different shapes and sizes. They can be broadly classified as rounded, irregular and tabular, or resembling a table top.

. . . FASCINATING FACT . . .
The part of an iceberg that is visible above water is only a small portion of its entire bulk. The enormous submerged part can cause great danger to ships. The saying 'tip of the iceberg' has its origins in this phenomenon.

Polar life

- **Extremely low temperatures** throughout the year make life difficult in the Polar regions. However, despite the cold, some plants and animals are able to survive in the Arctic and in Antarctica.

- **Antarctica** is covered with a thick layer of ice throughout the year, making it impossible for large land animals to survive. However, microscopic organisms and small insects thrive here.

- **Marine life** flourishes in the polar regions. Apart from numerous species of fish, animals such as jellyfish, starfish, squid and sea anemones live in the Antarctic and Arctic oceans.

- **Whales**, sharks, dolphins and seals are also found in these regions.

- **Several species** of albatross, gulls and petrels are found in Antarctica. However, this region is best known for its penguins. Arctic birds include puffins, gulls, snow owls, petrels, auks and guillemots.

- **Polar bears and reindeer** are found only in the Arctic region. Beluga whales and narwhals also thrive in the Arctic Ocean.

- **The Arctic** is home to several other land animals. The Arctic fox, brown bear, moose, wolf, ermine, musk ox, hare and squirrel also live there.

- **The lack of moisture** and low temperatures limit vegetation in the coldest parts of the polar regions. In Antarctica, land vegetation consists of algae, lichens and moss.

- **Coastal seaweeds** thrive in the southern waters of the Antarctic Ocean, along with some forms of marine algae.

- **In the Arctic**, the tundra supports a wide variety of plant life, especially during spring. This includes shrubs, grass, moss, lichen and certain species of flowering plants. Tall trees are unable to survive in these extreme conditions.

▲ *Coniferous trees can be found on the edges of the Arctic region where the permafrost ends. However, the icy polar regions are not suitable for trees.*

Penguins

▲ *A penguin and chicks. These social birds like to live in large groups.*

- **Penguins** are big sea birds that cannot fly. There are about 17 species of penguins, most of which live in the Antarctic region.

- **Some species** are found as far north as the Galapagos Islands. Smaller penguin species are found in warmer waters.

- **Larger penguins** are better at retaining heat, so they can live closer to the South Pole. The emperor penguin is the tallest at 1.2 m, while the smallest is the fairy penguin, or the little blue penguin, which is less then 40 cm in height.

- **Penguins** have a thick layer of fat that protects them from the freezing temperatures of the region. Their coats are waterproof.

- **These flightless birds** have black heads and wings, and a white underside. They have sharp bills and a short tail.

- **Penguins** do not use their wings for flying. Instead the wings act like flippers that help them swim. These birds are good divers and swimmers and can move in water at great speeds in search of small fish and krill.

- **On land**, penguins waddle about clumsily. They are often seen sliding down slopes on their bellies.

- **Adélie penguins** are known to waddle over 300 km every year to reach their breeding grounds. These birds depend on the Sun to navigate across the ice. Once the sun sets they are at risk of losing their way.

- **Rockhopper penguins** have a tuft of yellow feathers on their head. They are called rockhoppers because they jump around from rock to rock.

- **Penguins** have been hunted extensively by man for their fat and skin. Their natural enemies are sharks, whales and leopard seals.

Emperor penguin

- **Emperor penguins** are the tallest of all penguin species. They are also the heaviest seabirds. An adult emperor penguin weighs about 45 kg.

- **They live** along the coasts of Antarctica and are well adapted to the freezing temperatures here.

- **In addition** to using their huge fat reserves, emperor penguins also huddle together in order to keep each other warm. They take turns to move to the centre of the group to warm up.

- **Their heads** and wings are black in colour, while the abdomen is white and the back is bluish grey. Emperor penguins also have bright orange or golden patches near their ears.

- **Emperor penguins** dive to great depths in search of food, which they catch in their sharp beaks. They can dive to depths of more than 250 m and hold their breath under water for almost 15 minutes.

- **Their diet** consists of fish, squid and crustaceans.

- **These are the only** penguins to breed in the harsh winter of the Antarctic. The male penguins have a warm layer of skin between their legs and lower abdomen called the 'brood pouch'.

- **Emperor penguins** do not build nests. After courtship, the female lays a single egg and leaves it in the care of the male. She then goes to sea to hunt for food. Meanwhile the male holds the egg on his feet and covers it with his brood pouch.

- **The egg** takes about 60 days to hatch. During this time, the male emperor penguin braves icy winds and fierce storms to protect the egg on his feet. He even starves himself through this period.

- **After about two months** of hunting at sea, the female returns with food. She throws up, or regurgitates, the food to feed the newborn chick. Soon the male goes out to sea, leaving the female to take care of the chick.

◄ *Emperor penguins get their dark colouring as they mature. Chicks are grey in colour.*

Puffins

- **Puffins** are closely related to murres. They are short water birds, found mainly around cold Arctic waters.

- **There are four species** of puffins: the rhinoceros auklet, the Atlantic puffin, the horned puffin and the tufted puffin.

- **The Atlantic puffin** is the most well-known. Also called the common puffin, this species is found along the west coasts of Europe and off Maine in North America.

- **The puffin** is known for its brightly coloured bill, the shape of which resembles the beak of a parrot. The puffin, therefore, is also called the 'sea parrot'.

- **The bill** may be bright red, orange, blue or green. However, in winter it becomes dull grey in colour.

- **Puffins** can store a number of fish and other small sea creatures in their bills and carry them back to their nests. On average they can carry about ten fish at a time.

- **The tongue** and the upper part of the bill have spikes that help puffins hold on to several fish at a time.

- **Puffins** have webbed feet that help them swim. They dive underwater to search for food. Each dive can last up to a minute.

- **These birds** have thick, waterproof feathers to protect them from wet and cold climates. This, coupled with their ability to drink salt water, helps puffins to live out at sea for months at a time.

- **Puffins** breed in colonies and are known to pair for life. They dig burrows on cliffs and in the ground using their bill and feet. The female lays a single egg in the burrow.

◄ *Puffins have short, dumpy bodies, and are clumsy on land and in flight.*

Polar bears

▲ *Unlike other Arctic mammals, the polar bear does not shed its coat in summer.*

- **Polar bears** are found in the Arctic region, along the icy northern shores of Russia, Greenland and Canada.

- **They are the biggest** meat eaters, or carnivores, that live on land. Male polar bears are bigger than females and can weigh over 650 kg.

- **Polar bears** are easily recognized by their thick white fur. The fur provides the bears with excellent camouflage in the snow. Underneath its fur the polar bear's skin is dark.

- **The fur is oily** and waterproof. The hair does not stick together when wet, allowing the animal to shake the water off its body.

- **Polar bears** have small heads and slender necks. Their long, streamlined bodies make them excellent swimmers.

- **Their front paws** are wide and help them paddle through water. Several tiny protrusions and suction pads under the paws give these animals a firm grip on the ice. They also use their front paws to stun prey.

- **Polar bears** feed mainly on seals. They are also known to scavenge on the carcasses of whales and walruses.

- **These animals** are skilled hunters. Sometimes they lie still on the edge of the ocean, waiting for a seal to surface. The moment the seal comes out, the polar bear pounces on it.

- **In summer**, polar bears prefer to stalk their prey on land. While stalking, they sometimes lie on their chest with their rump in the air. They then lunge forward using their powerful hind legs, grabbing the seal before it escapes.

- **Polar bears** often cover their black nose with their paws while waiting for prey. This helps them to blend into the snow and remain unseen.

...FASCINATING FACT...

Polar bears do not drink water. It is believed that they get the water they need by breaking down fat, and from the animals that they eat.

Arctic seals

- **Arctic seals** include harp seals, ringed seals, hooded seals, bearded seals, spotted seals and ribbon seals.

- **Ribbon seals** are named for the light-coloured ribbon stripes around the head, the front flippers and the posterior. These ribbon stripes start to appear at the age of four. They are more distinct in males than in females.

- **These seals** have internal air sacs above their ribs. However, the use of these air sacs remains a mystery. Ribbon seals are the only species to have such air sacs.

- **Most Arctic seals** pull their front flippers together while moving on ice. Ribbon seals, however, move one flipper at a time.

- **Hooded seals** are named for the inflatable 'hood' on the top of their head. These hoods are found only in males, who also have inflatable nasal sacs. The male hooded seals inflate these sacs through one or both nostrils during courtship.

- **Bearded seals** get their name from their prominent white whiskers, which they use to find food at the bottom of the ocean.

- **Ringed seals** are the smallest of all pinnipeds. They do not grow longer than 1.5 m.

> ...**FASCINATING FACT**...
>
> Bearded seals are known as *mukluk* in Yupik, a language spoken by Alaskan Inuit. According to a story, some foreigners asked an Inuit what he was wearing. Thinking that they had asked him what his boots were made of, the Inuit replied "*mukluk*," meaning that they were made from a bearded seal. Today the term *mukluk* is used to describe all kinds of footwear made by the Inuit.

▲ *Arctic seals bang their heads against ice on the water's surface to create breathing holes.*

- **Ringed seals** are named after the ring-shaped marks on their body. These are the most abundant Arctic seals.

- **Spotted seals** were once thought to be the same as harbour seals. Both these seals were referred to as 'common seals'.

- **Later it was realized** that both species were different. Harbour seals are found only in ice-free water, while spotted seals inhabit pack ice. Moreover, spotted seals are the only seals that breed in China.

Arctic terns

▲ *Arctic terns live for at least 30 years, during which time they would have flown more than one million kilometres.*

- **Like all terns**, the Arctic tern is a member of the gull family. This seabird is known for its long migratory trips.

- **The Arctic tern** is found in the Arctic and sub-Arctic regions of Asia, Europe and North America.

- **In autumn**, these birds travel south all the way to the Antarctic region. This trip from the Arctic to the Antarctic and back measures over 40,000 km.

- **The distance** that Arctic terns cover during migration is the longest for any bird. It takes the species more than eight months to complete this journey.

- **After spending** the northern summer in the Arctic, the bird flies to Antarctica for the southern summer. Because of this, the Arctic tern experiences more daylight than any other creature.

- **Arctic terns** are not very large birds. However, some can grow to over 40 cm in length, from bill to tail.

- **They are usually grey** with a white underside and a black-topped head. The bill and feet are dark red. The webbed feet of Arctic terns are also fairly small, because of which these birds cannot swim too well.

- **Arctic terns** stay away from the water as far as possible. They plunge into the water in search of small fish to eat, quickly swooping down to catch fish that are close to the surface of the water. Arctic terns also eat squid, krill, shrimps and insects.

- **Most Arctic terns** nest in colonies on coasts and islands. They lay eggs on open ground, and like all terns they protect their young and nests.

- **Arctic terns** are often confused with common terns. However, the bill of the Arctic tern is much sharper and its feet and legs are smaller.

Greenland sharks

- **Greenland sharks** are found in cold Arctic waters. They live in the region throughout the year. They prefer to feed in shallow waters during winter.

- **These sharks** are extremely lazy and are hence known as sleeper sharks. Greenland sharks are also called gurry sharks.

- **They are one** of the bigger shark species. Their average length is about 5 m, but some of them can grow to over 6 m. The largest recorded specimen was 6.4 m long.

- **Greenland sharks** are greyish brown and have small fins. The dorsal fin is smaller than in most other sharks. This helps them swim under sheets of ice. They have a rounded snout.

- **These sharks** feed on a wide variety of prey. Their diet includes fish, seals, squid and dead whales. They use their short but sharp teeth to dig into the flesh of their prey.

- **Despite their sluggish nature**, they are known to hunt fast-swimming fish such as salmon. They are ambush hunters and wait until their prey is close enough before they attack.

- **Most Greenland sharks** have parasites called 'copepods' clinging to their eyes. Until recently, it was believed that these copepods glow in dark waters and attract prey.

- **The meat** of the Greenland shark is poisonous and has to be dried or boiled thoroughly before consumption.

- **The shark's flesh** contains high concentrations of chemicals such as urea and trimethylamine oxide. These induce an alcoholic effect on those who have consumed the meat without cooking it properly. For this reason, the Greenlanders call people who are drunk, 'shark-sick'.

● **The Inuit** hunt Greenland sharks for their skin, which is used for making boots. The teeth of these sharks are used to make knives.

▼ *Although, the Greenland shark prefers icy waters, some have been sighted off the coast of Maine in USA.*

The first boats

- **Based on drawings and models** found in Egypt, there is evidence that boats date back as far as 6000BC. In fact, recent studies suggest that boats were common in Asia and Africa even before that.

- **Wood** was the most popular material used to build boats in ancient times. In some ancient civilizations, such as Mesopotamia, boats were made of animal skin stretched over bones.

- **Later coracles**, or round boats covered with animal skin, were developed. These boats had wicker frames and were used mainly for fishing.

- **Kayaks** were another type of skin boat. They were used by the Inuit in Greenland for whaling. Kayaks are used even today, but mostly for recreation.

- **Dugouts** soon replaced skin boats. At first, dugouts were merely hollowed-out tree trunks. Later these hollows were made watertight by either inserting a separate piece of wood, called a transom, on both ends, or by sealing the ends with clay.

- **The Egyptians** built rafts by tying papyrus reeds together. These lightweight boats were used for fishing and for transporting light goods on the Nile. Later, the need to transport heavier cargo led the Egyptians to build stronger wooden boats.

> ...FASCINATING FACT...
> The Chinese made strong ships, known as 'junks'. These ships had a number of large sails usually made of linen, and were steered by rudders, or movable blades on the stern. The junks were largely used to transport cargo. However, in several parts of China, they also served as houses and schools.

- **Egyptian rafts** were made from planks of wood tied together. Unfortunately they were not very sturdy and were used only for trips along rivers and coasts.

- **Gradually sails** were developed, which could harness wind energy and move boats at a greater speed. Sails were first developed by the Egyptians, in 3500BC. They equipped their reed boats with square sails.

- **The Phoenicians** developed the sail further. They were mainly traders and needed to travel long distances. During the period 1500–1000BC, they developed excellent sail boats.

- **Shipbuilding** received a boost during the age of exploration, from AD1000 to 1500. The Vikings and the Portuguese and Spanish sailors went on long voyages, which required fast, sturdy and dependable ships.

▲ *The word 'junk' is said to have come from the Chinese word* jung, *meaning 'floating house'.*

271

Viking voyagers

- **Vikings** came from the Scandinavian countries of Denmark, Sweden and Norway. They were great travellers and spent much of their life at sea. They also invaded several countries.

- **The name 'Viking'** means 'pirate raid' in the Norse language. Although some Vikings were indeed pirates, most of them were farmers who sailed from their countries in search of better agricultural lands.

- **Their passion** for sailing made the Vikings the best shipbuilders of their time. They built two kinds of ships, the longship and the *knarr*, also called *knórr*.

- **The longship** was a long and narrow vessel, mainly used as a warship. On average the longship was 30 m long, and was powered by a single, square sail.

- **The sails** were made of sheep's wool or linen and often cost more than the rest of the ship.

- **Viking women** were responsible for making the sails. They first made small, diamond-shaped pieces and trimmed them with leather strips. These pieces were then sewn together to make a large, square sail.

- **The *knórr*** was a heavy cargo ship. It was about 17 m long and wider than the longship. It was used to carry cargo, such as wool, timber, grain and even livestock.

- **When building a ship**, the Vikings first erected the keel, a large beam around which the hull of the ship was built. The keel ran the entire length of the ship, from the bow to the stern, and was made of a single piece of wood.

- **Wooden planks** were affixed to the sides of the keel in an overlapping pattern. The planks were then fastened with iron nails. This technique made the ships sturdy and flexible. The floor was set on the keel, and bars were put across to make a deck and seats for oarsmen. The ships were steered by oars at the stern.

- **The bow** of the longship sometimes had an ornate carving of a snake or a dragon head. These ships, therefore, were often referred to as 'dragon ships' by the Vikings' enemies.

◀ *Viking ships are believed to be the first vessels to have crossed the Atlantic Ocean. The Vikings discovered Iceland around AD860 and settled in the new land.*

Erik the Red

- **Erik the Red,** born in AD950 in Jaeren, Norway, was one of the first European explorers to reach North America. He was born Erik Thorvaldson, but was known as Erik the Red because of his red hair.

- **When Erik** was a little boy, his father, Thorvald, was exiled on charges of murder. Thorvald and Erik left Norway and settled in Iceland.

- **Around AD982,** Erik was banned for three years from Iceland for manslaughter. During this time he explored Greenland, which had been discovered by his fellow countryman, Gunnbjorn Ulfsson almost 50 years before.

- **After his three-year exile,** Erik returned to Iceland to relate stories about the new land he named Greenland. He then sailed back to Greenland with several other Vikings who joined him to settle in this new land.

- **Erik's son,** Leif Eriksson, was born around AD980. He is popularly known as 'Leif the Lucky'. Like his father, Leif also was a great seafarer.

- **Leif** was only 24 years old when he led his first voyage. On this trip, he sailed to Norway carrying gifts for King Olaf. When he landed in Norway, Leif was invited to be the king's guest.

- **During his stay,** Leif learnt about Christianity and adopted the religion. He also took a priest back with him to Greenland in order to spread the message of Christianity.

- **As a boy,** Leif had heard the story of a trader named Bjarni Herjolfsson, who had spoken about sighting a new land to the southwest of Greenland. Soon after his return from Norway, Leif set sail in search of Bjarni's land.

On his way, Leif landed on Baffin Island in present-day Canada. He named it Helluland, which meant 'flat rock land'. From there he travelled south to Labrador, finally arriving at the land Bjarni had spoken about.

Leif named this new land Vinland, meaning Wineland, after discovering grapes on this land. The remains of a Vinland settlement can be seen at L'Anse aux Meadows in Newfoundland, Canada.

▼ *Vikings settled on Greenland's coastline. Inland areas were covered in ice.*

Marco Polo

- **Marco Polo** is one of the most famous explorers in history. He was born in Venice, Italy, in AD1254 and died in AD1324.

- **He was the first European** to travel across the entire Asian continent and reach China. He later published a popular book entitled *The Travels of Marco Polo*.

- **Marco Polo's** father, Niccolo, and his uncle, Maffeo, were great explorers too. In AD1260, the two men set off on their first journey to China, where they met Kublai Khan, the Mongol emperor.

- **Around AD1269**, the Polo brothers returned to Italy. However, towards the end of AD1271, the brothers once again embarked on another journey to China. This time, Marco Polo accompanied them.

▶ *It is believed that Marco Polo governed the city of Yangzhou during his stay in China.*

- **At first**, they planned to take the sea route from the Persian Gulf to China. However, the ships available were not good enough so they decided to travel by land.

- **On their way**, the trio crossed Afghanistan and the Pamir Mountains, before taking the Silk Road to China.

- **During his long journey**, Marco Polo recorded all that he saw. He also gave a detailed account of the rise of the Mongols and the life of Kublai Khan.

- **Finally**, three and a half years after they had left Venice, the Polos arrived at Cambaluc, the capital of the Mongol empire. The trio had travelled a gruelling 9000 km to reach their destination.

- **Marco Polo** was impressed with the Chinese, their means of communication, and their use of paper money and coal. In fact, he was so involved with the matters of the emperor that Marco Polo spent 17 years in the court of Kublai Khan before finally returning home.

- **Marco Polo** opted for the sea route on his return journey. He sailed through the South China Sea and the Indian Ocean. Several of his crew members died during the voyage, probably of scurvy or malaria. Marco Polo gave little account of his return journey.

...**FASCINATING FACT**...
Some historians doubt Marco Polo's journey since his journals do not contain any mention of the Great Wall and common Chinese customs such as the use of chopsticks.

Bartolomeu Dias

- **Bartolomeu Dias** (*c.* AD1450–1500) was a Portuguese explorer who travelled to the unexplored shores of Africa. Little is known about his birth and childhood.

- **Portugal** was one of the foremost seafaring countries in Europe during the 15th century. The king often commissioned voyages in search of new lands. In 1486, King John II sent Dias on a voyage to find a trade route around Africa leading to Asia.

- **After ten months** of preparation, Dias finally set sail from Lisbon, the capital of Portugal, in August 1487. He took two caravels, or sail boats, and one supply ship.

- **Dias** took with him six Africans who could convey the Portuguese king's goodwill to the native people. They were also to convey the king's message of peace and his wish to meet Prester John, the king of Ethiopia.

- **In 1488**, Dias became the first European to sail around Cape Agulhas, the southernmost tip of Africa.

- **On February 3, 1488**, Dias landed at Mossel Bay, located to the east of the Cape of Good Hope. He carried on until he reached the Indian Ocean by sea, a discovery that also opened a sea route to India.

- **During this journey**, Dias also sighted the Cape of Good Hope. He originally named it *Cabo Tormentoso*, meaning Cape of Storms.

- **According to a legend**, King John renamed it *Cabo da boa Esperanca*, or the Cape of Good Hope, since it opened up a world of commercial opportunities.

- **In 1497**, Dias accompanied the Portuguese explorer Vasco da Gama on the latter's expedition to India. He followed da Gama up to Cape Verde islands, where he left the expedition at Sao Jorge de Mina, the Portuguese fortress on Gold Coast, the present-day Ghana.

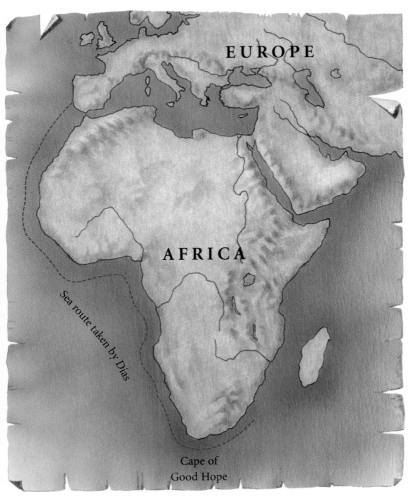

EUROPE

AFRICA

Sea route taken by Dias

Cape of
Good Hope

◄ The Cape of Good Hope is a headland near Cape Town, South Africa. It is often incorrectly regarded as the southernmost tip of Africa. However, Cape Agulhas is actually the southernmost tip.

279

Christopher Columbus

- **Christopher Columbus** (1451–1506) was an Italian explorer who sailed across the Atlantic Ocean to establish a westward sea route to Asia. Instead, this great mariner landed in the Americas.

- **Columbus** was only 14 years old when he first set out to sea. He worked on various ships and even led voyages to Tunisia and Anjou in Africa.

- **After settling in Portugal** for a few years, Columbus moved to Spain with his son. Columbus was driven by a passion for exploring new lands. He made repeated pleas to the Spanish monarchs to fund his expeditions.

- **Initially**, Columbus received no support. The Christian rulers of Spain were more concerned with battling the Moorish kingdom of Granada, than with funding overseas exploration. However, once victory against Granada became certain, they became more receptive.

- **Columbus** once again approached King Ferdinand and Queen Isabella of Spain. This time he convinced them that he would find a trade route to the Far East.

- **On August 3, 1492**, the Italian mariner finally set sail from Palos, Spain with three ships, *Niña*, *Pinta* and *Santa Maria*. The ships carried over 100 men, ship repairing equipment and other supplies.

- **After sailing** for five long months, Columbus and his crew sighted land. They set foot on an island that they thought was in Asia. But it was actually a part of the Bahamas. Columbus named this island San Salvador.

- **Columbus** continued his journey to Cuba, Haiti and the Dominican Republic. He named the natives 'Indians', since he thought that he was, in fact, in the Indies.

On March 15, 1493, Columbus returned to Spain, where he was accorded a hero's welcome. He was given the title of Admiral of the Ocean Seas and made the governor of all the lands he had discovered.

Convinced that Asia was located beyond the islands he had discovered, Columbus made three more trips to the west between 1493 and 1502. During this period he discovered Jamaica, Trinidad and Tobago, Grenada, Venezuela and Central America.

◀ Santa Maria *was wrecked when it ran into rocks off the coast of present-day Haiti. Its remains were used to build a fort on the island.*

Amerigo Vespucci

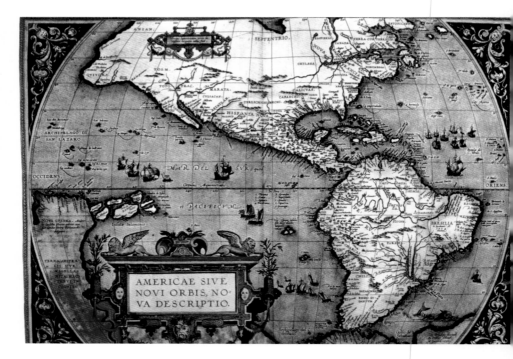

▲ *An early map of the Americas. Vespucci was not the first European to sight these continents, but he was the first to identify the New World as separate from Asia.*

- **The continents** of North and South America were named after the Spanish explorer Amerigo Vespucci.

- **Vespucci** was born in Florence, Italy in 1454. Even as a boy, Vespucci was interested in geography, the study of stars and the exploration of new lands.

- **He was the first** to dispute Columbus' claim that he had landed in a part of Asia. Instead, Vespucci firmly believed that the landmass discovered was a 'new world' and not in Asia.

- **In 1492**, Vespucci left Florence. He settled in Sevilla, Spain, where he became the director of a shipping company that provided resources for the expeditions of Columbus.

- **Vespucci** is said to have obtained the support of King Ferdinand of Spain for an expedition and set sail in 1497. Although little is known about this voyage, it is believed that he must have sailed along the coasts of Mexico and North America.

- **Vespucci** embarked on a second voyage in 1499. This was the first conscious voyage to the Americas. During this trip Vespucci explored the north eastern coast of South America and also landed in Cuba and the Bahamas.

- **In 1501**, he led another expedition to the Americas, this time funded by King Manuel I of Portugal. Although this voyage was not as successful as the others, Vespucci still managed to discover parts of Brazil.

- **In his fourth voyage**, in 1503, Vespucci went further south along the South American coast and spotted the Falkland Islands, off Argentina.

- **Vespucci** was one of the earliest explorers to describe South America as a continent. In his accounts published in 1507, the terms 'New World' and 'America' were first used with reference to the lands Vespucci visited.

- **Vespucci** made maps of coastal South America that were sold to a German cartographer. According to one theory, the maps were reproduced with Vespucci's name on that area of the map. Many people misunderstood this to be the name of the land, and it came to be called America.

Vasco da Gama

- **Vasco da Gama** (c. 1460–1524) was a Portuguese explorer who discovered a sea route to India.

- **In 1488,** Bartolomeu Dias had opened up the possibilities of a new route to the East by discovering the southern tip of Africa. He established that India could be reached by water, but his work was only half done.

- **Arab traders** held the monopoly of trade with the Eastern countries at that time. In order to outflank them, King João II of Portugal commissioned Estevão da Gama, Vasco's father, to complete Dias' journey.

- **Estevão** died before he could complete the voyage. Moreover, a shortage of funds put an end to further Portuguese expeditions for a brief period.

- **Following the death** of King João II in 1495, his cousin, King Manuel I ascended the throne of Portugal. King Manuel I decided to renew João's efforts to reach the East and put Vasco da Gama in charge of the expedition.

- **Vasco da Gama** planned his journey thoroughly and stocked four ships with supplies. He was accompanied by Goncalo Alvares, his brother Paolo da Gama and his companion Nicolao Coelho, who often sailed with Vasco da Gama.

- **On July 8, 1497,** da Gama set sail from Lisbon. His crew consisted of 170 men, many of whom were convicts.

- **By December,** Vasco da Gama's fleet had reached the southernmost part of Africa. From there, the fleet continued to sail along the east coast of Africa.

- **Vasco da Gama** stopped at coastal towns like Mozambique and Mombassa to replenish his stocks. Throughout his journey he faced opposition from Arab traders. Vasco, however, met an Arab guide at Malindi, in what is now Kenya. The guide agreed to lead the Portuguese across the Arabian Sea.

- **On May 20, 1498**, Vasco da Gama finally reached the Indian port of Calicut, which was then the main trading centre for spices and precious stones.

◀ *In 1524, Vasco da Gama was made the Portuguese viceroy to India and he set off on his third and final voyage. This great explorer, however, died soon after arriving in the city of Cochin, India.*

285

Ferdinand Magellan

- **Ferdinand Magellan** was born in 1480, into a noble Portuguese family. He led the first sea voyage around the globe. He was also the first European to cross the Pacific Ocean.

- **Like Columbus**, Magellan believed that a westward sea passage to Asia existed. He also realized that he would need to cross the New World, or the Americas, to do so.

- **Having fallen** out of favour with of the Portuguese monarch, Magellan gave up his nationality and left for Spain. There he approached King Charles I and told him of his plans to approach the Spice Islands in Asia from the west.

- **The king** granted him funds and on September 20, 1519, Magellan set sail with a fleet of five ships and over 200 men. He sailed along the coast of Africa towards Brazil.

- **On December 6**, Magellan sighted Brazil. After stocking up on supplies at Rio de Janeiro, the crew continued down the coast of South America towards the Pacific Ocean.

◀ *Magellan's journey not only proved that the Earth was round, but also showed that the oceans of the world were linked.*

- **Finally**, in October, 1520, they found a strait. Magellan named it the Strait of All Saints. Later this strait was renamed Magellan's Strait.

- **Conditions** in the strait were so difficult that one of the ships turned back. It took the remaining ships nearly 40 days to cross the narrow strait. At night, the crew saw an island where fires from Indian camps glowed through the dark. The crew named this island Tierra del Fuego, meaning 'land of fire'.

- **It took the fleet** four months to cross the Pacific Ocean. During this time, members of the crew suffered because of the lack of food and fresh water. Many came down with scurvy. Finally, the fleet arrived at the island of Guam in the South Pacific, where it managed to stock up on supplies.

- **The crew** continued to sail. On March 28, 1521, they reached the Philippines, where Magellan was killed in a tribal war. However, his crew carried on with the voyage under the leadership of Sebastian del Cano, one of Magellan's most skilled navigators.

- **On May 1, 1521**, Sebastian del Cano arrived at Moluccas, or the Spice Islands. After stocking up on valuable spices, del Cano and his men started on their return voyage. Finally on September 6, 1522, one ship carrying 18 crew members arrived in Spain, becoming the first to circumnavigate the globe.

Sir Francis Drake

- **Englishman Sir Francis Drake** (c. 1540–1596) was a skilled navigator. His remarkable achievements demonstrated the growing power of the English navy, which was competing with Spain and Portugal to gain a monopoly over international trade.

- **Drake** commanded his first ship in 1567 and travelled to the Caribbean on a slave-trading mission. During this expedition his fleet was ruthlessly attacked by the Spaniards. After suffering huge losses, Drake set out to replenish the stolen goods.

- **In 1572**, Drake led another expedition. On reaching the Isthmus of Panama, the land liking the Atlantic and Pacific Oceans, Drake became the first Englishman to see the Pacific Ocean. He also led some journeys to the Caribbean, attacking the Spanish ports there.

- **In 1577**, Drake was secretly sent by Queen Elizabeth I to capture the Spanish colonies on the western coast of the Americas. He set sail with five ships on December 13.

- **Drake** did not reveal the intended destination to his crew. When he turned south from Brazil, he faced opposition from his crew members.

- **Drake** disposed of two unfit ships at Rio de la Plata in present–day Argentina. He also gave a remarkable speech to cheer up his crew, and renamed his ship the *Golden Hind*.

- **The journey** proved to be difficult. When the fleet entered the Pacific Ocean after crossing the dangerous strait between the South American landmass and Tierra del Fuego, a violent storm destroyed one ship. Another turned back to England.

Drake, however, did not give up. He continued to sail north, hoping to find a passage through the Americas. It is believed that Drake must have crossed California and reached the United States–Canada border.

Unable to find a passage through the Americas, Drake turned west towards the Pacific Ocean. He visited Moluccas, Celebes, Java and finally the Cape of Good Hope.

When Drake returned home to England in September 1580, he had become the first Englishman to have sailed around the world.

▲ *Queen Elizabeth I visited Drake aboard the* Golden Hind *and knighted him for his efforts.*

Voyages to Australia

- **European sailors** might have found a sea route to the East through the Pacific Ocean. But it was not until the late 1600s that they discovered Australia and New Zealand. However, the maps made after 1540 indicated that a 'southern land' did indeed exist.

- **It is believed** that Chinese traders were in contact with the native inhabitants of this 'southern land', which we now know as Australia.

- **Arabs**, too, are believed to have traded with the natives, later known as Aborigines, in north Australia.

- **Willem Jansz**, a Dutch explorer, was the first European to sight Australia. In 1606, he sailed along 320 km of the Australian coast, all the time under the impression that it was an extension of New Guinea. He called the land Nieu Zelandt. According to certain reports, this name was not adopted. However, another Dutch explorer, Abel Janszoon Tasman, later used it to name New Zealand.

- **The first known landing**, however, took place in 1616. This time another Dutchman, named Dirk Hartog, landed on the west coast of Australia, after his ship was blown off course on route to Java.

- **In 1642**, Abel Tasman explored the southern coast and sighted the island of Tasmania, which was later named after him.

- **William Dampier**, a pirate, was the first Englishman to land in Australia. He explored the northern and western coasts.

- **Captain James Cook** was sent by British royalty in 1768 to discover the east coast of Australia. Sailing on the *Endeavour*, he went around the north coast and sailed along the east coast of the continent.

- **Cook** made a map of the east coast and discovered and named Botany Bay on the southeast of the island continent.

- **In 1786**, the British government decided to colonize Australia. On May 13, 1787, Captain Arthur Phillip of the British Royal Navy set sail for Botany Bay with more than a thousand people, mostly convicts. On January 26, 1788, Captain Phillip established the first European settlement in Port Jackson, what is now Sydney, in Australia. Although the Aborigines initially opposed it, the colonization of Australia was complete by the second half of the 19th century.

► *As well as studying the planets, Cook took wildlife experts with him on his explorations. They collected plants that weren't known in Europe, and drew sketches and made notes about them.*

Maori land

▲ *The Maoris were the first settlers of New Zealand. They are believed to have sailed all the way from Polynesia about 1000 years ago.*

- **Dutch explorer** Abel Tasman (1603–1659) was sent on a mission in 1642 to find the unknown 'southern land', referred to as Terra Australis Incognita. It was believed that this land extended across the Pacific Ocean.

- **On August 14, 1642**, Tasman began his journey from Batavia, present-day Jakarta in Indonesia. After reaching Mauritius, Tasman sailed east, missing Australia completely. In December 1642, he finally spotted the land we now know as Tasmania.

- **Tasman** named the island 'Van Diemen's Land' at the time. It was only later that the British colonists changed the name in honour of the explorer.

- **After investigating the island**, Tasman continued his voyage further east and discovered New Zealand. He named it *Staten Landt*, thinking that it was connected to a land located near the southern tip of South America.

- **Tasman** looked for a bay to moor his ship, but faced opposition from the Maoris, the natives of New Zealand. He lost four of his crew members in this encounter.

- **In 1766**, British explorer Captain James Cook had set sail in the *Endeavour* to observe the transit of planet Venus from Tahiti. He also had a secret mission – to find the unknown 'southern land'. He sailed south with the Tahitian chief Tupaia.

- **In 1769**, Cook reached New Zealand and claimed it for the British Empire. Gradually, settlers from Great Britain started moving to New Zealand.

- **Other Europeans** and Americans also arrived in New Zealand to make it a base for whaling and sealing. Missionaries followed to preach Christianity.

- **The early settlers** faced resistance from the Maoris. In February 1840, they signed the Treaty of Waitangi to settle land disputes, but a battle erupted in 1860. With this, the colonization of New Zealand began.

- **The Maoris** could not match the firepower of the settlers, whom they called Pakehas. Their defeat marked the beginning of European domination.

Cook's mission

- **James Cook** was born on October 27, 1728 in Yorkshire, England. He was famous for his voyages in the Pacific Ocean and is credited with the discovery of the Hawaiian Islands.

- **In 1755,** Cook joined Great Britain's Royal Navy. Soon after, the Royal Society of London chose Lieutenant Cook to lead a scientific voyage to the Pacific island of Tahiti.

- **The mission** involved the observation of a rare astronomical phenomenon, the passing of the planet Venus between the Earth and the Sun. It was believed that this would help scientists calculate the distance between the Earth and the Sun.

- **There was another motive** behind the voyage. The British Empire wanted to gain more information about Australia, a continent that had been sighted by Abel Tasman.

- **Cook** set sail from Plymouth on the *Endeavour*. On April 11, 1769, Cook and his team of scientists reached Tahiti after sailing around South America. They observed the Venus transit from there.

- **He then sailed** in search of the 'southern land' and reached New Zealand. On his return, he sailed along the eastern coast of Australia. Back home in England, Cook was commended for his achievements and made a naval commander.

> **... FASCINATING FACT ...**
> Fearing an outbreak of scurvy among his crew, Cook fed them citrus fruits, carrots andmarmalade. Later, it was discovered that citrus fruits, rich in Vitamin C, helped to prevent scurvy.

▶ *Captain James Cook's historic ship the* Endeavour *was built in 1764 in Whitby, Yorkshire, Britain. The ship was originally named the* Earl of Pembroke *and was first used to transport coal.*

- **Cook's** second voyage was more ambitious. Having concluded that neither New Zealand nor Australia was a part of the southern continent, Cook set off in search of this elusive land.

- **On January 17, 1773,** Cook became the first to cross the Antarctic Circle. Although Cook had sailed farther south than any other explorer, he never sighted land. However, he did discover a group of islands in the Pacific, which were later named the Cook Islands.

- **On his third voyage,** Cook wanted to prove the existence of the Northwest Passage, which was thought to exist as a link between the Pacific and Atlantic oceans. During this journey, he discovered the Hawaiian Islands. He named them the Sandwich Islands after his friend, the Earl of Sandwich.

- **Initially the natives** gave Cook and his crew a warm welcome. But their trust soon wore off, and they became hostile towards the foreigners. On February 14, 1779, Cook was stabbed to death by the natives.

295

In search of El Dorado

- **El Dorado**, a Spanish term meaning 'the golden one', was probably first used by 16th-century Spanish explorers to describe a legendary golden city in South America.

- **Stories of the vast wealth** of this city reached Europe, and 16th century Spanish explorers were determined to find this land.

- **It was believed** that whenever a new ruler was appointed to the Chibcha tribe of South America, his entire body was covered with gold dust. He then washed it off in a sacred lake, called Guatavita.

- **It was also thought** that the chosen leader threw a pile of gold and other precious stones into the lake. In the legends, the city was also referred to as Manoa.

▲ *It is believed that Sir Walter Raleigh first heard about El Dorado from Pedro Sarmiento de Gamboa, the famous Spanish explorer of the 16th century.*

- **According to a recent theory**, the city was called Paititi by the Incas. It is believed that when the Spaniards invaded their land in 1532, the Incas fled to Paititi with their treasures.

- **Several European expeditions** were carried out to find this golden city. Even today, the search for El Dorado continues.

- **One of the famous Spanish voyages** in search of El Dorado was that of Diego de Ordaz around 1531. In 1541, another famous Spanish adventurer, Francisco de Orellana, sailed down the Amazon River in search of the fabled city.

- **At the same time**, Philip von Hutten, a German explorer, also tried his luck. Although each explorer had a tale to tell, none of these voyages could conclusively prove the existence of El Dorado.

- **In 1595,** Sir Walter Raleigh, a British explorer, embarked on a similar mission. He returned and declared that Manoa was a city on Lake Parima in Guiana, present-day Venezuela.

- **German naturalist and explorer** Alexander von Humboldt finally dismissed this myth of a land of gold on a lake.

▶ *Alexander von Humboldt was the first to sail down the Casiquiare Canal, the only natural canal connecting two – the Orinoco and the Negro rivers. It was during this voyage that Humboldt discovered the truth about El Dorado.*

297

Diving deep

- **Man crossed the oceans** to reach far-flung new lands. Soon, the same oceans started to draw his interest. Adventurers began exploring the ocean depths. This quest produced some great divers and explorers in the 20th century.

- **Charles William Beebe** (1872–1962) was a famous deep sea explorer. In 1934, he set a record by diving to a depth of over 920 m off Nonsuch Island, Bermuda.

- **The simple**, hollow, deep-sea diving vessel that Beebe used was called the bathysphere. It was invented by Otis Barton, a wealthy engineer, who accompanied Beebe in one of the most dangerous expeditions ever.

- **Another renowned** deep sea explorer is Dr. Robert Ballard. He is best-known for discovering two of the most famous wrecks – the *Titanic* and the *Bismarck*. The former was found in 1985, while the latter was discovered four years later.

- **With over 100** deep-sea expeditions to his name, Ballard has also written several books on his discoveries. His other findings include *Yorktown*, the American aircraft carrier that was sunk in the Battle of Midway during World War II.

- **Ballard** also led the team that discovered hydrothermal vents in the seafloor off the Galapagos Islands in 1977. His recent achievements include the discovery of two Phoenician ships off the Israeli coast. Dating back to about 750BC, these are the oldest shipwrecks ever to be found.

- **Marine biologist** Sylvia Earle is famous for her expeditions that focus on researching marine ecosystems. She has numerous records and achievements to her credit. Sylvia also holds the depth record for solo diving by a woman.

- **Emile Gagnan** and Jacques Cousteau contributed to the field of deep-sea exploration through their invention, the aqualung. This device helped divers stay underwater for several hours. It was successfully used during the removal of mines after World War II.

- **Hans Hass** was a pioneer in scuba diving and underwater expeditions. His film, *Red Sea Adventure*, was judged the best underwater documentary at the Venice Film Festival in 1950.

- **Undersea still photographers** and filmmakers such as David Doubilet, Stan Waterman, Michele Hall and Howard Hall have also contributed to our knowledge of the ocean depths.

▲ *An underwater photographer taking photographs of a great white shark.*

299

Ships today

- **Modern ships** and boats have come a long way when compared to those used in ancient times. Today, we have a wide choice of ships and boats suited for all purposes, from pleasure boats to cargo ships and battleships.

- **The sailboats** of yesteryear have given way to sophisticated fuel-driven vessels. Iron, steel and fibreglass hulls have replaced wooden hulls to provide greater speed and durability.

- **Modern commercial ships** are of various types. However, they are broadly classified into cargo and passenger ships. Cargo ships are used to transport goods, while passenger liners carry people.

- **Among the different kinds** of cargo ships, tankers are most widely used. These ships are used to transport crude oil, petroleum or chemicals, and are the largest ocean-going vessels.

- **Reefers**, or refrigerated container ships, are used for transporting perishable goods, such as fruit, vegetables and meat.

- **Boats**, too, are of different types. These include high-speed jet boats, motorboats, iceboats, rowboats and sailboats.

- **Oars and sails** are still extremely popular. However, motorboats are more common now. These vessels have an internal-combustion engine that provides both speed and power.

- **Modern navies** have a variety of warships. These include cruisers, destroyers, aircraft carriers, frigates and various support vessels.

- **Our knowledge** of marine life and resources depends heavily on research vessels. Fitted with state-of-the-art equipment, these ships undertake study expeditions.

▲ *Frigates are an important part of modern navies. They are used to protect trading ships as well as other warships. They are also a major constituent of anti-submarine warfare.*

● **Specialized ships** and boats are used for fishing, patrolling, repairing and rescue operations. Sophisticated vessels like trawlers, long liners, seiners and lobster boats that use a variety of fishing gear have replaced old wooden fishing boats.

301

Ancient cargo ships

- **In ancient Mesopotamia**, which is in modern-day Iraq, the earliest boats were of three types. These were wooden boats with triangular sails, tub-shaped boats called *Guffa*, which were made from reeds and animal skins, and rafts made of timber and inflated animal skins, called *kalakku*.

- **The *kalakku*** did not have sails. Instead, it relied on currents to float downstream. Once the boat reached its destination, the cargo was offloaded and the boat, dismantled. It was then transported upstream on donkeys.

- **Massive clay pots** were used as floats. Animal skins were stretched across the inner and outer surfaces of the pots to keep them waterproof.

- **Reeds were used** by ancient Egyptians to make rafts that could carry goods across the Nile. These boats did not last long but were easy to build.

- **The earliest wooden boats** were simple structures. They were either pieces of log tied together or hollowed-out tree trunks. They could only carry a small amount of cargo.

- **With the need to transport** more cargo, the simple wooden boats were modified. Sails were first developed in Egypt in about 3500BC and were used in reed boats built to transport large stones.

- **The invention of the sail** revolutionized shipbuilding as it resulted in the ability to move large boat hulls. This allowed the transportation of large quantities of cargo at one time.

- **The Phoenicians** were the most skilled shipbuilders of ancient times. They made huge merchant vessels, with strong wooden hulls, capable of carrying large amounts of cargo.

- **While most ancient boats** were small and used to transport cargo down rivers, ocean-going vessels were being made in Asia.

▶ *Ancient Phoenician trading ships had broad beams, a sail and two stern oars. A large clay amphora containing drinking water was attached to the stem posts of these ships.*

● **People of the Indus Valley civilization** are believed to have used ships to trade with other civilizations such as Mesopotamia, while Chinese cargo ships called 'junks' are known to have travelled as far as Africa.

Modern cargo ships

▲ *Cargo ships that have fixed routes and charges are known as liners. Tramps are ships that do not operate on any definite route or schedule. These vessels arrive at any port where cargo is available.*

- **Cargo ships**, also called freighters, are usually huge and are used to transport cargo such as cars, trucks, food products, petroleum, textiles, minerals, gas and metals.

- **There are two main kinds** of cargo ships – container ships and bulk carriers. Tankers and supertankers are also cargo ships, but considered a separate category due to the nature of their cargo.

- **Container ships** carry their cargo in large containers. They are sometimes referred to as 'box boats'. These ships carry all kinds of dry cargo, from computers and televisions to furniture and foodstuffs.

- **Bulk carriers** are single deck vessels that are used to carry unpackaged, free-flowing dry cargo, such as grain, ore and coal. These ships have one large container or space. Products such as grain and coal are poured into this large container through openings in its roof.

- **Small container ships** called 'coasters' carry small amounts of cargo from minor ports to major ports. They are also known as feeder vessels, since they 'feed' cargo to bigger container ships.

- **Coasters** are named after the fact that they travel along the coast. These ships usually make more than one stop per trip.

- **With the advent** of container ships, huge cranes became a standard feature at cargo ship docks. Some cargo ships have onboard cranes called derricks. Cranes and derricks speed up the process of loading and offloading cargo.

- **Roll-on-roll-off**, or RORO vessels, and lighter aboard ships, or LASH, are popular alternatives to container ships. RORO ships have openings on their sides and stern, or the back of the ship, through which cars, trucks and even wheeled containers can be driven aboard.

- **The LASH vessel** is also called a barge carrier. It is a long cargo ship with a crane mounted on its deck. In this system, cargo is placed in flat-bottomed boats, or barges, that are loaded into a mothership, or LASH carrier.

- **The vessel** can load or offload several barges near a port and move on without wasting time. Barges that have been left behind are towed into the docks and offloaded at leisure.

Sailing ships

- **Sailing ships** use the energy of the wind to move. A sail is made up of pieces of cloth stitched together and tied to long poles called 'masts'.

- **The Egyptians** are believed to have first developed sails. Their reed boats were simple flat-bottomed structures with a huge square sail. Since these vessels did not have a keel, the mast was attached to the edge, or the gunwale, of the boat.

- **The Phoenicians**, during the period 1500–1000BC, modified the sailboats further. They also created a small space in the hull, called the 'deck,' to protect sailors from bad weather.

- **New sailing vessels** were developed for use at war. These were known as 'galleys' and had rows of oarsmen as well as sails. These gave way to the bireme, a big vessel that had two decks of oarsmen, followed by the trireme.

- **In China**, shipbuilders built a superior cargo boat called the 'junk'. This boat had a number of sails and was steered by rudders, or movable blades on the stern.

- **The Vikings** developed the longship, which was later replaced by 13th-century cargo vessels, called 'cogs', as the major carrier of goods in Europe.

- **In the 15th century**, sturdy boats called 'caravels' were developed in Spain and Portugal. They had four sails and were up to 25 metres in length.

- **Galleons** had long, slender hulls and were quite fast. The Spanish Armada used this vessel. The famous *Mayflower*, which took pilgrims to America in 1620, was a galleon.

- **With the British Empire** beginning to spread its wings in the 19th century, ships became larger and more fortified. They were often used to carry back riches from India and Africa.

● **The advent of steam** ships gradually led to the demise of sailing ships. Sailing is now a leisure activity, and sailboats are used for cruising, racing or fishing.

▶ *Egyptian sailboats are called* fellucas. *The earliest record of a ship under sail is depicted on an Egyptian pot dating back to 3200BC. These boats were made of either native woods or conifers from Lebanon.*

Tankers

- **Tankers** are huge ships used for transporting petroleum or natural gas. Some tankers also carry chemicals.

- **All countries** depend on oil and oil products, but few have these natural resources. Oil therefore needs to be transported from oil-rich countries to other parts of the world.

- **Oil pipelines** and tankers are the only two modes of transporting oil around the world. Tankers are, in fact, one or more tanks designed like a ship.

- **Tankers are divided** into various groups depending upon the nature of their cargo. The different types of tankers include Liquid Natural Gas (LNG) carriers, Very Large Crude Carriers (VLCC), Ultra Large Crude Carriers (ULCC), Medium Range carriers, SUEZMAX and PANAMAX.

▼ *Some tankers have caused huge environmental damage. Oil spills and other accidents can adversely affect the environment and marine life.*

- **The largest** of all tankers are the supertankers. They are alternatively known as VLCCs or ULCCs. These tankers are about 400 m long and mainly carry crude oil.

- **Supertankers** are bigger than even aircraft carriers, making them the biggest ships in the world. Since they are too large to approach most ports, these ships often have to offload their cargo into smaller vessels. Today, however, some ports have deepwater offloading facilities that are connected to the mainland by pipelines.

- **Tankers** carry millions of litres of oil. Even the smallest accident can cause the oil to spill and result in extensive damage to the environment. Hence, tankers require extremely strong hulls to prevent such accidents.

- **Tankers** with single hulls are at the most risk, since the hull is also the wall of the oil tanks. A breach in the hull would lead to a major oil spill.

- **Double-hulled tankers** are now becoming the norm. These vessels are considered safer because there is a space between the hull and the tanks. Very few oil tankers, however, have double hulls.

- **Tankers** also have sophisticated fire-fighting equipment, along with modern pumps to load and offload their liquid cargo.

...FASCINATING FACT...
The Norwegian-operated tanker, the *TT Jahre Viking*, formerly known as *Seawise Giant*, is the largest ship in the world. It is 458 m long and 69 m wide.

Container ships

- **In the 1950s**, Malcolm Mclean, an American trucker, came up with an alternative for the time-consuming and expensive process of manually loading and offloading cargo.

- **McLean** suggested that ships be loaded with big ready-made containers. These containers would be filled with cargo and lifted by cranes onto ships directly from trucks.

- **This process** of using containers to carry cargo is called 'containerization'. It is believed that the idea struck Mclean while waiting for the cargo from his truck to be loaded onto a ship.

- **Container shipping** integrated the movement of goods from trucks, trains, ships and even planes. Today, almost 90 percent of the world's cargo is moved in containers.

- **The first container ship** was the *Ideal X*, which sailed from New Jersey in 1956. The world's first terminal exclusively for containers was constructed in Port Elizabeth, New Jersey.

- **The OOCL SX-class vessels** are the world's largest container ships. The first to be built, the *Shenzhen*, is 323 m long and over 40 m wide. The vessel was launched on April 30, 2003.

- **Over the years**, container ships have also been modified to better suit the products they carry. Some carry sophisticated refrigerated containers for transporting perishable commodities such as fish, meat and fruit. These are called refrigerated ships, or 'reefers'.

- **Reefers** contain heavily insulated compartments. These ships have several locker spaces that can carry different products at a variety of temperatures. The cargo is moved about on conveyor belts or by electric fork-lift trucks.

- **Reefer equipment** has been modified to keep the goods they carry as fresh as possible. Most reefer containers have their own refrigeration units, which can be plugged into the ship's power source. If necessary, some reefers can even provide a humid environment for protecting sensitive products from dehydration.

- **Some reefers** are used to transport medicines, while others are used to keep goods from freezing in harsh climates.

▲ *Cargo is loaded onto container ships by huge cranes that can lift 20–30 containers per hour.*

Fishing vessels

- **People have used boats** for fishing since the beginning of civilization. Commercial fishing may be carried out by a single fisherman who takes his boat out to sea, or by huge fishing fleets.

- **Fishermen** in some countries still go out to sea in small wooden boats to cast their nets and wait for the catch. However, traditional fishing boats and methods have given way to bigger, more advanced vessels and new techniques that produce a very large haul.

- **There are three main** fishing vessels that can be found across the world. These are trawlers, seiners and long liners. All these vessels are more than 40 m long.

- **Trawlers**, also known as 'draggers', drag heavy nets, called trawls, across the seabed or through the water. These vessels are mainly used to catch shrimp, salmon and other edible marine creatures.

- **Whereas earlier trawlers** had sails, the modern ones are powered by diesel. They are often large and can measure up to 120 m in length.

- **Unlike trawls**, the mouths of seiner nets are closed before hauling them aboard. Seiners target fast-swimming fish like tuna and herring. The nets are allowed to float on water to catch these fish.

- **Long-liners** do not use nets at all. Instead, they have long lines with numerous baited hooks along their length. These lines trail behind the ship, hooking tuna, cod and even small sharks.

- **Other less common** fishing vessels include shrimp or lobsters boats, head boats and dive boats.

- **The sophistication** of modern fishing vessels has created its own problems. The use of modern equipment has increased the size of the catch but not without greatly reducing the fish populations in many regions. Most countries now regulate hauls in order to prevent the decrease in fish populations.

...FASCINATING FACT...
'Bycatch' is a term used to describe sea creatures that are not meant to be caught but are trapped inadvertently in fishing nets. Often the bycatch is not returned to the water despite the fact that it is unsuitable for commercial use.

◄ *Trawlers also have refrigeration facilities, allowing them to keep the catch fresh. Hence these vessels can also stay out at sea for several days.*

Luxurious liners

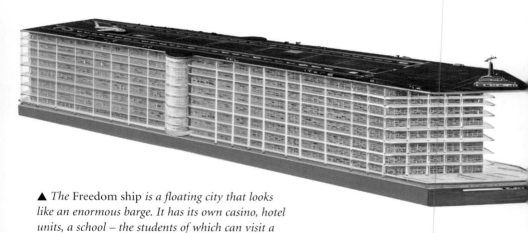

▲ *The* Freedom ship *is a floating city that looks like an enormous barge. It has its own casino, hotel units, a school – the students of which can visit a different country every week – and business units.*

- **Ships in ancient times** were not only used to carry goods, but were also a popular mode of transportation for people. Until the invention of the aeroplane, ships were the only way that people could cross the seas to new lands.

- **Ships that carry people** are called 'passenger ships'. These can vary in sizes. Smaller vessels are used for short, coast-to-coast journeys, while large ships with lavish amenities, called cruise ships, are used for pleasure trips.

- **Cruise ships** appeared only towards the latter half of the 20th century. Before that, intercontinental voyages were undertaken in large, motorized ships known as ocean liners.

- **Ocean liners** thrived towards the end of 19th century, when millions of people each year were emigrating from Europe to the United States. Some of the most famous ocean liners are the *Titanic, Mauretania, Normandie* and *Lusitania*.

- **The increased use** of ocean liners led to the establishment of several shipping companies. The better known of these included the White Star Line and the Cunard line.

- **The Cunard Line** is a British company that today owns the famous cruise ships, *Queen Elizabeth 2* and *Queen Mary 2*. It was set up by Samuel Cunard, the Canadian shipping pioneer, who along with a few others formed the British and North American Royal Mail Steam Packet Company.

- **The Cunard Line** was the first regular steamship service between Europe and the United States. Two huge Cunard liners, *Mauretania* and *Lusitania*, were launched in 1906. They were both around 240 m long. The latter was sunk by a German submarine in 1915.

- **The Cunard liners** were not the fastest or the largest. In fact, the company's rivals, the White Star Line, owned the fastest ships of that time. However, Cunard ships were known for their safety – a feature that set the company apart.

- **World War I** severely disrupted the transatlantic service. Some liners were taken over and used to transport troops. After the war, the transatlantic services recovered and boomed.

- **France launched the *Normandie*,** a liner famous for its luxury and modern art. Cunard followed with the launch of the *Queen Mary*, which was 310 m long. The revival, however, did not last long. World War II and the advent of jet aeroplanes in the 1950s effectively put an end to the transatlantic ocean liners.

The Titanic

- **The *Titanic*** was the pride of the White Star Line, a British shipping company. Built in Belfast, Northern Ireland, the luxury ocean liner was one of the largest passenger steamships of the time.

- **The ship** belonged to the company's Olympic-class liners. The others in this line were the *Olympic* and *Britannic*. The *Britannic* sank in 1916 after striking a mine laid by a German submarine in the Aegean Sea.

- **Like all transatlantic liners**, it was meant to transport passengers between Europe and the United States. It was about 260 m long and 28 m wide

- **The ship had about 900** crew members and could carry over 3000 passengers. Since the *Titanic* also carried mail, it was categorized as a Royal Mail Steamer, or RMS.

- **The *Titanic*** was the ultimate name in luxury at the time. Its most striking feature, the grand staircase, was immortalized in James Cameron's epic film based on the ship's tragic voyage. The ship had 16 watertight compartments in its hull and was thought to be unsinkable.

◀ *After its collision with an iceberg, the renowned* Titanic *took only three minutes to break apart and start sinking.*

...FASCINATING FACT...

Violet Constance Jessup, one of the crew members who survived the *Titanic* sinking, was aboard all three Olympic-class liners when disaster struck. She was a stewardess on the *Olympic* during the ship's collision with HMS *Hawke* in 1911. She was a nurse aboard the *Britannic* when it sank in the Aegean Sea in 1916.

- **At noon on April 10, 1912**, the *Titanic* began her maiden voyage. She set sail from Southampton, England, towards New York, United States. Among the passengers were several famous personalities including the American businessmen Benjamin Guggenheim and John Jacob Astor IV, and the writers Jacque Futrelle and Francis Davis Millet.

- **Four days later**, on April 14, the ship struck an iceberg off the coast of Newfoundland. It was almost midnight when the disaster occurred.

- **The iceberg** ripped through the hull, causing the first six watertight compartments to flood. Soon, the ship broke in two and the bow sank almost immediately. It was followed by the stern, which hit the ocean bottom at high speed, severely damaging the hull.

- **Another steamship**, called *Californian*, was anchored nearby when the disaster struck. The crew members of the *Californian* had seen the white rockets being fired from the *Titanic*. However, they failed to recognize these as distress signals.

- **By the time** the Cunard liner *Carpathia* came to the rescue, almost 1500 passengers had died. Only 712 passengers lived to tell the story.

Cruise ships

- **By the end of the 1950s,** ocean liners were completely replaced by jet planes as a popular mode of transport. More and more people chose to fly in order to save time. However, some still preferred the leisurely aspects of sailing the oceans.

- **Pleasure voyages** aboard ships soon became popular, beginning a new era in cruising. Today, cruise ships are an integral part of the tourism industry.

- **Like ocean liners**, modern cruise ships also boast lavish decor and comforts. Cruise ships, however, give more importance to amenities as compared to ocean liners, which put speed above all.

- **Ocean liners** undertook long voyages across the Atlantic Ocean, and even travelled as far as South America and Asia. However, modern cruise ships mainly operate on shorter routes and make more stops.

- **In addition to the crew**, these liners also have a separate hospitality staff. Some cruise ships have more staff than passengers in order to offer superior service.

- **Until the 1980s**, cruise ships were not as huge as the ocean liners. Knut Kloster, the director of Norwegian Caribbean Lines, changed that when he bought one of the biggest ocean liners, the *SS France,* and renovated it. He converted it into a cruise ship and renamed it *SS Norway*.

- **Soon large cruise vessels** became the norm. Today, most modern cruise ships are over 300 m in length. The longest is the *Queen Mary 2*, at 345 m.

- **Today**, there are several shipping companies that offer cruise voyages. The best-known include the Carnival Cruise Lines, Celebrity Cruises, the Cunard Line, Royal Caribbean International and Holland America.

● **The Caribbean Islands** and the Mediterranean region attract the most cruises. Some liners also offer trips to the icy waters of Antarctica.

▼ *Modern cruise ships are like floating hotels. They come complete with restaurants, bars, lounges, theatres, libraries, sport centres, mini golf courses, swimming pools, clubs, shopping malls and casinos.*

The Queen of luxury

- **One of the most famous** cruise liners today is the *Queen Mary 2*. It is the flagship of the Cunard Line and was built to replace the earlier Cunard flagship, *Queen Elizabeth 2*.

▲ Queen Elizabeth 2, *docking in Sydney, Australia. Prior to the launch* of Queen Mary 2, *the* Queen Elizabeth 2 *was the largest cruise liner.*

- **The *Queen Mary 2*** was named after another old Cunard liner, *Queen Mary*, which sailed the Atlantic Ocean from 1936 to 1967. The original *Queen Mary* now serves as a hotel off the California coast.

- **The *Queen Mary 2*** is around 34 m longer than the original *Queen Mary*. At 345 m, it is the longest cruise liner in the world.

- **Unlike its predecessors**, the *Queen Mary 2* is not a steamship. Instead, it has gas turbines and diesel generators that power its electric motors.

- **The ship was christened** by Queen Elizabeth II of the United Kingdom on January 8, 2004. It can carry over 2600 passengers, and boasts one crew member per couple.

- **This grand liner** has 14 decks of sports facilities, five swimming pools and ten restaurants. Apart from the usual amenities such as a library, theatre and internet access, the ship also displays over 300 valuable works of art.

- **One of the features** that sets the *Queen Mary 2* apart is its onboard planetarium, which at times serves as a cinema and a broadcasting studio.

- **The liner** made its inaugural voyage from Southampton, England to Fort Lauderdale, Florida, USA on January 12, 2004. It carried 2620 passengers on this voyage.

- **Apart from the transatlantic route**, *Queen Mary 2* also undertakes cruises to almost every part of the world including the Caribbean Islands, the Arctic regions and exotic locations in the Mediterranean.

- **During the Athens Olympics in 2004**, *Queen Mary 2* docked at the port of Athens as a floating home to dignitaries and celebrities.

Ferries

- **Ferries** usually have fixed routes, schedules and destinations. They most commonly operate from towns and cities near rivers and seas, and are an important means of public transport.

- **They mainly run** across rivers or bays, or from one point in a harbour to another. Long-distance ferries connect coastal islands with each other, or with the mainland.

- **The Staten Island Ferry** in the New York City harbour is a famous harbour ferry. The most well known long-distance ferry operates in the English Channel, between Great Britain and the rest of Europe.

- **Large ferries** also operate between Finland and Sweden. Some of these ferries carry hundreds of cars in their car decks. Some even transport railcars.

- **When a ferry** makes several stops it is called a waterbus. Such motorized vessels are common across the major water channels of Venice, Italy.

- **Ferry boats dock** at a specially designed ferry slip. If the ferry transports vehicles, the slip usually has an adjustable ramp called an 'apron' to facilitate loading and unloading.

- **Many ferry services** in Europe use hydrofoils, which are boats with wing-like foils mounted on struts below the hull. As the vessel picks up speed, the foils lift the hull out of water. This ensures a speedy service.

- **The Spirit of Tasmania** ferries form one of the best-known ferry services in the world. It carries passengers and vehicles across the Bass Strait between Tasmania and mainland Australia.

- **The world's largest ferry** operations can be found in the Strait of Georgia in British Columbia, Canada and Puget Sound in Washington, United States. Each operation comprises about 25 ferries.

▲ *A ferry is a boat or a ship that transports passengers over short distances.*
Some also carry vehicles and animals.

Patrolling the seas

- **The oceans** can be hostile at times. Danger can threaten those who venture into the deep waters. Many countries spend a lot of money to ensure the safety of people sailing the oceans and visiting the beaches.

- **The open waters** are constantly patrolled by authorities like coast guards, who keep a close watch on the activities on and off the coast.

- **Coast guards** help those in trouble at sea. They co-ordinate search and rescue missions, and are also responsible for protecting the coastal environment. They enforce maritime laws and are responsible for national security.

- **Coast guards** have their own fleet of cars, boats, lifeboats, ships, helicopters and planes. They use patrol boats to survey the surrounding waters of a coast and keep a vigil on all activities.

- **Floating hospitals,** or 'hospital ships', are large ocean-going vessels with medical staff and equipment. They are mainly used during a war.

- **Two of the largest hospital ships** are the USNS *Mercy* and USNS *Comfort*, both of which are operated by the United States Navy. All modern hospital ships are protected under the laws of war and display the Red Cross symbols.

- **A lifeboat** is an important rescue vessel. Lifeboats are of two kinds. One is carried by huge passenger ships, while others are launched from the shore.

- **Onboard lifeboats** usually carry three days' supply of food and water, medical supplies, oars and basic navigational equipment. Some lifeboats include electric heaters, rainwater catchments and sailing and fishing equipment.

- **Lifeboats** launched from the shore are called rescue lifeboats or rescue boats. Modern rescue boats are powered by diesel, while older ones, powered by sails, are also in use. All rescue boats have radios that help the crew to locate ships and onboard lifeboats set on sail. They also carry first-aid equipment and food.

● **The *Titanic* disaster** led to the formation of an ice patrol. The International Ice Patrol locates icebergs in the way of ships and boats.

▶ *Coast guards are mainly devoted to maintaining maritime law and saving people who are in danger at sea. However, during wars they are also responsible for harbour defence, port security and coastal patrols. In fact, in some countries coast guards are a part of the navy.*

325

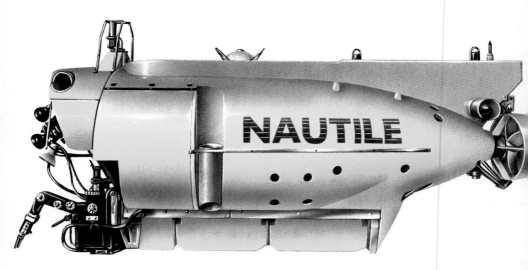

▲ *The submersible,* Nautile, *made more than 90 dives into the ocean depths to recover artefacts from the ill-fated* Titanic.

- **Specialized vessels** such as submersibles, tugboats, icebreakers and dredgers often lend ships a helping hand and perform tasks that other ships are unable to perform.

- **The submersible** is an underwater research vessel. It is primarily used to conduct underwater scientific research and for military and industrial purposes.

- **Submersibles** aid in studies of undersea geological activity, marine life, and mineral deposits. They also help to check on oil rigs. Submersibles involved in research usually accompany a huge research vessel.

- **Navies** use submersibles for a variety of tasks, including submarine rescue and repair, and mine detection.

- **Wreck divers** use submersibles for salvage operations, such as recovering ships, planes or valuable equipment that have sunk to the ocean depths.

- **Pressurized submersibles** are designed to operate in very deep waters. They can withstand the high pressure near the seabed.

- **The most sophisticated** of all submersibles are the remotely operated vehicles. These vessels do not need a pilot and are equipped with video and still-cameras and sensors.

- **Tenders are ships or boats** that service other ocean-going vessels. There are various types of tenders, including ships' tenders and submarine tenders. Tenders of smaller boats are called dinghies.

- **A ship's tender** helps to transport people or supplies to and from the shore or another ship. A submarine tender is a ship that carries supplies like food, fuel and other equipment to submarines. However, these are not very common nowadays.

- **Some modern cruise liners** have lifeboat tenders. In addition to serving as tenders, they also act as lifeboats. These vessels are bigger than normal lifeboats.

Tugs and icebreakers

- **Tugs, or tugboats**, are small but extremely powerful motorized ships. They are mainly used to guide ships into the docks. They also tow defective ships, barges and heavy equipment across open seas.

- **Although they are known** as tugboats, these are actually small ships and are quite strong despite their size. Modern tugs have diesel engines and can move at a reasonably good speed of 20 km/h.

- **Tugs are also used** to haul oil rigs to new locations. In addition, they can steer huge tankers in and out of oil ports.

- **Tugboats** can be divided into two main groups: habour tugs and ocean-going tugs. Harbour tugs, or short-haul tugs, are used to move ships in the vicinity of the harbour.

- **Ocean-going**, or long-haul, tugs are used to salvage ships from open seas and guide them to the dockyards for repair, or to tow floating docks and rigs to different locations.

- **Dredgers** are ships that collect sand and other sediments from the seabed. They are often used to deepen channels in harbours to prevent them from getting blocked. The material that is scooped up is used for commercial purposes.

- **Icebreakers** are tough, specialized vessels that are used to clear ice in rivers and seas in order to create a passage.

- **They are very sturdy** and usually quite heavy. They have an armoured body to withstand shocks experienced during collisions with ice.

- **They ram into ice sheets**, or masses of hard ice, and shatter them. Sometimes they crack open an ice sheet by weighing it down with their sheer bulk.

- **Icebreakers** help clear the way so that ships can follow. They are also used for exploration in the polar regions.

328

▼ *Tugboats are powerful ships and are used to guide ships,*
such as this aircraft carrier, to new locations.

Finding the way

- **Marine navigation** involves guiding a boat or ship safely through the waters to its destination.

- **In ancient times**, mariners stayed close to the shore so that they would not lose their way. In such instances, sailors used coastal navigation to determine their position. They kept in sight of land and used landmarks as reference points.

- **When they finally** ventured into the open seas, these early seafarers depended on the positions of the Sun, stars and other celestial bodies to determine directions. Several instruments, including the sextant, were designed for this purpose.

- **Modified versions** of some of the basic navigational tools from yesteryear are still in use. The most well-known is the magnetic compass, which is crucial in determining the direction at sea.

- **A compass consists** of a moving needle that automatically points towards the Earth's magnetic north. The instrument has been in use since the 12th century. The mariner's compass was an early form of the magnetic compass.

- **The mariner's compass** consisted of an iron needle and a lodestone. The needle was rubbed against the lodestone, then stuck in a piece of straw and floated in a bowl of water. The needle would come to a rest pointing towards north.

...FASCINATING FACT...
To calculate ship speed, early mariners dropped overboard a log tied to a reel of rope, knotted at regular intervals. The faster the ship travelled, the more the rope was unwound from the reel. The mariners counted the number of knots pulled off the reel in a given period of time and determined the speed of the ship in knots.

- **Other primitive tools** of navigation included the jackstaff. This instrument was used to measure the Pole Star's distance from the horizon and thus determine the position of the vessel at sea.

- **Ancient navigators** also used a line with a piece of lead on one end to measure the depth of the water, thereby determining how far into the sea the vessel has sailed.

- **Dead reckoning** was another popular method of determining the position of a vessel. For this, navigators calculate the ship's position, or the 'fix', with its speed, time and direction.

- **Nautical charts** provided details about bodies of water, like their depth of the water and the location of islands, shores, rocks and lighthouses.

▲ *A sextant is a navigational instrument used to measure the angle and distance between two heavenly bodies such as the Sun and the Earth.*

Modern navigation

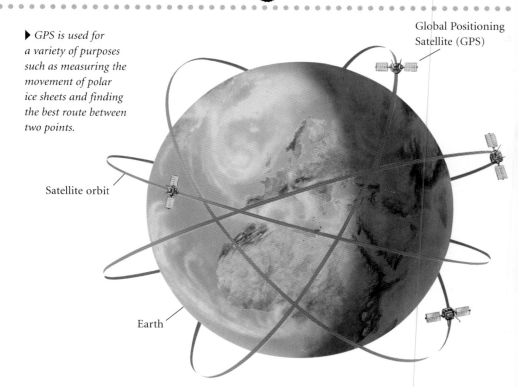

▶ *GPS is used for a variety of purposes such as measuring the movement of polar ice sheets and finding the best route between two points.*

Global Positioning Satellite (GPS)

Satellite orbit

Earth

- **The navigation equipment** used in the early days of seafaring has undergone a major change. Electronic navigation has replaced manual techniques, and advanced high-tech gadgets are now being used worldwide.

- **Modern navigational tools** provide data that are more accurate than ancient, manual methods. Some of the most important inventions are radio direction finding, long-ranging navigation and radar.

- **One of the first forms** of radio navigation was radio direction finding, or RDF. With this method, navigators tuned in to a particular radio frequency to determine their position. Some specific signals also had their own Morse code.

- **Long-range navigation**, or Loran, helps to fix the position of the ship by measuring the time taken by different radio signals to reach the receiver from fixed onshore transmitters.

- **The most popular form** of Loran is Loran-C, which uses two land transmittors simultaneously. This system is now being replaced by the global positioning system, or GPS.

- **GPS is a type of modern** satellite navigation, or satellite positioning system. This process uses 24 artificial satellites orbiting the Earth, the first of which was launched in the early 20th century.

- **With this system**, the navigator has a GPS receiver. A control device keeps track of the satellites, which send signals and the exact time. Comparing data from more than one satellite, the receiver calculates the ship's exact position.

- **The traditional** dead-reckoning system (DRS) has been modified into the inertial guidance system. This has the same function as the earlier DRS, but is more accurate.

- **Radio detection and ranging**, popularly called radar, is another commonly used navigational technique. Radar helps to locate faraway objects by bouncing radio waves off them.

- **A radar uses a scanner** to determine the location of objects, and has a display that shows its findings. It can not only locate the presence and position of an object but also determine its shape, size, speed and direction of movement.

Shipwrecked!

- **In modern times**, sophisticated navigational equipment has reduced the number of shipwrecks to a large extent. But until the 20th century, seafarers were completely dependant on dead reckoning and the magnetic compass.

- **One of the best-known** shipwrecks is the *Titanic*. It sank after colliding with an iceberg. Today, with the aid of navigational instruments like the GPS and the radar, such disasters can be averted.

- **Wars have claimed** several ships. Both naval and civilian vessels have been sunk by torpedoes fired from warships and submarines. In fact, the majority of the existing wrecks were a direct result of war. Most of them were sunk during the first and second World Wars by German submarines.

- **One of the famous casualties** of war was the *Lusitania*. This passenger liner belonged to the Cunard Line and was sunk during the First World War by a torpedo from a German submarine off the coast of southern Ireland. Around 1200 people were killed.

...FASCINATING FACT...

The Cunard liner, *Queen Elizabeth*, was the largest passenger steamship ever built. Launched in 1938, the ship was used to transport troops during World War II. The ship survived the war and dominated transatlantic passenger service until 1969, when it was finally declared unfit for the seas. The ship was docked off Hong Kong and refurbished as a floating university. However, the docked ship caught fire and capsized in 1972.

◀ Ships are lost at sea due to several reasons, such as bad weather, poor navigation and war.

- **On July 19, 1545,** the Tudor warship *Mary Rose* sank unexpectedly during a battle with the French. The ship went down at Solent, near Portsmouth, killing almost all its crewmembers.

- **The actual reasons** behind the sinking of the *Mary Rose* continue to be a mystery. But it is believed that overloading and human error, not French cannons, could have sealed the ship's fate.

- *Bismarck*, the pride of the German navy during World War II, was responsible for several attacks on both merchant and naval vessels. The most noteworthy of these was the sinking of the British warship *Hood*, in May 1941.

- **The *Bismarck*,** in turn, was sunk by British ships hungry for revenge. After a long battle, Hitler's most dreaded weapon finally sank three days after the *Hood*, taking with it over 2000 sailors. The remains of the *Bismarck* were discovered in 1989, off the coast of Ireland.

- **The famous Argentine battleship** *Belgrano* became the first ship to be sunk by a nuclear-powered submarine during a conflict. The British submarine *Conqueror* sank the vessel during the Falklands War of 1982, killing over 300 people. The wreck of the *Belgrano* is yet to be discovered.

The ancient Greek navy

- **Ever since they were first developed,** ships have played an important role in times of both war and peace. However, the vast differences between these two roles led to the manufacture of vessels solely for warfare.

- **As maritime trade flourished** in ancient times, neighbouring countries began to compete with each other for dominance. Realizing that the existing merchant vessels were inadequate for battles at sea, these nations started to build warships.

- **The Phoenicians** were the first to develop a war galley. However, the most advanced and practical warships were built by the ancient Greeks, who revolutionized the art of naval warfare.

- **The war galleys** of the Phoenicians were sailing ships with oars that could be manoeuvred even in the absence of wind.

- **The Greeks** went one step further and equipped their galleys with a bronze-tipped spike. This spike could ram into enemy ships and sink them.

- **The first war galley** to use the spike was the penteconter, a fast vessel with 50 oars. A penteconter was about 35 m long.

- **About 700BC,** the penteconter gave way to the bireme. This war galley had two levels of oarsmen, which gave the ship more power without the need to lengthen it.

> ### FASCINATING FACT
> In the 7th century AD, the Byzantines developed a flaming substance that could be catapulted at enemy ships to set them afire. This substance was known as Greek Fire.

- **As with other ships of its kind**, the oars on the lower level of the bireme were cut into the side of the vessel. However, the second level of oarsmen rowed from the deck.

- **The success of the bireme** eventually led to the creation of the trireme. This was the most effective warship of the time. It had three levels of oarsmen, with as many as 170 oarsmen in one ship.

- **The Greeks used triremes** to devastating effect in the Graeco-Persian wars. The triremes were invincible and played a major part in establishing Greece as a naval power.

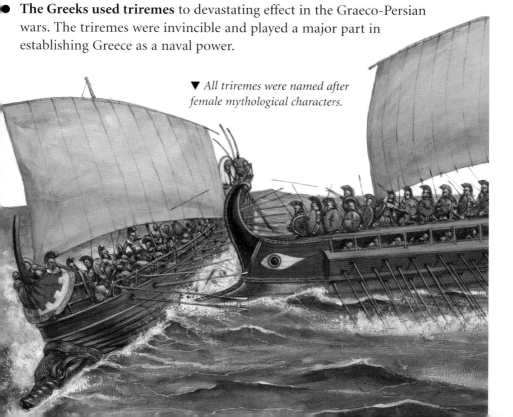

▼ *All triremes were named after female mythological characters.*

The ancient Roman navy

- **The earliest Roman navy,** first established about 311BC, was not a very powerful one. The Romans took pride in land warfare and the small navy they had was under the control of the army.

- **Their navy** mainly consisted of a few triremes, which were larger than the Greek ones. But even this small navy was decommissioned a few years later.

- **The Romans developed** a powerful navy about 261BC during the First Punic War against Carthage. But by that time the powerful triremes had lost their place as the dominant warships. So, the Roman navy had to find new ways of countering their enemies.

- **The Roman navy** did not have any experience in building ships. Hence, they based the design of their vessels on quadriremes and quinqueremes captured from Carthage.

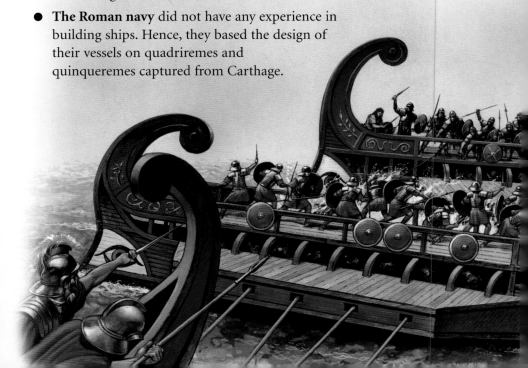

- **Contrary to popular belief,** quadriremes and quinqueremes did not have four and five levels of oarsmen. Instead, they probably had one or two rows of oars, with four or five men rowing each oar.

- **These ships** often carried about 100 soldiers and stone-throwing catapults to attack port towns.

- **The Romans** also developed a device called the *corvus*. This was a raised board with a spike on the underside.

- **The *corvus*** was used to board enemy ships. Once on board, the superior Roman infantry easily defeated the enemy.

- **The weight** of the *corvus*, however, made the Roman ships unstable. The device caused many a Roman vessel to capsize, incurring heavy losses. It also prevented the smooth manoeuvring of the ships.

- **The Roman navy** was very innovative and some of its strategies are followed even today. The Romans also built harbours at strategic points.

◄ *The ancient Romans often recreated gladiator battles. However, these naval battles were extremely expensive to stage, so they took place only rarely.*

The Spanish Armada

◄ *On its return voyage, the Armada ran into terrible storms. Many ships were wrecked off the rocky coasts of Scotland and Ireland.*

- **The Spanish Armada** was a great fleet launched in 1588 by Philip II of Spain to invade England and overthrow the queen, Elizabeth I.

- **Commanded by the duke of Medina-Sidonia**, the Armada comprised about 130 ships, largely Spanish. Some ships were from Portugal and Naples.

- **The preparation of the Armada** had actually begun in 1586, under the command of marqués de Santa Cruz. But the English troops commanded by Sir Francis Drake managed to attack Cádiz in 1587 and destroy over 30 ships docked at the harbour.

- **The huge fleet** finally set sail for England on May 28, 1588 with 30,000 men aboard. It was the largest fleet ever to be launched at the time and was considered invincible.

- **In July 1588**, an English fleet commanded by Lord Charles Howard engaged the Armada near Plymouth.

- **The battle** between the Armada and the English fleet continued for a week, but the English were unable to break through the Armada's crescent formation.

- **When the Armada** anchored near Calais, France, Lord Charles Howard ordered some ships to be set on fire and sent them against the huge Spanish fleet, hoping to set them on fire.

- **The English fire ships** caused panic among the Spanish and the Armada's formation broke. The English took advantage of this and moved in for the final assault.

- **On July 29, 1588**, the English fleet finally defeated the Armada in the Battle of Gravelines. About 15,000 Spaniards died in the battle.

- **Due to the terrible storms**, only 67 badly damaged ships of the Armada managed to return home.

...FASCINATING FACT...
Known for their experimentation, the English had equipped around 10,000 of their troops with firearms, while the Spaniards mostly depended on bows and arrows.

Ironclads

- **The first ironclad** was the 16th century Korean *geobukseon*, or 'turtle ship'. It was designed by Korean admiral Yi Sun-sin to fight Japanese invaders. However, such vessels became popular only in the mid-19th century, when they replaced wooden ships.

- **In 1855**, during the Crimean War, the French navy deployed steam-powered vessels called 'floating batteries' against the Russians.

- **These 'floating batteries'** were mounted with cannons and protected by iron armour. The armour was, however, brittle and could not withstand more than two cannon hits.

▶ *Ironclad warships, or ironclads, were developed in the United States and Europe in the 19th century. These ships had thick iron armour that protected them.*

> ...**FASCINATING FACT**...
> The biggest conflict involving ironclads was the Battle of Lissa,
> fought between the Austro-Hungarian and Italian navies in 1866.
> It was one of the largest European naval battles with both sides
> pitting huge ironclad warships against each other. The battle, won
> by Austria-Hungary, established the empire as one of the biggest
> naval powers in the Mediterranean.

- **Not to be outdone,** the British developed similar ships. But true ironclads were built only after the Crimean War. The French built the *La Gloire* in 1858, while the British came up with the HMS *Warrior*. The Russians also joined the race with their first ironclad, the *Prevenetz*.

- **Steam-powered ironclads** were first used in a conflict during the American Civil War, between the United States of America and the Confederate States of America.

- **The first of these ironclads** was called CSS *Manassas*. This turtleback ironclad steam tug was put to effective use against the US Navy.

- **Ironclad warships** were first used in combat in the Battle of Hampton Roads in 1862. These vessels, the Confederate ironclad CSS *Merrimack*, and the Union ironclad USS *Monitor*, heralded the age of armoured warships.

- **Ironclads** were mainly of two kinds – casemates and monitors. A casemate was a typical ironclad ship, powered by steam and with sloping sides.

- **A monitor** was a shorter steam-powered ship with guns that fit in a small turret. Its low height made it safer against enemy fire. The turret could be rotated to aim the guns.

Battleships

▲ Chih Yeun, *the mighty Chinese battlecruiser, was one of the heaviest and most dreaded battleships of its time.*

- **Battleships** dominated navies in the first half of the 20th century. They were large and heavily armoured ships that carried powerful guns.

- **Historically**, the name 'battleships' referred to the line-of-battle ships used during the age of sail, about 1571-1862.

- **During the age of sail,** ships carried heavy cannons, most of which were placed on the sides of the vessel. Since these cannons could only fire straight, the ships fell into lines, one behind the other. This popular battle formation was called the line of battle.

- **Battleships** were rated according to the number of guns they carried. First-rate ships had three decks with over 100 guns, while second-rate ships carried about 90 guns. Third-rate ships, with about 60 guns, were rated the lowest. At times, fourth-rate ships also carried guns.

- **Battleship design** underwent major changes during the 19th century. Wooden sail ships were heavily armoured and refitted with steam engines. Turreted guns were also first used during this period. This helped to considerably reduce the number of guns onboard.

- **Towards the end of the 19th century,** battleship design had become stable and one single design was being followed across the world. Most ships in this period had two turrets, four 12-inch guns and smaller, secondary guns. These ships travelled at a maximum speed of 18 knots.

- **By the end of the 19th century**, ships resembling modern battleships started to appear. The first of these ships were HMS *Devastation* and HMS *Thunderer*.

- **Countries** started to spend a lot of resources on building more and more powerful battleships. Although dreadnoughts came to the fore during World War I, the typical battleships were back in action in World War II.

- **Well-known battleships** deployed in World War II were the *Bismarck*, the *Misssouri*, the *Prince of Wales* and the *Yamato*.

- **Before the start of World War II**, battleships were the rulers of the seas. However, in World War II they became secondary to aircraft carriers, which offered greater effective range of attack than the battleships.

- **Several battleships** were decommissioned after World War II. Those retained were largely used as escorts to aircraft carriers or for the bombardment of shores. Even these were eventually scrapped in the early 1990s.

Dreadnoughts

- **The launch of the HMS _Dreadnought_** in 1906 revolutionized battleship design. The _Dreadnought_ was equipped with 10 large guns mounted on five turrets.

- **The HMS _Dreadnought_** was also the fastest warship of the time. The ship's armour was strong enough to withstand multiple hits.

- **The wing turrets** of the ship were, however, flawed. The turrets strained the hull during firing. Moreover, when the ship was fully loaded, its thickest armour belt sank into the water.

- **The drawbacks** in the design of the _Dreadnought_, however, did not hinder the success of this popular warship. On the contrary, all battleships before the HMS _Dreadnought_ came to be known as pre-dreadnoughts and the ones that followed were termed dreadnoughts.

- **The new dreadnoughts** were modelled on their parent ship. All were powered by steam engines, and had turrets and armour plates. Later, they were also equipped with underwater missiles, or torpedoes.

- **This battleship** soon started a naval arms race between Great Britain and Germany. The United States and France also set about building their own dreadnoughts. World War I was a testing ground for the new dreadnoughts.

...FASCINATING FACT...

The British Navy was once fooled by a group of five Englishmen and author Virginia Woolf dressed as Abyssinian princes. They fooled the crew into allowing them to inspect the HMS _Dreadnought_.

◀ *The USS* Iowa *was one of the most famous US dreadnoughts in World War II. She supported airstrikes against the Japanese.*

- **By 1914**, the British navy owned 10 dreadnoughts, while Germany had 13. In 1915, the British came up with the first super-dreadnought, *Queen Elizabeth*. This battleship had eight 15-inch guns as compared to the ten 12-inch guns used in the previous dreadnoughts.

- **An epic battle** involving dreadnoughts was fought off the coast of Jutland, Denmark. The British navy deployed 28 dreadnoughts, as compared to the 16 dreadnoughts of the Germans. The British also used their four super-dreadnoughts during the conflict.

- **The battle** was inconclusive with neither side posting a clear victory. The British navy lost 14 ships and over 6500 men, while the Germans lost only 11 ships and over 3000 men.

- **The dreadnoughts**, however, emerged the winners, with more and more nations adopting these new battleships.

347

Submarines

- **Submarines** are warships that operate underwater. Although the term usually refers to military vessels, there are also scientific and commercial submarines. The first submarine was built in 1620 by the Dutch inventor Cornelius Jacobszoon Drebbel. This vessel was propelled using oars.

- **The early submarines** were largely used for underwater exploration. But soon the importance of the submarine as a military vessel was recognized. The first submarine built exclusively for military use was named the *Turtle*.

- **Built in the 1770s,** the *Turtle* was a manually-operated, spherical vessel that could accommodate only one person. Designed by David Bushnell, an American inventor, the *Turtle* was first used during the American War of Independence.

- **Over the next century,** several kinds of submarines were developed. However, they were not put to effective military use until the 20th century. Diesel submarines were first used during World War I.

- **Nuclear-powered submarines** did not enter the scene until well after World War II. With nuclear energy, the vessels could stay submerged for longer periods.

- **The earlier submarines** did not have periscopes. These were added in the mid 19th century. Periscopes offer a view of what's happening above water.

- **Submarines also carry** weapons that include mines, torpedoes, cruise missiles and nuclear-tipped ballistic missiles.

- **Submerging and surfacing** is done with the help of ballast tanks. When a submarine has to dive into the water, its ballast tanks are filled with water. When it needs to resurface, compressed air is forced into the tanks to push out the water.

◄ Submarines are designed to approach a target undetected, making as little noise and movement as possible. Modern subs are mostly cigar-shaped and they rarely surface.

- **Modern navies** use two basic types of submarines: attack and ballistic missile submarines. Attack submarines are also known as hunter-killer submarines. They usually use torpedoes and are designed to attack warships and other submarines.

- **Ballistic missile submarines** have nuclear warheads to attack land targets such as strategic cities. They are built as back-ups in case all land-based missiles are destroyed.

U-boats and Q-boats

▼ *The U-47 was one of the most successful U-boats of World War II. It was involved in about 10 combat patrols for a total of 238 days at sea, sinking 30 enemy supply ships.*

- **The German U-boats** were the first military submarines that played a vital role in conflict. These diesel-powered vessels revolutionized naval warfare.

- **They were called U-boats** because the German navy named all its submarines with a 'U', followed by a number. The 'U' stood for *Unterseeboot*, meaning 'undersea boat' in German.

- **The U-boats gained** notoriety due to the aggression of German captains who were instructed to attack warships as well as merchant vessels and passenger liners.

- **These submarines** were long boats that ran on rechargeable batteries when submerged. Their main weapon was the torpedo. However, the U-boats operated mainly on the water surface, submerging only during attacks.

- **In May 1915,** torpedoes from a German U-Boat sank the passenger liner, *Lusitania*. Several American civilians died in this attack. This event was one of the main reasons why the US became invovled in World War I.

- **Q-Boats** were decoy ships introduced by the Allies, particularly the British, during World War I to counter the German U-Boats. Q-Boats were usually trawlers and cargo ships armed with hidden guns.

- **The Germans** targeted all ships that were bound for Britain. Their strategy was to cut Britain off from the rest of the world and thus defeat her. As a countermove, Q-Boats were used to lure the U-Boats into attacking them. They would then open fire without warning.

- **The Q-Boats** had some initial success, but soon the Germans caught on to the strategy and started to attack the ships with long-range torpedoes.

- **During World War II**, the Germans came up with another brilliant strategy to use their U-boats effectively. They developed a tactic of mass attack, wherein a group of U-boats, called a pack, would travel and attack together.

- **Soon technological** advances aided easy detection of submarines, making their attack tactics ineffective. By the end of World War II, the German U-Boat fleet lost over 30,000 crew members and around 750 boats.

. . . FASCINATING FACT . . .
The countries involved in World War II discovered several methods of detecting submarines. Radar was the most common method used. One of the most ingenious techniques was employed by the Allies, who used chemical sensors to detect the smell of submarine exhausts.

Ships of World War I

- **It is an accepted theory** that World War I (1914–1918) was a direct result of the naval arms race between Britain and Germany and their allies.

- **Great Britain's** powerful HMS *Dreadnought* triggered the arms race. The success of the *Dreadnought* inspired all the other powerful nations to develop similar warships.

- **Dreadnoughts** and early battleships were the mainstay of most of the countries involved. These ships were armed with the most powerful guns of the time.

- **Later during the war**, sleek battlecruisers like the HMS *Renown* of Britain were developed. These ships were capable of high speeds and could make short, swift attacks.

- **The best known** battlecruisers of the time, HMS *Inflexible,* HMS *Invincible* and HMS *Indomitable*, belonged to the British navy. Both HMS *Inflexible* and HMS *Invincible* proved effective in the Battle of the Falkland Islands during World War I. They destroyed a German cruiser squadron in the South Atlantic Ocean.

- **The British navy** also owned about 20 dreadnoughts and over 30 battleships and battlecruisers along with an array of destroyers, aircraft carriers and submarines, making it the most feared naval power during the period. The British navy also consisted of seaplane tenders, one of which, the *Engadine*, served in the Battle of Jutland.

- **The most feared warships** of World War I were the German U-boats. To counter their threat, Britain developed decoy ships called 'Q-boats'.

- **The US Navy** developed underwater explosives, known as depth charges, which could destroy submarines. This and other anti-submarine measures helped neutralise the German naval threat in World War I.

● **British passenger liners** were converted into armed merchant cruisers to relieve the strain on the regular cruisers. They were used to escort civilian and merchant vessels.

At the outbreak of World War I, the British navy used light cruisers to enforce a blockade on Germany by sinking trade ships. But towards the latter half of the war, the light cruisers were soon replaced by armed merchant cruisers, which were better suited for the purpose.

▼ *Dreadnoughts played a vital role in World War I. They were responsible for the naval arms race between Great Britain and Germany, and for the subsequent dominance of the British navy.*

Ships of World War II

- **World War I** was dominated by land battles and territorial warfare. In World War II, however, naval power became a very important factor.

- **Battleships and aircraft carriers** were built in large numbers. Aircraft carriers gave the flexibility of attacking from the sea, the land or the air.

- **The carriers** performed three types of operations. These were air raids, battles with rival carriers, and landing support for amphibious attacks.

- **In the 1930s**, the Japanese had developed a number of large battleships in order to gain control over the Pacific Ocean. The *Yamato* and her sister ship *Musashi* were the largest battleships ever built.

- **Work on the *Yamato*** began in 1937 at a specially prepared dock at the Kure naval dockyards. The ship was launched on August 8, 1940, and put into service on December 16, 1941.

- **The *Musashi*** was launched in November 1939 and put into service in August 1942. Both the *Yamato* and the *Musashi* played key roles in the Japanese successes during World War II.

- **On October 22, 1944**, the *Musashi* was sunk by American aircraft, armed with bombs and torpedoes, at the Battle of Leyte Gulf, one of the largest naval battles in history. More than 1000 of the total 2900 crew members died.

- ***Yamato's* final mission** was the 'Ten-Go' operation following the invasion of Okinawa by US troops. On April 6, 1945, the *Yamato*, along with the light cruiser *Yahagi*, and eight destroyers set sail to take on the US naval forces.

- **The US Navy**, however, launched an aggressive air raid against the enemy ships. The *Yamato* was repeatedly hit by torpedoes and was eventually destroyed about 200 km off Okinawa.

● **Twenty-two US Navy fleet carriers** and nine small aircraft carriers served in World War II. Eight ships were built before the war started and the rest were built during the war.

▲ *Over 300 warships, of which about 12 were aircraft carriers, were either sunk or damaged by Japanese suicide pilots known as* kamikaze *bombers towards the end of the war. The US aircraft carrier* Intrepid *was one of them.*

The Bismarck

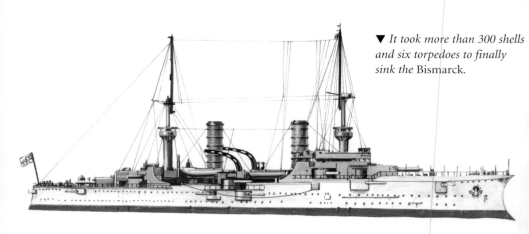

▼ *It took more than 300 shells and six torpedoes to finally sink the* Bismarck.

- **The German battleship** *Bismarck* was named after Otto von Bismarck, the first chancellor of the German empire.

- **This huge ship** posed the biggest threat to the Allied forces during World War II. It entered service in 1940 under the command of Captain Ernst Lindemann.

- **The German Nazi leader** Adolf Hitler was keen to upstage Britain as the dominant naval power. With this objective in mind, he ordered the German navy to target merchant ships of the Allied forces. The *Bismarck* spearheaded this mission.

- **On May 18, 1941**, the *Bismarck* set off on her maiden voyage. In order to stop the *Bismarck*, the British Prime Minister, Winston Churchill, gave orders to sink the ship. On May 24, she was engaged in a fierce battle with two British vessels, the *Hood* and the *Prince of Wales*.

- **During the conflict**, the *Bismarck* managed to strike a fatal blow. One of its shells penetrated the *Hood's* armour, leading to a massive explosion. The British battlecruiser sank immediately, taking down all but three of her 1418 crew members.

- *The Prince of Wales*, on the other hand, escaped under a smokescreen, but not before causing considerable damage to the *Bismarck*.

- **The German ship** was chased relentlessly by the *Prince of Wales, the Norfolk* and the *Suffolk* while on her way to France for repairs.

- **A massive air attack** was launched by British torpedo planes from HMS *Ark Royal*, an aircraft carrier. After a particularly damaging hit on the steering gear, the *Bismarck* was in serious trouble.

- **Allied destroyer ships** mounted a series of attacks, but the *Bismarck* fought on. On May 27, 1941, she was again engaged in a long battle with HMS *King George V*, HMS *Rodney*, HMS *Dorsetshire* and HMS *Norfolk*.

- **Unable to survive** this last onslaught, the crippled German warship finally sank with over 2000 crewmembers. It is believed that the *Bismarck's* crew deliberately sank the ship to avoid being captured.

> ...FASCINATING FACT...
> Sir Winston Churchill's famous order to sink the *Bismarck* at all costs inspired the popular song, *Sink the Bismarck*. The song was written by Johnny Horton and Tilman Franks.

Protecting the convoy

- **A naval convoy** is a group of ships travelling together and relying on each other for defence, supplies and other aid.

- **Capital ships** are the main ships in a convoy, with the heaviest fire power. These include ships like heavy cruisers, aircraft carriers and battleships. They usually require a troupe of smaller ships to protect them.

- **A convoy** may also be formed by a group of merchant ships being escorted by one or more armed vessels.

- **In ancient times,** such convoys were very effective against pirates. Ships came to the defence of one another when they were attacked.

- **Convoys** are prime targets because of their size. Hence they need specialized and fast vessels to protect the heavier ships.

- **Convoy-protecting ships** are particularly effective against submarines. A protector ship, such as a destroyer, engages rival submarines to give the other convoy members time to escape.

- **Frigates** are warships that protect and escort other warships and merchant ships. They engage in anti-submarine warfare, but are less heavily armed than destroyers.

- **In areas** where mines have been planted, minesweepers move ahead of a convoy to clear the waters for the ships coming behind.

- **The corvette** is another escort ship. It is a lightly armed, small and manoeuvrable warship. Corvettes are smaller than frigates.

- **Escort carriers** are small aircraft carriers. They were introduced by the US Navy during World War II. Their functions included ferrying aircraft, hunting out submarines, patrolling and escorting convoys.

▲ *Naval convoys were first developed to guard against pirate attacks. Today, naval convoys are an important part of the naval strategy of most countries.*

Aircraft carriers

▲ *Most modern aircraft carriers are powered by nuclear energy.*
The heavier and bigger ones can support over 85 planes.

- **Aircraft carriers** are massive warships that carry military aircraft. These ships have flight decks to support the take off and landing of fighters and bombers.

- **Apart from enabling** military planes to take off and land at sea, aircraft carriers also provide air cover to other warships.

- **Most aircraft carriers** have a flat top deck that serves as a strip for take offs and landings. Although it is quite long, it is small compared to normal runways. Hence, steam-powered catapults are used to launch the planes into the air.

- **These catapults** help the planes accelerate from 0 to 240 km/h in just two seconds to attain take off speed.

- **Landing on the carrier** requires great skill. The planes have tailhooks that snag one of four arresting cables stretched across the deck, stopping the aircraft within 100 m.

- **Aircraft carriers** are over 300 m long, with a huge crew. They are expensive, owned only by a few countries. The United States owns the most carriers. As of 2004, the US Navy has 12 carriers, the most famous being the *Abraham Lincoln*.

- **There are several types** of aircraft carriers, including seaplane tenders, assault carriers, light carriers, escort carriers, fleet carriers and supercarriers. Some of these, such as seaplane tenders, are no longer in use.

- **Most countries today use light carriers**, which can support helicopters and jump jets, or other vertical take off and landing planes. Such aircraft can take off and land with almost no forward movement, and so do not need catapults.

- **Aircraft carriers** are accompanied by many other ships that either provide protection or carry supplies. Together they are called a 'carrier battle group'.

...FASCINATING FACT...
American pilot Eugene Fly was the first to take off from a stationary ship. He did so from the US cruiser USS *Birmingham*. On May 12, 1912, British commander Charles Samson became the first pilot to take off from a moving warship. He did so from the battleship HMS *Hibernia*.

Destroyers

- **A destroyer** is a long-endurance warship that is light and very fast. These naval vessels are known for their speed, manoeuvrability and weaponry.

- **Destroyers** usually escort larger vessels during a battle. They defend the rest of the battle formation against short-range attacks.

- **These ships** are equipped with anti-surface, anti-air and anti-submarine weapons. These include guns, missiles and torpedoes. Some destroyers are also reinforced with naval helicopters.

- **The destroyer** was developed to counter-attack small and swift torpedo boats used in the Chilean Civil War of 1891 and the Sino-Japanese War of 1894–95.

- **The small torpedo boats** were so dangerous that defending navies had to use ships meant for targeting larger ships to counter the small boats. This led to the birth of the torpedo-boat destroyer.

- **Destroyers** had to be as fast as torpedo boats, and equipped with guns as well as torpedoes. However, they were much larger than the torpedo boats.

- **The destroyer evolved** through the years after its birth as a torpedo destroyer. During World War I, a new threat emerged in the form of submarines. Destroyers now had to be equipped with sonar facilities to counter this threat.

- **In World War II**, the primary attackers at sea were aircraft. To counter these, destroyers had to be equipped with anti-aircraft guns.

▲ *Fletcher class destroyers were the mainstay of the US Navy during World War II.*

Minesweepers

- **Minesweepers** are highly specialized ships that are used to find and destroy naval mines placed in the sea.

- **Naval mines** are used against ships and submarines. Like landmines, they are stationary weapons placed at strategic spots and are triggered when a ship or submarine approaches them.

- **These mines** are designed to explode underwater, and have proved to be very effective. According to official statistics, mines have destroyed more ships than any other weapon since World War II.

- **The work of a minesweeper** is extremely dangerous. A mine may detonate merely at the sound of an approaching vessel. Hence, minesweepers are specially designed to produce much less noise than other ships.

- **For further protection**, minesweepers have hulls made of wood, plastic or steel with low magnetic properties. These ships are also equipped with sonar and radar to help detect mines.

- **As minesweepers are so vulnerable**, helicopters with long, sweeping underwater cables and wires are sometimes used to assist in minesweeping activities.

- **Minesweepers** are usually over 55 m in length and clear underwater mines with the help of massive winches.

- **Special mortars** and torpedoes designed to destroy mines are also used. As in many other naval vessels, minesweepers also have anti-aircraft and other weapons on board.

- **Minesweepers** are generally used to clear an area where a large number of simple mines have been planted. Their sweeping wires cut loose floating mines. Sometimes these vessels use electric pulses to detonate magnetic mines.

- **Minehunters** are slightly different from minesweepers. They are equipped to handle more complicated modern mines. These include seabed mines that need to be located and destroyed one by one.

- **Both minesweepers** and minehunters are together known as mine counter-measure vessels, or MCMVs.

▲ *The same minesweepers used to deactivate mines are sometimes also used to lay them.*

365

Battle of Salamis

- **The Battle of Salamis** is considered to be one of the most important chapters in the history of naval warfare. This naval battle, fought during the Graeco-Persian Wars (492–449BC), turned the tables in favour of the Greeks.

- **The Graeco-Persian Wars** began with the Battle of Marathon in 490BC. King Darius, the Persian ruler of the time, invaded Greece with ambitions of capturing the country. However, his efforts were thwarted.

- **In order to avenge** his father's defeat at the Battle of Marathon, Darius' son, Xerxes, invaded Greece in 480BC. He defeated the Greeks at the Battle of Thermopylae.

▼ *The Greek victory at the Battle of Plataea in 479BC brought an end to the threat of Persian attack*

- **Xerxes conquered Athens**, forcing its inhabitants to flee to Salamis, a small island near Athens. The Persians continued to pursue their enemy.

- **The Athenian fleet** in Salamis was soon joined by the rest of the Greek fleet. The Athenian general, Themistocles, wanted a naval battle. His allies disagreed at first but they eventually consented when Themistocles threatened to advance with his navy with or without the support of his allies.

- **The Greek navy** was heavily outnumbered by the Persian navy. The Greeks owned about 350 ships, including triremes and penteconters, while the Persian fleet consisted of over 1000 ships.

- **The Persians** were so confident of defeating their enemy that King Xerxes had a throne set up on a cliff overlooking the Bay of Salamis to watch the battle.

- **Using a clever ploy** to tackle the large Persian fleet, Themistocles sent Sicinnus, a slave, to meet Xerxes. As planned, Sicinnus told Xerxes that the Greek navy had decided to retreat during the night.

- **Fooled by this message**, the Persian navy advanced into a narrow strait near Salamis. The Greeks went back further, drawing the entire Persian fleet into this strait.

- **This made the Persians** easy targets since their ships could not move easily in the narrow strait. The lighter Greek triremes rammed into the Persian ships and sank them. The Greek army also swung into action and jumped on board the ships for hand-to-hand combat, defeating the mighty Persians.

Battle of Aegospotami

- **The Battle of Aegospotami** was the decisive conflict of the Peloponnesian War (431–404BC), involving the Greek city-states of Athens and Sparta and their allies. The powerful Athenian navy was destroyed in this battle, which ended the state's supremacy.

- **The Greek city-states** of Sparta and Corinth formed an alliance against Athens.

- **In the beginning**, none of the states involved in the war made any gains. Soon, a terrible plague spread through Athens, killing hundreds of people, including the great leader, Pericles.

- **Following the death of Pericles**, Athenians split into groups. One of these groups, the oligarchs, negotiated a 30-year truce with Sparta. However, the truce lasted only seven years and in 415BC, Pericles' nephew, Alcibiades, led an Athenian assault on Sicily, an ally of Sparta and Corinth.

- **The mission** failed and Athens lost a huge part of its fleet in the battle. But the city-state continued to fight valiantly and even won some key battles.

- **After one such victory**, in the Arginusae Islands, the Athenian general, Conon, led his fleet to the Aegospotami River. Realizing that the Spartan fleet commanded by Lysander was also nearby, Conon tried to engage them in a battle.

- **Meanwhile, Lysander** was busy plotting the downfall of Athens. He ordered his men to be patient and wait for the right time before striking.

- **Five days after** they first arrived at Aegospotami, the Athenian fleet dispersed in search of food, leaving their ships unguarded. Seizing the moment, Lysander attacked and burned nearly all their ships.

▲ *Before the Peloponnesian War, Athens was a great naval power.*
Athens used her powers to expand her territories.

- **Only nine** of the 170 ships managed to escape. After destroying the Athenian navy, Lysander sailed to the port of Piraeus in Athens to cut off the food supply to the city.

- **Finally, in 404BC**, Athens surrendered to Sparta, which then set up an oligarchy of Athenian nobles that came to be known as the Thirty Tyrants because of their brutality.

Battle of Actium

- **The Battle of Actium** was the famous naval battle of the Roman Civil War (32–30BC), which saw the downfall of the great Egyptian queen, Cleopatra, and the Roman hero, Mark Antony.

- **After the murder of Julius Caesar in 44BC,** the Roman Empire was divided into three separate administrations called a triumvirate. They were led by Caesar's nephew, Octavian, Mark Antony and Marcus Lepidus.

- **In 36BC,** Lepidus was excluded from the triumvirate, which was eventually dissolved in 33BC, just before the civil war broke out.

- **Antony's relationship** with Cleopatra and his defeat at the hands of the Parthians turned the Romans against him making the civil war imminent.

- **Octavian** further incited the Romans against Antony. This angered Antony and he began preparing for a full-scale war with Octavian.

- **Octavian's fleet** was led by his able general, Marcus Visparius Agrippa. He was up against the mighty armies of Antony and Cleopatra, the queen of Egypt.

- **It is believed** that Antony's generals tried to persuade him not to go to war against Octavian, but Cleopatra convinced him otherwise. On September 2, 31BC, the rival navies met in a bay off the coast of Actium in Greece.

- **Antony started the combat** with his fleet of nearly 220 heavy ships, equipped with missile-throwing devices.

- **Octavian's ships** were smaller but more manoeuvrable. They dodged Antony's onslaught and engaged the enemies in a fierce battle. The battle raged on with no conclusion in sight.

- **Tired of waiting in the wings**, Cleopatra suddenly withdrew her fleet from the battle. Antony followed her, creating panic among the sailors.

● **Seizing the opportunity,** Octavian launched an all-out attack and burnt Antony's ships, thus ending the war.

▼ *A year after the Battle of Actium, both Antony and Cleopatra committed suicide.*

Napoleon versus Nelson

- **One of the most** well-known battles in European naval history is the Battle of Trafalgar, fought between a British fleet and the combined fleets of France and Spain.

- **The British fleet** was commanded by Viscount Horatio Nelson. He was appointed commander of the British Mediterranean fleet when war broke out in 1803 between England and France after a brief ceasefire.

- **Nelson's job** was to block French ports so as to stop merchant trade. He was in charge of blocking trade activity at Toulon in France.

- **This blockade** effectivly kept the French from invading Britain. Napoleon Bonaparte, emperor of France, was nurturing ambitions of conquering Britain.

- **Frustrated** with the blockade, Bonaparte sent orders to the French navy to break it. The mission was handed over to Charles de Villeneuve of France.

▶ *Horatio Nelson, one of Britain's greatest naval admirals, was blinded in his right eye during a battle in 1794. He also lost his right arm during another battle in 1797.*

- **He reached Cape Trafalga**r near Cadiz in Spain. Villeneuve formed his ships into a single battle line so as to break open the blockade.

- **Nelson**, however, had different plans. He divided his fleet into two. He then caught Villeneuve completely off-guard by charging at right angles to the line of French and Spanish ships.

- **Villeneuve** was not prepared for this. The British fleet had an easy advantage and demolished the fleet.

- **So masterly** was the plan that the battle was over in a few hours. It began before noon and ended by late afternoon.

- **Nearly 20** French and Spanish ships had been destroyed, and Villeneuve was taken a prisoner along with thousands of others.

...FASCINATING FACT...
Admiral Nelson spent about 30 years at sea and fought bravely in a number of battles. Yet it is believed that there was one problem he could never overcome – his seasickness! He is said to have planned his battles days in advance, so that he had time to adjust to the sea by the time he had to fight.

World War I at sea

- **World War I** has become synonymous with trench warfare. However, while the war was mainly fought on land in Europe, naval warfare also played a very important role.

- **In fact**, some historians believe that the naval arms race between Germany and Great Britain was responsible for the outbreak of World War I.

▼ *The Allied forces and Germany signed the armistice treaty on November 11, 1918, thus officially marking the end of World War I.*

- **There were two main fronts** in the maritime war of 1914–18. They were the North Sea and the Atlantic Ocean. Some battles also took place in the Mediterranean Sea.

- **The mainstay of the British Navy** was its fleet of large battleships. It also had destroyers, battlecruisers and light cruisers. The Germans countered these with submarines, or U-boats.

- **During this war**, both Germany and Great Britain used sea blockades to stop each other's trading activities. The British fleet in the North Sea was especially effective in preventing supply ships from reaching Germany.

- **The Germans** retaliated by using their dreaded U-boats to target not only British naval vessels but also their merchant ships.

- **The most well-known victim** of the U-boats was the passenger liner *Lusitania*. A few months later another liner, *Arabic*, was also sunk by the U-boats.

- **One of the most important naval battles** of World War I was fought between the British and German fleets in 1914 at Heligoland Bight, off the northwest coast of Germany. British submarines and destroyers managed to sink three German cruisers and a destroyer in the battle.

- **In 1915**, a British fleet commanded by Vice Admiral David Beatty defeated a German fleet under the command of Rear Admiral Franz von Hipper at the Battle of Dogger Bank.

- **Other noteworthy naval battles** of the war included the battles of Coronel (November 1, 1914) and the Falklands (December 8, 1914). The most famous battle, however, was the one fought off the coast of Jutland, Denmark, in 1916.

375

Battle of Jutland

- **The Battle of Jutland** was an important naval conflict between German and British fleets. The action began on May 31, 1916, when the two fleets met at about 121 km off the coast of Jutland, Denmark.

- **The battle** was known as the Battle of Skagerrak in Germany. It was the largest naval battle ever fought using only surface ships.

- **The British Grand Fleet** was commanded by Admiral John Rushworth Jellicoe. Vice Admiral Reinhard Scheer led the German High Seas Fleet.

- **Meanwhile**, the British Vice Admiral, David Beatty, lined up his battle cruisers and destroyers against a squadron of German battle cruisers led by Rear Admiral Hipper. Both sides opened fire simultaneously.

- **The German squadron** tried luring the British ships into the firing line of their main force. Beatty, who was waiting for his main fleet, led by Admiral Jellicoe, to arrive, had to resort to delaying tactics. The British suffered heavy losses as both HMS *Indefatigable* and HMS *Queen Mary* were blown up.

- **Jellicoe finally arrived** with the rest of the Grand Fleet. The clash of the main forces soon led to the destruction of the British battle cruiser HMS *Invincible*. The German flagship *Lutzow* was also severely damaged.

- **In a bold move,** Jellicoe commanded his fleet to form a V-shape. This gave them more angles to fire from at the advancing German fleet. Faced with the superior British fleet, the Germans started to retreat.

- **Taking advantage** of poor intelligence reports and a series of other mistakes on the part of the British, the Germans made a retreat plan. Scheer manoeuvred the German fleet behind the Grand Fleet and escaped at night, ending the battle.

▶ *Admiral David Beatty was promoted to the rank of Rear Admiral in 1910, at the age of 39. Following his show of outstanding courage and leadership in the Battle of Jutland, Beatty was appointed the commander of the Grand Fleet in November 1916.*

● **The British** lost 14 vessels, including three battlecruisers and eight destroyers, and over 6000 men. The Germans, on the other hand, lost only 11 ships and around 1500 men.

● **The battle** might have been inconclusive and the British might have suffered heavy losses. But it proved to be a strategic victory for the British, since it gave them undisputed control of the North Sea.

D-day landing

- **D-day**, one of the most well-known military terms, refers to a date and time for which any event, usually an attack, is scheduled.

- **The most famous D-day** in history was the landing of the Allied forces on the coasts of Normandy, France, during World War II, which combined the military strength of Great Britain, the United States and their allies.

- **Germany** had become very powerful under Hitler and by 1940 had occupied a large part of the European continent, including France. At the outset of World War II, Hitler was also extending Germany's boundaries to the east.

- **France** was a strategic location. The Allied forces realized that to win the war the Germans had to be driven out of France. Plans were carefully drawn up and on June 6, 1944, the Allied Forces landed in France.

- **Allied navies** had already encountered the German U-boats. Realizing that a naval approach would prove insufficient in the face of an onslaught from the U-boats, an immense build-up of ground and air power was also set in motion to back the Allied navies.

- **Around 152,000 soldiers** from the United States, Britain and Canada were involved in the attack, which took place at Normandy in northern France. The Germans were taken by surprise as they thought the attack would be near Calais to the east, the narrowest part of the English Channel.

- **During the attack,** the Allied ground forces were supported by 23,000 paratroopers. Air raids pounded the German defences.

- **This combined air, sea and land attack,** which became famous as the D-day landing, was the largest sea-borne invasion in history.

- **The German gunners** put up a tough fight but the sheer size of the attack and the Allied air superiority made it difficult for the German commander, Erwin Rommel, to mount a successful counterattack.

- **The Allied attack** pushed back the German forces. A similar attack in southern France finally liberated the country, and the victory at Normandy paved the way for the German defeat.

▼ *The D-day landing was code-named 'Neptune' and the entire operation was called 'Operation Overlord'.*

War in the Pacific

- **The Pacific War** began long before World War II. But some of the biggest campaigns of the conflict took place during World War II and had an immense effect on its outcome.

- **During World War II**, Japan forced Thailand to join forces with it against the Allies, which included the United States, Great Britain, China, Australia and allies. Germany and Italy also came to the aid of the Japanese.

- **Political instability** in China during the 1920s encouraged Japan to expand its control to Chinese territories. After capturing Korea in 1910, the Japanese soon set their sights on China, particularly Manchuria. Several significant events over the next few years eventually sparked off the Sino-Japanese conflict in 1937.

▼ *US navy vessels near Mount Fuji in Japan, on their way to accept the Japanese surrender.*

- **During the war**, Japan began a reign of terror across China in an attempt to control the Chinese. However, the Japanese brutality succeeded in turning many other countries against Japan.

- **The United States**, the United Kingdom and the Netherlands enforced an oil and steel blockade on Japan. The country reacted by launching an offensive against these nations, targeting especially the United States.

- **On December 7, 1941**, Japan attacked Hong Kong, the crown colony of Britain, and also invaded the Philippines, which was controlled by the United States. On the same day, Japan also targeted Thailand and Malaya.

- **Japan's greatest fear** was the US Pacific Fleet, based at Pearl Harbor, Hawaii. Hence, it planned a surprise air attack to destroy the entire fleet. On the same day that they attacked Hong Kong and other Southeast Asian countries, the Japanese relentlessly bombed Pearl Harbor.

- **The incident** brought the United States into the war. Japan had hoped that the shock of Pearl Harbor would force the United States to negotiate and allow the Japanese to continue their campaigns in China, but this did not happen.

- **The Pearl Harbor** attack only served to provoke the Americans, who had earlier chosen to stay out of the Asian conflict. After the attack, public opinion on the war changed overnight and the United States entered the fray.

- **The Japanese** encountered their first defeat at the hands of the US Navy in the Battle of the Coral Sea (May 7, 1942). Isolated battles like the one for Rabaul in Papua New Guinea and Guadalcanal in the Solomon Islands also did not go Japan's way. Finally, the Battle of Midway (June 4, 1942) made US the dominant force in the Pacific Ocean.

Pearl Harbor

- **Pearl Harbor** was one of the largest attacks in naval history. In fact, the Japanese attack on the US base proved to be the turning point in World War II.

- **The Japanese** felt threatened by America's Pacific Fleet, based in Hawaii. They were also angered by the oil blockade imposed on them by the United States.

- **The Japanese Imperial Navy** put in place the most powerful aircraft carriers and planned a massive surprise attack.

- **On the morning of December 7, 1941**, Japanese fighter planes took off from a fleet of aircraft carriers towards Pearl Harbor. Backed by submarines, these fighter planes bombed the US Pacific Fleet.

- **The Japanese** used six aircraft carriers, 441 warplanes, including fighters, torpedo-bombers, dive-bombers and fighter-bombers for the surprise attack.

- **Many battleships** were destroyed by simultaneous torpedo attacks and aerial bombings. The battleship USS *Arizona* blew up and sank, killing over 1100 men. This ship remains a memorial to those who died that day.

- **Within a few hours of the attack**, the Japanese had destroyed four US battleships and damaged four more. Many American naval and military personnel were either killed or wounded.

- **The Pearl Harbor attack** united the Americans who were divided on the issue of joining the war and the American president, Franklin D. Roosevelt, declared war on Japan the following day.

- **The attack**, however, had left the US navy crippled, and the country could not play a significant role in the Pacific Ocean.

- **Having put the US Pacific Fleet** out of action, Japan was free to conquer southeast Asia, southwest Pacific and extend far into the Indian Ocean.

▲ *The American destroyer USS* Shaw *was hit by three bombs and was completely destroyed during the Pearl Harbor attack.*

Battle of the Coral Sea

▲ *Fleet Admiral Chester W. Nimitz was the chief architect of the victories achieved by the US Navy during the Pacific War. He represented the United States at the Japanese surrender ceremony on September 2, 1945, aboard the USS* Missouri. *Here he is seen signing the Instrument of Surrender.*

- **After the Pearl Harbor attack**, Japan was virtually unchallenged. It started occupying territories to the south, and within a few months it had conquered almost all of south Asia.

- **Since the US navy** had suffered extensive losses during the Pearl Harbor attack, it needed time to reorganize itself before launching an attack on Japanese naval forces.

- **The Battle of the Coral Sea**, fought in May, 1942, for the control of the Solomon Islands, was the first American campaign after the Pearl Harbor incident.

- **In April 1942**, Japanese forces left their stronghold of Rabaul and launched a sea attack on Port Moresby and Tulagi in the Solomon Islands.

- **The capture** of these islands made the Japanese more dominant in the Pacific Ocean, encouraging them to plan an attack on Australia.

- **After taking over Tulagi**, the Japanese moved forward to take over the Louisiade Archipelago, southeast of New Guinea and Port Moresby. By this time the American fleet had arrived on the scene.

- **Better communications technology** helped the US Navy to learn about the Japanese plan. It countered with two of its own carriers and additional cruisers, destroyers, submarines, land-based bombers and patrol seaplanes.

- **They intercepted the Japanese** in the Coral Sea and a fierce battle began. The Japanese navy suffered heavy losses and casualties, and was forced to retreat.

- **The Battle of the Coral Sea** was important as it weakened the Japanese navy and stopped it from gaining control of Australian waters.

Battle of Midway

- **The Midway Island**, also known as the Midway Atoll, is located in the Pacific Ocean, between the Hawaiian Islands and Japan.

- **During World War II** the atoll, which was then a US naval and air base, was of great strategic importance. Capturing it would have given the Japanese protection against US attack from the Hawaiian Islands.

- **A month** after suffering losses at the Battle of the Coral Sea, a large Japanese fleet of aircraft carriers sailed towards the Midway Island.

- **The Battle of Midway** was a battle between aircraft carriers. Aircraft took off, launched bombing raids, and went back to the carriers.

- **Japan's Admiral Isoroku Yamamoto**, the naval chief, had clever plans. He sent a smaller fleet towards Alaska to mislead the US navy. Yamamoto was known for his complicated battle plans.

- **US reconnaissance planes** had watched the movement of ships and the US was prepared for an attack. In June 1942, the Americans launched an aerial attack on the advancing Japanese fleet.

- **Japan counterattacked** and bombed the airstrips in Midway. The damage was not severe enough to prevent the American planes from flying.

- **While the Japanese aircraft** were refuelling and reloading, American ships approached them. The Japanese stopped the refuelling operations and abandoned their planes stacked with bombs on board the aircraft carriers.

- **The Japanese** prepared for a ship-to-ship battle. This soon proved to be a tactical blunder as the bombs and the fuel lines made the Japanese carriers highly explosive targets.

- **After a fierce battle** in which it lost four aircraft carriers, two cruisers and three destroyers, Japan was forced to retreat. Although the US Navy emerged from the battle almost unscathed, it lost one of its most precious aircraft carriers, the *Yorktown*.

▼ *Soldiers aboard the* Yorktown *flee after the ship was bombed by the Japanese. Although the ship sank following the attack, there were no casualties as it was abandoned.*

Rowing boats

▲ *Rowing can be categorized into sweeping and sculling. In the first type, each rower uses one oar, while in the latter each rower uses two oars.*

● **Since ancient times,** boats have been used for fun and sporting activities. Such boats include yachts, sailboats, canoes, powerboats and rowing boats.

388

- **Rowing boats** are moved with oars or paddles. They have been around for centuries. The row boats used for sporting activities consist of a long, slender vessel called a shell. Although shells used to be made from wood, materials such as fibreglass and carbon fibre are more commonly used today.

- **Rowing** east to west across the Atlantic Ocean is tougher than rowing west to east because of ocean currents and so, takes about twice as long.

- **Some rowing boats** are steered by a coxswain, or cox, who sits in the stern, facing the crew. The cox steers the boat and encourages the rowers. Rowing boats that do not have a cox are called 'coxless', or 'straight'.

- **Kayaking and canoeing** have also gained a great deal of popularity in recent years. In both sports, rowers use paddles instead of oars. Unlike oars, paddles are not used in pairs.

- **Both canoes and kayaks** are small vessels that are pointed at the ends. Canoes are mostly open-topped, while kayaks are completely covered, except for an opening for the rower to sit in.

- **Canoes and kayaks** can be paddled by one or more persons. Kayaks have double-ended paddles, while canoes have paddles with single blades. Despite their differences, the word 'canoe' is often used to describe both vessels.

- **There are several sporting competitions** involving canoes and kayaks, including slalom canoeing, rodeo canoeing and canoe polo.

- **Rowing single-handed** across the Atlantic Ocean is a tough task. In 1969, an Irish rower managed to make the crossing from west to east in just 70 days.

- **Polynesian peoples** once travelled from island to island across the Pacific Ocean in large canoes fitted with outriggers to make them more stable at sea.

Powered for fun

- **With the development of steam** and internal combustion engines in the 1800s, sails and oars became less common and soon motorboats were fashionable. Motorboats are fitted with inboard or outboard motors.

- **Some motorboats** use inboard motors, in which the engine is located within the hull. In outboard motorboats, the motor is attached to the stern of the boat and can be seen at one end.

- **Perhaps the most revolutionary** propulsion system for high-speed was the water-jet engine. In this system, water from under the boat is drawn into a pump-jet and then expelled through an opening at the stern.

- **High-speed boats** are used in search, rescue and salvage operations. They are also used for racing and leisure. Boats like hydroplanes and tunnel boats are especially popular among racing enthusiasts.

- **The streamlined hydroplanes** have projections called sponsons at the front. When a hydroplane picks up speed, it is lifted out of the water and supported by these sponsons.

- **The flat-bottomed tunnel-boat** also has a pair of sponsons, one along each side of the hull. Like the hydroplane, the tunnel boat rises out of the water supported on its sponsons.

- **The runabout** is a high-speed motorboat, which can hold around eight people.

- **Runabouts** can be used for racing but they are more commonly used for fishing and water skiing.

- **Most modern boats** are usually made of plastic and reinforced with fibreglass. These vessels are lightweight, fast and easy to manoeuvre.

● **The most popular** kinds of powerboat racing include jet sprint and offshore powerboat racing. In jet sprint boat racing, boats powered by water-jet propulsion race in shallow watercourses with several sharp turns. Offshore powerboat racing takes place in the open seas.

▲ *Over 14 kinds of high-speed boats are currently used in powerboat racing.*

Surfing

- **Surfing** involves riding the waves using a surfboard. Surfing is usually done where massive breaking waves are common.

- **Since the 1960s,** the sport has grown in popularity. The dangers involved have only enhanced the excitement and glamour of this sport.

- **Surfers** usually lie on their boards and paddle out to wait for a suitable wave. The idea is to ride a wave as soon as it starts to break.

- **There are several** intricate movements and manoeuvres in surfing. A surfer may ride the crest, or top, of a wave or its breaking curve.

- **The best surfers** can perform manoeuvres in the air. These moves, called aerials, were inspired by skateboarding and snowboarding. In a 360 aerial, a surfer does a 360 degree airborne spin.

- **Surf boards** may be long or short. The longboards are over 2.5 m in length, while shortboards are 2 m or less. Both have small fins to help with stability and steering.

- **Long considered** merely a local recreation, surfing is now an official sport. Professional surfers generally use the shortboard.

- **Surfing** is believed to have originated in Hawaii. Today, it is a highly popular activity worldwide, especially in Australia, South Africa, the United States and Brazil.

- **In competitions,** surfers are judged by the size of the waves and the distance they ride. Skills shown while performing manoeuvres are also considered.

◀ *Surfing requires great strength and agility and lots of practice. A good surfer has to be extremely fit and be able to swim well.*

393

Riding the waves

- **Water skiing** is another popular water sport. In this, the skier is towed behind a motorboat at great speed. Water skiing can be enjoyed on large, relatively calm expanses of water such as rivers, lakes and bays.

- **The sport** was invented by an American teenager named Ralph Samuelson in 1922. Samuelson believed that it was possible to ski on water as on snow. He chose Lake Pepin in Lake City, Minnesota for his first skiing attempt.

- **A water-ski** run begins with the skier crouched low, holding the tow rope attached to the motorboat. Upon acceleration, the skier stands up straight and starts to skim across the surface of the water.

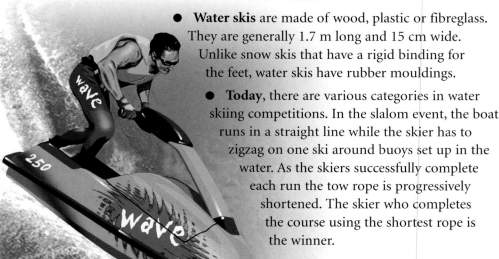

- **Water skis** are made of wood, plastic or fibreglass. They are generally 1.7 m long and 15 cm wide. Unlike snow skis that have a rigid binding for the feet, water skis have rubber mouldings.

- **Today**, there are various categories in water skiing competitions. In the slalom event, the boat runs in a straight line while the skier has to zigzag on one ski around buoys set up in the water. As the skiers successfully complete each run the tow rope is progressively shortened. The skier who completes the course using the shortest rope is the winner.

◀ *Jetskis first went on sale in 1973. They can travel at nearly 100 kilometres per hour.*

- **Trick skiing** is performed using either two short skis or a single ski. In this category participants perform tricks, similar to gymnasts, while skiing. Skiers are judged depending upon the difficulty of their tricks and performance.

- **In the jump event**, a pair of long skis is used. Skiers achieve maximum speed before hitting a ramp floating in the water. They use the ramp to launch themselves into the air before falling back into the water again.

▲ *Water skiing is now one of the most popular of all water sports.*

- **Show skiing** involves elaborate preparations. With music and colourful costumes, skiers perform dance acts and ballets. Troupes also form complex human pyramids.

- **Wakeboarding** is an offshoot of waterskiing, which also combines surfing techniques. Instead of skis, the rider stands sideways on a board to 'surf' on the waves created by the boat's wake.

- **Jet skis** are also popular. These are motorized personal watercraft that look like motorbikes and travel at high speeds. Most jet skis can accommodate two or three people. The rider sits or stands on the jet ski.

395

Underwater diving

- **Underwater diving** is of two kinds: recreational and professional. Recreational diving is a favourite pastime of tourists and amateur divers who like to explore the ocean floor for fun.

- **Professional divers** are those who dive underwater for specific purposes, such as conducting scientific studies, repairing oil rigs and retrieving wrecks or military equipment.

- **Coral reefs** are ideal spots for amateur divers. The Caribbean is one of the most popular places for diving.

- **Snorkelling** is one of the oldest forms of recreational diving, and does not require any specialized gear. A swimsuit, a mask, flippers and a snorkel, or breathing tube, is the only equipment required.

- **Snorkellers** swim face down on the surface of the water with their snorkels above the surface. This helps them to breathe while they observe life underwater.

- **While many children and adults** enjoy snorkelling, the more adventurous prefer scuba diving. SCUBA stands for self-contained underwater breathing apparatus.

- **Scuba divers** wear a metal tank filled with compressed air on their back for breathing. The air pressure is controlled by a regulator. Air from the tank flows through a hose into the diver's mouth.

- **Scuba divers** also wear a heavy weight-belt around their waist. This helps them to stay underwater. When they want to surface, they release the belt.

▶ *Today, diving has become one of the most popular water sports. People can explore an amazing underwater world and study marine life.*

● **There are two kinds** of scuba equipment: open circuit and closed circuit. Both types consist of a tank filled with oxygen and connected to a diving regulator. In the open circuit the exhaled gas is lost, while in the closed circuit the exhaled gas is recycled.

● **Emergency equipment** such as a knife, signalling instrument and a light are essential for scuba divers. Some also carry a stun gun to protect themselves against sharks.

Mermaids

● **Mermaids** are legendary creatures of the sea. It is believed that mermaids have a woman's head and the body of a fish. A male mermaid is known as a 'merman'.

● **Sirens** are the Greek equivalents of mermaids. According to Greek mythology, these sea nymphs lived on an island surrounded by cliffs. Unlike mermaids, sirens were supposed to be half-woman and half-bird.

◄ *According to Greek mythology, one of the perils faced by Jason and the Argonauts included passing the Siren's Island. When the ship approached the island, Orpheus, one of the Argonauts, played his flute in order to drown the sweet yet deceptive voices of the Sirens. Thus the Argonauts escaped the clutches of the Sirens.*

- **They were considered** to be the daughters of Achelous, god of the Greek river by the same name. The sirens were believed to sing very sweetly.

- **These sea nymphs** lured lost sailors with their enchanting songs. The spellbound sailors often wrecked their ships on the cliffs near the island and drowned.

- **The most common** image of a mermaid was first seen during the Middle Ages. It shows a mermaid sitting on a rock, combing her hair with one hand and holding a mirror in the other.

- **The legend** of mermaids and mermen can be traced back to the times of ancient Babylon and Syria. Both these peoples were known to worship gods who took the form of merfolk.

- **Oannes**, the Babylonian sea god, was said to have the top half of a man and the tail of a fish. Similarly, the Syrian moon-goddess, Atargatis, is shown as a mermaid. In fact, Atargatis is one of the first mermaids to have been illustrated.

- **Several other folklores** also talk about mermaid-like creatures. However, not all of them have the body of a fish. Most of them appear human in form. Some of these creatures include the Nix and Nixie from German folklores, the Russian Rusalka and Vodyany, and the Indian Apsaras.

- **There have been plenty** of reports of mermaid sightings, even as late as the 20th century. But most scientists believe that these sightings are of sea mammals called manatees or dugongs.

- **The legend** of the mermaid has spawned a number of films and stories, including *The Little Mermaid*, a fairy tale by Hans Christian Anderson.

Gods of the seas

- **Over the years**, man has feared and revered the mighty oceans. Many religions and cultures across the world have worshipped sea gods and goddesses since ancient times.

- **Perhaps the most famous** of all deities of the sea are the ones in Greek and Roman mythology. Poseidon, the Greek god of the sea, was regarded as the most powerful god after his brother Zeus, the king of all Greek gods.

- **Poseidon** was also the god of earthquakes. It was believed that he lived in a beautiful palace under the ocean and caused earthquakes when he was angry.

- **Sailors** offered their prayers to Poseidon before setting sail. He was called Neptune by the Romans.

- **Proteus** was another ancient sea god. He was believed to be the herdsman of Poseidon's seals. He had the gift of prophecy and could change his form at will.

- **Amphitrite,** the wife of Poseidon, was a sea-goddess in ancient Greece. To the Romans she was known as Salacia. Her name is used to refer to the seas.

- **The Greek goddess Aphrodite** was the protector of sailors as well as the goddess of love and beauty. Aphrodite's Roman equivalent was Venus. She was also known as Ishtar in Mesopotamia, and Astarte and Turan in other cultures.

- **Apart from the popular ones**, there were also a number of gods and goddesses belonging to the lower order. Glaukos, or Glaucus, and Palaemon, were all minor Greek sea gods, and Okeanides, or Oceanids, was a goddess.

- **The ancient Celtic culture** included a number of sea gods. The Welsh god Dylan was the most famous. His symbol was a silver fish.

- **Dylan**, it was believed, could swim like a fish and was loved by all sea creatures. Lir and Shoney were also Celtic sea gods. The ancient Babylonians worshipped Ea, a sea god associated with the Persian Gulf.

▶ *It is said that the Greek goddess Aphrodite rose fully formed from the waves, and this image is famous in literature and art.*

Heroes of the oceans

- **Most legendary heroes** have at one time or the other faced the perils of the oceans. Ancient folklore and tales are full of mythological characters setting sail to prove their worth.

- **Some of these great heroes** include Beowulf, King Gilgamesh, Aeneas and Perseus. But the adventurous voyage of Jason and the Argonauts is perhaps the most well known tale of all.

- **In Beowulf**, the Scandinavian prince Beowulf fought to free the Danes from the evil monster Grendel and his mother. For 12 years, Grendel had terrorized the Danes.

▼ *Beowulf dives into the lair of Grendel's mother, deep within the ocean.*

- **Grendel** killed King Hrothgar's men every time they gathered at Heorot, the king's mead hall, to celebrate. Beowulf slew Grendel to put an end to his reign of terror.

- **The fight** between Grendel's mother and Beowulf is a memorable one. The hero, a great swimmer, dived deep into the ocean to enter Grendel's mother's lair and kill her. Grendel's mother represented the horrors of ocean depths.

- **The adventures** of King Gilgamesh of Uruk are recounted in the *Epic of Gilgamesh*, considered to be the oldest literary work. In this Middle Eastern story, written in about 2500BC, King Gilgamesh went in search of immortality.

- **The death** of his dear friend, Enkidu, saddened Gilgamesh, who started to fear his own death. Not wanting to die, Gilgamesh set off on his quest for immortality. He approached Utnapishtim, the only human who had been granted eternal life by the gods.

- **Utnapishtim** told the king that it was not possible to attain immortality. However, he spoke of a plant found under the sea which would keep him young for the rest of his life. Gilgamesh dived into the sea and found the plant, only to lose it.

- **Greek mythology** tells the story of another legendary hero, Perseus. He was the son of Zeus and he killed Medusa, the snake-headed gorgon. This great hero also saved Princess Andromeda of Ethiopia from the sea monster sent by Poseidon, the much-feared sea god.

- **The famous Trojan hero**, Aeneas, also had to endure a gruelling journey through the oceans. After the Greeks lay siege to Troy, Aeneas fled the city with his family. It is believed that the gods told him to go to Italy, where Aeneas eventually laid the foundation for the Roman Empire.

Jason and the Argonauts

- **Jason is famous** in Greek mythology as the leader of the Argonauts, who went on a quest for the Golden Fleece. He was the son of Aeson, a Greek king whose throne was grabbed by his half brother, Pelias.

- **Jason** grew up and claimed his right to the throne. But his uncle asked him to first prove himself by returning the Golden Fleece, which had been stolen from their kingdom.

- **Jason** gathered together a crew of young noblemen and set sail on a ship called the *Argo*. This group of 50 heroic men came to be known as the Argonauts after their ship.

- **Among the Argonauts** who braved the perils of the ocean were Hercules, Orpheus and Peleus.

- **Their destination** was Colchis, a kingdom located at the eastern end of the Euxine, or Black, Sea. It was ruled by King Aeëtes for whom the Golden Fleece was like a lucky charm and hence, he valued it greatly.

- **The route of the *Argo*** was from Iolcus in Thessaly to the island of Lemnos, on to the Euxine Sea along Mysia to the east of the Aegean Sea, and then Thrace.

- **On the way**, they saved the life of a Thracian king called Phineus. Grateful to the Argonauts, Phineus told them how to pass safely through the Symplegades, the rocks at the entrance to the Euxine Sea.

> ...**FASCINATING FACT**...
> According to legend, the Golden Fleece belonged to a ram owned by Hermes, the messenger of the gods. A fierce dragon is supposed to have guarded this fleece.

▶ *Jason and the Argonauts sailing through the Symplegades. These were a pair of cliffs that clashed together, destroying the ships that passed between them. The Argonauts, however, survived the ordeal.*

- **When he arrived at Colchis,** Jason faced a number of tough challenges thrown at him by Aeëtes. Eventually Jason managed to get hold of the Golden Fleece with the help of Aeëtes' daughter, Medea.

- **Medea returned with Jason** on his voyage back home on the *Argo*. On the way, the crew encountered the six-headed monster, Scylla, and the deadly whirlpool, Charybdis. But the brave men managed to survive all these dangers.

- **At one point**, sea nymphs saved the ship during a fierce storm and Jason and his Argonauts eventually arrived home safely.

Journey of Odysseus

- **Homer's epic poem**, *Odyssey*, begins where the *Iliad*, the poem depicting the Trojan War, ended. The poem deals with the adventures of the Greek hero, Odysseus, on his way home to Ithaca after the Trojan War.

- **Days after leaving Troy**, the crew came upon the island of the Lotus-Eaters. On eating the lotus plant the crew members were so happy that they forgot all about their families and returning home. However, Odysseus forced them to continue their journey.

- **The next obstacle** came from the one-eyed giants called Cyclops. One of them, Polyphemus, devoured several of Odysseus' crew who had landed on the island for provisions.

- **Odysseus** hatched a clever plan to blind Polyphemus with a burning stake. He then led his men back to the safety of their ship and set sail towards the island of Aiolia, where Aeolus, the keeper of the winds, lived.

▲ *Homer was believed to have lived in Ionia, Greece, around 700BC, and was thought to have been blind.*

- **Unfortunately for Odysseus**, Polyphemus was the son of Poseidon the sea god. Poseidon stirred up fierce storms to make Odysseus' journey more difficult.

- **Finally Odysseus arrived** at the island of King Aeolus, who had the power to control winds. The king was kind to the visitors, and tied up all the dangerous winds in a small bag and gave it to Odysseus.

- **When they set off**, the sea and wind were fair but some of Odysseus' crew were tempted to open the bag. Out came the most violent winds and hurled the ship back to the island of Aiolia.

- **At the next stop**, the tribe of Laestrygonians killed most of Odysseus' crew and destroyed their ships.

- **At the Aeaean Island**, some of Odysseus' crew were transformed into swines by Circe, the sorceress, until he rescued them. Later, Circe instructed him to seal his sailors' ears with wax so that they were not tempted by the magical songs of the Sirens, the beautiful sea nymphs.

- **Towards the end** of his journey, some of Odysseus' crew were carried off by Scylla, a six-headed monster, after which a violent storm hit the ship. The vessel fell apart and at the end of the long and perilous journey, only Odysseus returned home safely.

Atlantis

- **Atlantis** is believed to have been an ancient island civilization that existed around 11,000 years ago. It is thought that it was a very advanced culture, which was drowned and is now under the sea.

- **According to legends,** Atlantis was swept away by tidal waves following a devastating earthquake. The island sank to the bottom of the sea with all its riches.

- **Many people** have searched for Atlantis over the years and there are many theories about where it is. But as yet there is no trace of the lost island.

- **Atlantis** was originally mentioned by the Greek philosopher Plato, in two dialogues, *Timaeus* and *Critias*. In these, he talks of the history of Atlantis and its ancient culture.

- **He describes Atlantis** as a flourishing commonwealth. The people, it seemed, were excellent engineers and architects. There were palaces, harbours and docks on the island.

- **Ships sailed on canals** that joined the sea. Plato also lists the wonders of the buildings with their fountains and precious ornaments.

- **Some people believe** that Atlantis did not exist but was created by Plato to illustrate his philosophy of the perfect government.

- **The exact location** of this lost land has been a topic of much debate. Atlantis has been linked to Crete, the Canary Islands, the Scandinavian Peninsula and many other places.

- **There is a theory** that Plato's story was inspired by the catastrophic events that may have destroyed the Minoan civilization on the islands of Crete and Thera.

- **Through the centuries**, a belief has evolved that Atlantis was an island-continent in the Atlantic Ocean. Another theory suggests that Antarctica was in fact, the lost Atlantis. But most geologists have argued against this theory.

▼ *A recent theory argues that Atlantis is actually Spartel Island, a mud shoal in the straits of Gibraltar that sank about 11,000 years ago.*

409

Sea serpents

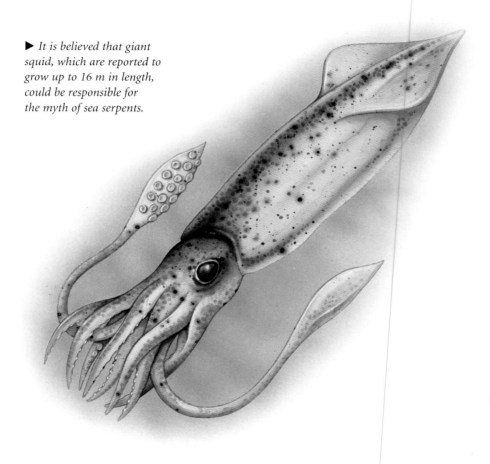

▶ *It is believed that giant squid, which are reported to grow up to 16 m in length, could be responsible for the myth of sea serpents.*

● **Like mermaids** and sirens, sea serpents are imaginary creatures. As the name suggests, they are supposed to be huge and snake-like.

- **In ancient times**, vessels that sank were thought to have been attacked by sea serpents.

- **It is believed a monster** similar to the mythical sea serpent lives in the waters of Loch Ness, a lake in Scotland that is 37 km long.

- **Several sightings** of the sea serpent have been reported. Many expeditions have been sponsored to find the monster, but its existence has not yet been proven. In fact, no scientific evidence supports the existence of sea serpents or of a Loch Ness monster.

- **Experts say floating seaweed** could have been mistaken for large sea serpents. Gulfweeds, especially brown gulfweed in the Gulf Stream and the Sargasso Sea, drift in large, floating masses, causing a number of accidents to ships.

- **Some scientists** believe that exaggerated details of the peculiar-looking oarfish or sea snakes have contributed to reports of sea serpents or monsters.

- **Many believe** that the tales of sea serpents reported by mariners and explorers originated from sightings of oarfish. Oarfish are the longest bony fish in the world.

- **Oarfish are rarely seen** by humans. They live at depths of over 200 m and only come to the surface if they are sick or injured. This factor could be responsible for reports of sea serpents.

- **Even sea snakes** could have been mistaken for sea monsters. Though most sea snakes are not very big, some, like Stokes' sea snake, can reach lengths of nearly 2 m.

- **A famous mention** of sea serpents is in Greek mythology: Laocoön, a priest who tried to warn the Trojans against the wooden horse, was killed by two powerful sea serpents sent by Poseidon.

The Bermuda Triangle

- **The Bermuda Triangle** is one of the greatest unsolved mysteries in the world. It is not shown on maps, but is thought to have its three corners in Bermuda, Florida and Puerto Rico, all in the western Atlantic Ocean.

- **A number of planes** and ships have disappeared with their crew from this area, which is also known as the Devil's Triangle.

- **Christopher Columbus** had reported that the area of the Sargasso Sea, with its floating weeds, was thought by sailors to be strange and dangerous.

- **The most famous disappearance** occured in December 1945. Flight 19, a squadron of five US Navy bombers called Avengers, vanished while on routine training.

- **A rescue plane** was sent after the five planes disappeared, but nothing was found. Subsequent investigations showed that the planes were running low on fuel.

- **The disappearance of Flight 19** continues to be a mystery. Reports state that the sea was calm when the planes vanished. Moreover, the Avenger bombers were designed to float.

- **Scientists** say that most of the disappearances in the Bermuda Triangle have logical explanations. For example, the enormous amount of entangled seaweed floating in the region could drag down aeroplanes that have crashed.

- **Various theories** have been provided to explain the mysteries of the Bermuda Triangle. Some even think that UFOs were responsible for abducting the missing aircraft and ships.

- **Some say** that the deepest point of the Atlantic Ocean is within the Bermuda Triangle, which could explain why some of the missing ships and aeroplanes have never been discovered.

● **Other theories** suggest that the disappearances were caused by vortexes, bad weather, sea currents, carelessness or the aircrews' lack of experience.

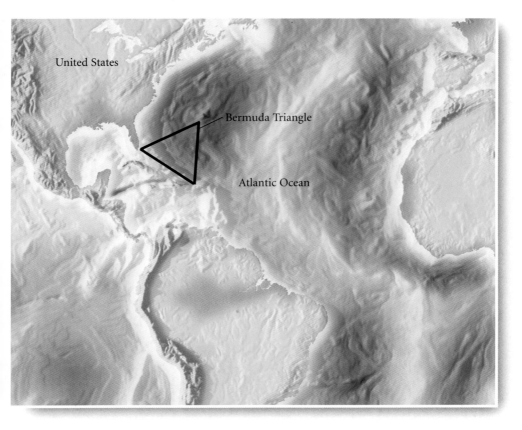

United States

Bermuda Triangle

Atlantic Ocean

▲ *Over 20 planes and 50 ships are believed to have disappeared in the Bermuda Triangle.*

Literary ocean

- **Throughout the years**, the oceans have captured the imagination of writers. The sea has been the subject and background of many works of fiction.

- **One of the most celebrated** ocean novels is the shipwreck adventure, *Robinson Crusoe* (1719), by Daniel Defoe.

◀ *In Daniel Defoe's novel, Robinson Crusoe is stranded on a desert island.*

- **In Gulliver's Travels** (1726), written by Jonathan Swift, the hero travels from one strange land to another across the oceans.

- **Oceans** have inspired several books in the science fiction genre. The most famous is Jules Verne's *20,000 Leagues Under the Sea* (1870). The charismatic captain of the submarine *Nautilus* makes the reader even more curious about the mysteries of the deep.

- **Oceans and voyages** play an important role in R L Stevenson's works, especially his two bestsellers, *Treasure Island* (1883) and *Kidnapped* (1886). Both books are about young boys experiencing the thrills and perils of sea life.

- **Another intriguing sea character** is Captain Ahab of Herman Melville's *Moby Dick* (1851). He fought against the perils of the oceans and refused to give up his search for a whale that bit off his leg.

- **The ocean** also forms the backdrop for the good-versus-evil theme in Melville's *Billy Budd* (1924).

- **The will to survive** against the perils of the ocean is the theme of Ernest Hemingway's *The Old Man and the Sea* (1952).

- **This simple tale** is the story of an old Cuban fisherman who ventures out into the open sea, with the hope of catching a big fish. The rest of the story relates the ensuing struggle between the old man and the mighty ocean.

- **Yaan Martel's** *Life of Pi* (2002) is about a boy who sails about in a lifeboat with the most unlikely of companions – a tiger.

Ocean movies

- **From adventures to war films**, pirate tales and tragedies, films have immortalised the oceans.

- *Battleship Potemkin* (1925), directed by Sergei Eisenstein, was one of the earliest films to depict the ocean, which forms the background as workers mutiny aboard the ship.

- **Fascinating aspects** of naval warfare have thrilled movie-goers for years. Films like *Tora! Tora! Tora!* (1970) and *Pearl Harbor* (2001) documented the realities of battles at sea.

- **The destructive power** of the ocean was portrayed through a tragic love story in James Cameron's *Titanic* (1997). In one of the highest box office earners of all time, the beautiful liner is seen sinking after crashing into an iceberg in the Atlantic Ocean.

- **Natural hazards** at sea have always inspired film makers. In *The Perfect Storm* (2000), a trawler is caught in a gigantic storm in the Atlantic Ocean and is tossed around by strong winds and towering waves.

- **The oceans** have also provided themes for science fiction films. *20,000 Leagues Under the Sea* (1954) was among the first science fiction films. More recently, *The Abyss* (1989) tells the story of an underwater rescue team plagued by aliens.

> ...FASCINATING FACT...
> Surfing movies have established a genre of their own often with a cult following. *Point Break* (1991), although not a typical surf film, is famous for its wave-riding scenes.

- **Another sci-fi movie**, *Waterworld* (1995) presented a futuristic tale, in which global warming melted ice caps, thereby flooding the Earth.

- **With the release** of Steven Spielberg's *Jaws* (1975), the fear of sharks also caught the imagination of filmgoers. The film was based on Peter Benchley's book of the same name.

- **A number of films** tried to copy this blockbuster. In *Shark Attack* (1999) sharks are used by people to frighten bathers away from a valuable seafront.

- **Being marooned** on a deserted island has always been a popular topic and both *The Blue Lagoon* (1980) and *Cast Away* (2000) were crowd-pullers.

▶ *In* Cast Away, *actor Tom Hanks plays a FedEx agent who is stranded on a deserted island after a plane crash. Hanks shed over 20 kg and grew his hair for the role.*

Sea special effects

- **Seafaring films** evolved further with the development of underwater photography and videography technology. Special effects were added to enhance the reality in such films.

- **The first ocean films** were difficult to make. The earliest underwater movie cameras and lighting equipment were crude.

▲ *The memorable submarine* Nautilus, *from Walt Disney's* 20,000 Leagues Under the Sea *was the brainchild of the famous art director Harper Goff.*

- **However**, with the development of computer technology, all aspects of underwater filming, like lighting, wide-angle picture composition, macro filming, editing and soundtrack mixing have changed dramatically.

- **Walt Disney's** *20,000 Leagues under the Sea* (1954) was one of the first films to use special effects in underwater action sequences.

- **With the popularity** of sea imagery in films, underwater studios have been created. Film crews are no longer exposed to the dangers of the open sea.

- **Modern technology**, particularly computer generated images, have now become the mainstay of films. The successful use of computer generated images are evident in the the runaway hits, *Finding Nemo* (2003) and *The Perfect Storm (2000)*.

- **In *The Perfect Storm*,** the film makers built a life size replica of the boat *Andrea Gail*. The live scenes involving the actors were filmed in a large tank. A blue cloth that served as the backdrop. Computer generated images, like the monstrous 100-foot wave, were later superimposed onto this blue background.

- **Walt Disney's *Finding Nemo*,** stretched the limits in animation. The life-like coral reef and the jellyfish forest were probably the biggest challenges ever faced by animators. It is no small wonder that the film was in the making for over two years.

- **Both *Titanic* and *The Abyss*** used massive water-filled tanks as oceans. Sophisticated lighting was used to make these artificial 'oceans' come alive.

- **A new audio system** allowed several layers of communication simultaneously. This enabled filmmakers to record scripted dialogue directly on tape during underwater filming. *The Abyss* was the first motion picture to make use of this technology.

Pirate aboard!

▲ *Marooning was a terrible fate. The pirate was left alone while his friends sailed away.*
He was given a few vital things – a pistol and ammunition, and a bottle of water.

● **The word 'pirate'** means someone who robs ships at sea. Plutarch, the ancient
Greek historian, was the first to define pirates in about AD100. According to
him, pirates were people who attacked ships and maritime cities illegally.

- **The practice of piracy** is thousands of years old. One of the first available documents on piracy was a carving on a clay tablet from 1350BC, which described attacks on ships in North Africa.

- **People turned to piracy** for many reasons. Some sailors became pirates after their ships were captured by other pirates, while many became pirates just for the money.

- **Pirates followed** the increase in trade across the world. Many of them established their own empires, and piracy posed a major threat to merchants and trading vessels.

- **Privateering**, which was allowed legally by several countries, also helped the rise of piracy. It was made popular in the 1500s by Sir Francis Drake, the famous British sailor and explorer.

- **Privateers were given** a special license to attack pirate ships. But many privateers realized that they could be wealthier if they became pirates instead.

- **The late 1600s to the early 1700s** marked the peak of piracy. This period, known as the Golden Age of Piracy, saw pirates flourish in the Mediterranean, Europe, Africa, Asia and the Americas.

- **The Island of Nassau** in the Bahamas played an important role during the Golden Age of Piracy. The island served as a resting point for pirates when they returned from their raids.

- **The Golden Age of Piracy** continued until early 1700s, when stern actions, such as torture and death sentences, were taken to suppress piracy.

- **It is believed** that ancient Chinese pirates were extremely organized. They were known to keep records and contracts of all their activities, and even maintained accounts of the payments made by their victims.

Pirate symbols

- **Pirates have always** been identified with certain symbols and icons. These include skull and crossbones motifs, black eye patches, parrots, hook hands, wooden legs and buried treasure.

- **The Jolly Roger** is perhaps the most famous symbol associated with pirates. It was a black flag with a white skull-and-crossbones pattern, which was meant to frighten victims.

- **The Jolly Roger** may have derived its name from *jolie rouge*, which was the French name for a red flag used by early pirates. *Jolie rouge* means 'pretty red', and it signified that no mercy would be shown to victims. It is also believed that the Jolly Roger may have acquired its name from Ali Raja, a famous pirate of the Indian Ocean.

- **The Jolly Roger** was first believed to have been used around 1700, when Emanuel Wayne, a French pirate, raised a black flag patterned with a skull, crossbones and an hourglass.

- **Pirates used flags** to warn ships of their intentions. This created fear in the enemy before attacking, making it easier to dominate their victims.

- **The Jolly Roger** was the most common pirate flag, but pirates used a variety of other flags. In fact, each pirate captain was identified with a special flag.

...**FASCINATING FACT**...
Bats were a common feature of early Chinese pirate flags.
This is because the Chinese considered the bat to bring
wealth and good luck.

- **Calico Jack**, an 18th-century pirate, was associated with a skull and a pair of crossed swords. Others added motifs like daggers to enhance their fearsome image.

- **Christopher Moody** added an hourglass with wings to his flag, a motif which signified that time was flying.

- **Blackbeard**, the famous pirate of all, used a flag with a skeleton that held an hourglass in one hand and a spear in the other, and stood next to a bleeding heart.

- **Merchant ships** had very few defences against pirates. Hence some used to raise the Yellow Jack flag, which warned of yellow fever on the ship, in the hope that the pirates would not then attack it.

▲ *When a pirate captain decided to attack, he raised a special flag. Black flags became popular in the early 1700s, with pirates adding their own initials or symbols.*

Types of piracy

- **Pirates in history** can be divided into many different types. Some were just ruthless mercenaries, while others were supported by their governments.
- **The Phoenicians** were largely peaceful traders of the Mediterranean, but some were the earliest pirates. They sometimes attacked merchant ships and towns.
- **Pirates were also active** in ancient Greece and Rome. It is believed that Julius Caesar was once kidnapped by pirates and held for ransom.

▼ *Corsairs operated mainly on the Mediterranean Sea and usually sailed in galleys.*

- **Privateers looted ships** without any fear because they were supported by their governments. They were given a license known as the 'letter of marque', which allowed them to seize the property of other pirates and merchant ships belonging to enemy countries

- **King Henry III of England** was the first to issue letters of marque, to allow privateers to attack enemy supply ships during wars.

- **Sailors known as corsairs** came from France and worked mostly on the Mediterranean Sea. Many of them were privateers, as they were permitted to attack enemy ships in the area.

- **Buccaneers were pirates** who were active in the West Indies. They mainly attacked French and Spanish ships and colonies.

- **Some vikings** were thought to be pirates. However, most were just farmers or warriors, who travelled from Scandinavia in search of land to settle on.

- *Vrijibuiter*, or plunderer, was the name given to a Dutch pirate. The word comes from *vrij*, meaning 'free' and *buit*, meaning 'loot'.

- **The word *vrijibuiter*** inspired the naming of English pirates as freebooters and of French pirates as *flibustiers*.

> **...FASCINATING FACT...**
> It is believed that Captain William Kidd was a privateer, but he was hanged as a pirate. This is because he was unable to provide his letter of marque to prove he was a privateer.

425

Buccaneers

- **Buccaneers** were 17th-century pirates who raided Spanish colonies and ships in the West Indies and the New World. Buccaneers were mostly English, French and Dutch.

- **The term 'buccaneer'** is said to have originated from the word 'boucan', a method which the buccaneers used for preparing meat.

- **Buccaneers** were originally hunters who settled on the islands of Hispaniola, particularly Haiti, and Tortuga, in the West Indies. They only became pirates later, eventually shifting their base to Jamaica.

- **Buccaneers** were not seen as typical pirates, and considered to be more like privateers. The British government commissioned them to attack French and Spanish ships and colonies. But they were never given a letter of marque to prove their association with the government.

- **A French buccaneer**, named Montbar, was one of the leaders of the buccaneers. He was known as the 'Exterminator', since he destroyed several Spanish ships and killed many Spaniards.

- **Sir Francis Drake** and Richard Hawkins acquired much of their wealth as privateers. Inspired by their prosperity, groups of unruly buccaneers began to attack Spanish colonies.

> **. . . FASCINATING FACT . . .**
> When the buccaneers settled on the Island of Hispaniola, the local Spanish people became worried. They sent hunters to kill the wild cattle on which the buccaneers depended for food. The need for food and money forced the buccaneers to become pirates, and move to the Island of Tortuga.

- **Henry Morgan** was perhaps the most renowned buccaneer. He led several raids against Spanish colonies. In 1671, he led a group of buccaneers to capture Panama. He did not evacuate the colony until he was paid a huge ransom.

- **Buccaneers** like William Dampier and Thomas Cavendish also became famous for their adventures at sea. Their voyages proved invaluable for the eventual exploration of the New World.

- **During the War of the Spanish Succession (1701–14)**, several buccaneers were hired by their governments to fight as privateers.

- **By the end of the 18th century**, buccaneering ceased to exist, as increasing numbers of buccaneers gradually turned to privateering.

▶ *Sir Henry Morgan is believed to have sued the publishers of the book* The Buccaneers of America *for slandering his name.*

Corsairs

▲ *The red-bearded Barbarossa Brothers, Aroudj and Kheri ed-Din, were the best-known corsairs.*

● **Corsairs** were French pirates who operated on the Mediterranean from the 1400s to the early 1800s.

- **Unlike the buccaneers**, some corsairs shared their booty with their countries to avoid being arrested. Like privateers, corsairs were initially allowed by their governments to rob enemy ships.

- **Corsairs** belonging to the Islamic religion adhered to North Africa's Barbary Coast. Called Barbary corsairs, these pirates established their own empires and built fortresses to protect the ports of Algiers, Tunis and Tripoli.

- **The Barbary corsairs** were the most well known of all corsairs. They were not loyal to their government, and raided any ship that crossed their path.

- **Christian corsairs** were based on the Island of Malta. They competed with the Islamic corsairs to capture merchant ships and passengers.

- **Barbary corsairs** were known for their barbaric acts. They brutally attacked Christian corsairs along the southern coast of the Mediterranean Sea.

- **These corsairs also** created their own pirate empire, the Barbary States, to reign over the pirates living in the region. Raises, or pirate kings, ruled the empire.

- **The most famous** of the Barbary corsairs were the Barbarossa Brothers. Named after their red beards, the brothers ensured their success by paying the Tunisian sultan for permission to use Tunis as their base of operations.

- **The Christian corsairs** of Malta were initially religious warriors who fought against the Barbary corsairs. They were, however, soon attracted by the riches of piracy and became pirates themselves.

- **The French government** decided to help harassed merchants and waged a war on the Barbary corsairs. In 1830, the French captured the base of the Barbary corsairs and ended their reign of terror in the Mediterranean.

429

Blackbeard

- **Edward Teach** (*c.* 1680–1718), who was better known as Blackbeard, was the most notorious pirate of all time.

- **Born in Bristol, England** as Edward Drummond, Blackbeard started out as an honest sailor before becoming a privateer. However, it did not take long for the wealth to be gained from piracy to attract Blackbeard.

- **In November 1717**, Blackbeard captured a French slave ship called *La Concorde* and renamed it *Queen Anne's Revenge*. He then wreaked havoc on the Caribbean Sea and the Atlantic Ocean until his death in 1718.

- **When Blackbeard** became a pirate, he changed his surname to Teach, which was often incorrectly spelt out in records as Thatch. Blackbeard, so nicknamed for his long and unruly black beard, became renowned for his eccentric ways.

- **He mixed gunpowder** in his rum and braided his beard with black ribbons. He was even known to weave hemp into his beard and set the strands on fire during attacks.

- **Blackbeard** often raised the national flag of the target ship, so that his crew would appear friendly. As soon as he came close enough to his target, he would raise his own pirate flag and take the target ship by surprise.

> ### ...FASCINATING FACT...
> Blackbeard was feared by one and all due to his ruthless and peculiar image. It is believed that on one occasion, when refuseda diamond ring on a passenger's finger, he sliced off the fingeritself. Legend has it that even Blackbeard's pet parrot mockedprisoners while they were tortured!

- **This notorious pirate** lived with unofficial protection on the Island of Nassau in the Bahamas, which was the base of his operations. But when Woodes Rogers, the royal governor of the island, carried out raids, Blackbeard had to go into hiding.

- **In 1718**, Blackbeard planned a party in Virginia's Ocracoke Island, his new hideout. When Alexander Spotswood, the governor of Virginia, heard about this, he decided to capture the dreaded criminal.

- **Spotswood** sent his men under the command of Robert Maynard. The team took Blackbeard's unsuspecting group by surprise. Blackbeard put up a fight, but he and his crew members were unprepared.

- **Robert Maynard** eventually killed Blackbeard and cut off the pirate's head. He hung Blackbeard's head from his ship to prove to everyone that Blackbeard was, indeed, dead.

▶ *One man was not afraid of Blackbeard – naval officer Robert Maynard. In 1718 he leapt aboard Blackbeard's ship and attacked.*

Captain William Kidd

- **Captain William Kidd** was one of the best-known figures of the pirate world. Beginning his life as a sailor and a ship-owner, he later turned to privateering.

- **Born in Greenock**, Scotland, in *c.* 1645, Robert Kidd sailed to America and married into a wealthy family. As a result, he inherited his wife's property and became a successful merchant.

▶ *During his execution, Captain Kidd had to be hanged thrice, as on the first two attempts the rope broke.*

- **On a journey looking for trade**, Kidd was offered a position as a member of a group of privateers whose job was to capture pirates. Kidd sold his ship so that he could raise the funds required to join the group.

- **Captain Kidd**, now a privateer, sailed off in his new ship, the *Adventure Galley*, to catch pirates. But his mission was a failure, and Captain Kidd had to cover his money in some way.

432

- **The law permitted Kidd** to capture only pirate vessels or those belonging to the French. But a desperate Captain Kidd began to capture all non-English ships. From 1697 to 1698, Kidd captured several ships off the east coast of Africa.

- **In January 1698**, Captain Kidd sighted a merchant ship, the *Quedah Merchant*, which is believed to have contained cargo worth over $100,000.

- Kidd raised the French colours on approaching the vessel. The merchant ship also signalled French colours, and Kidd attacked. By the time he realized that he had attacked an English ship, it was too late.

- **An arrest warrant** was issued for Captain Kidd. On his return to America, he was taken into custody at the Stone Prison in New York. Later, he was sent to England, tried in court and subsequently found guilty of piracy.

- **On May 23, 1701**, Captain Kidd was hanged in London and his body was left hanging in an iron cage over the River Thames.

- **Buried pirate treasure** was first associated with Captain William Kidd. Stories like Edgar Allan Poe's *The Gold Bug* and R.L.Stevenson's *Treasure Island* only contributed to the belief that Kidd had buried a large amount of treasure. In fact, the legend of Kidd's buried treasure has led to several treasure hunts on Oak Island in Nova Scotia, Canada.

> **...FASCINATING FACT...**
> According to legend, whenever Captain Kidd buried his booty, he killed a fellow crew member and buried him with the treasure. He believed that the dead pirate's soul would guard the valuables and keep treasure hunters away.

Alexander Selkirk

- **Born in Fife, Scotland, in 1676,** Alexander Selkirk was a rebellious boy and ran away to sea at an early age. After going on buccaneering expeditions for some time, Selkirk became a sailing master on the galley *Cinque Ports* in 1703.

- *Cinque Ports* was on one of the ships being used for a privateering expedition led by William Dampier, the English navigator. A year later, Selkirk quarrelled with the ship's captain about the safety of the vessel.

- **When they stopped** at the Juan Fernández Islands off the coast of Chile, Selkirk asked to be marooned, or left alone, because he was not willing to sail any further on the *Cinque Ports*.

- **Selkirk** regretted his decision soon after he made it, but he had to wait until a ship came to his rescue. However, he became famous as a castaway who spent more than four lonely years (1704–09) on the island.

- **In the meantime**, Selkirk learnt how to survive the hardship and used his possessions carefully and cleverly. He carved trees with his knife and built two huts.

- **He also hunted goats** with the weapons he made and sewed new clothes for himself from goatskin. He used nails to stitch the skin together.

> ### ...FASCINATING FACT...
> Alexander Selkirk left the *Cinque Ports* after he argued with the captain about the vessel's unsafe condition. He was proven right because it is believed that the ship eventually did sink, taking most of its crew with it.

- **In 1709**, Selkirk was finally rescued by Woods Rogers, the captain of a British privateering ship named *Duke*. Selkirk continued his sailing career until he died in 1721, aboard the *Weymouth*.

- **One of the Juan Fernández Islands** was subsequently named Alejandro Selkirk to honour the famous castaway.

- **Alexander Selkirk** is considered to be the inspiration behind author Daniel Defoe's 1917 novel, *The Life and Strange, Surprising Adventures of Robinson Crusoe, of York, Mariner*.

▶ *Alexander Selkirk was left on the deserted island of Más a Tierra with only a musket, some carpentry tools, gunpowder, a knife, a copy of the Bible and his clothes.*

Other famous pirates

- **The Golden Age of Piracy**
  produced many famous pirates.
  One of them was Black Bart.
  It is believed that he captured
  over 400 ships and looted riches
  worth over £50 million.

- **Born in Wales in 1682**,
  Bartholomew Roberts came to
  be known as Black Bart or the
  Great Pirate Roberts. Black Bart
  was one of the last pirates of the
  Golden Age.

- **As he sailed** along the coasts of
  North and South America, Black
  Bart created such a reputation for
  himself that his name alone struck
  terror in the hearts of sailors.

- **Black Bart** was a very well-dressed
  pirate, sporting a crimson
  waistcoat, breeches and a feathered
  hat. He also wore a golden chain
  with a diamond pendant around
  his neck and was known to carry
  four pistols across his shoulder,
  on a silk sling.

▲ *Black Bart is
believed to have
discouraged
gambling aboard
his ship.*

436

- **Among the buccaneers**, Sir Henry Morgan was the most successful. He was also a privateer in the Caribbean on behalf of the English, and was also known to plunder land.

- **A point on Andros Island** in the Bahamas was renamed Morgan's Bluff in his honour. It is said that he once placed a lantern there to misguide a merchant ship onto the rocks. Once the ship was wrecked, Morgan stole its cargo.

- **Another famous pirate** was the English Major Stede Bonnet. He was regarded as the most unlikely pirate, given his prosperous background. Bonnet was popularly called the Gentleman Pirate, and was perhaps the only pirate who bought ships instead of stealing them!

- **Bonnet** spent some time with Blackbeard, who it seems was amused with the well-dressed gentleman. When captured, Bonnet pleaded for a pardon but was hanged in 1718.

- **One of the cruellest pirates** was Edward Low from the Caribbean. He was known to slice off the lips and ears of his victims to punish them.

- **Jean Lafitte** also features in the pirates' hall of fame. This famous privateer from America eventually turned to piracy, and became renowned for smuggling slaves. Henry Avery, or the Arch Pirate, was also a famous slave trader.

...**FASCINATING FACT**...
Jean Bart, the French corsair, attacked vessels that sailed in the English Channel and the North Sea. He was famous for his daredevil ways and it is believed that he once single-handedly rowed over 240 km in a tiny boat to escape his English enemies.

Bonny and Read

- **Women pirates** have a significant place in the history of piracy. Ann Bonny and Mary Read, who lived during the 1600s, are among the most famous women pirates.

- **Ann Bonny** began her life as a pirate when she joined a pirate ship dressed as a man. She eventually became one of the fiercest pirates of all time.

- **Born in Ireland as Ann Cormac**, she was brought up by her father in South Carolina, USA. She later married James Bonny, a poor sailor, and moved to Nassau in the Caribbean.

- **The marriage** did not last for long, and Bonny's life changed forever after meeting 'Calico' Jack Rackham, a pirate captain. Deciding to run away with Calico Jack, Bonny disguised herself as a man to join his crew.

- **By the 1720s**, Ann Bonny had become the first female pirate to sail in the Caribbean.

- **It was on Calico Jack's ship** that Bonny met Mary Read, another dynamic female pirate. Read, also disguised as a man, had been a pirate much longer than Bonny and was already respected for her fearless exploits.

- **When both Bonny and Read** became pregnant, their real identities were revealed to their fellow crew members. The two began dressing as women, except during battles.

...FASCINATING FACT...
It is popularly believed that Ann Bonny fell in love with Mary Read, who was also disguised as a man aboard Calico Jack's ship. When Read later revealed her true identity, the two became the best of friends.

- **It is believed that Bonny and Read** were the only two on board to put up a fight when the British captured Calico Jack's ship.

- **During trial**, both women were sentenced to death by hanging. They then revealed themselves as women and pleaded against their execution as they were pregnant.

- **Little is known** about what became of Ann Bonny and Mary Read. Both escaped the death sentence, but Mary Read was said to have died in prison before giving birth, due to a fatal fever.

▲ *Both Bonny and Read (right) were renowned for their courage and ferocious battle tactics.*

Other women pirates

- **Besides Ann Bonny and Mary Read**, there were many other women who became famous as pirates. In fact, women pirates have ridden the waves since the earliest times.

- **One of the earliest women pirates** was Queen Artemisia of Halicarnassus, Greece, who attacked ships in the Mediterranean.

- **Alvilda**, a Scandinavian princess, was one of the first female pirate captains. Alvilda established an all-woman pirate crew and sailed to sea, in order to avoid marrying a Danish prince. She eventually married the prince and became queen of Denmark.

- **Cheng I Sao of China** was another famous woman pirate. It is believed she led more than 50,000 pirates in the early 1800s.

- **Grace O'Malley**, another famous woman pirate, was born to wealthy Irish parents in 1530. She went to sea at a young age with her father, who commanded a fleet of ships.

▼ *Grace O' Malley was also known as the 'Pirate Queen of Connaught'.*

- **Grace** eventually took to piracy, raiding merchant ships. After the death of her first husband, she settled on Clare Island in Clew Bay, with a band of about 200 men under her command.

- **She was imprisoned** twice in her lifetime, but convinced Queen Elizabeth I to pardon her. Grace even wrote to the Queen, requesting an annual wage to live on so that she could retire from piracy.

- **Charlotte de Berry** disguised herself as a man to join the Royal English Navy. During a battle at sea, Charlotte's true identity was discovered and she was forced aboard a ship to Africa. The captain of the ship assaulted Charlotte, so she beheaded him. After assuming control of the ship and its crew, Charlotte turned to piracy, raiding gold-laden ships off the African coast.

- **In 1896, Gertrude Imogene Stubbs** was refused a job in her dead father's steam engine company solely because she was a woman. Poverty and a thirst for vengeance eventually drove Gertrude into piracy. She soon became famous as Gunpowder Gertie and the Pirate Queen of the Kootenays.

- **French noblewoman** Jane de Belleville took up piracy after her husband, accused of spying, was executed. Jane helped the English to invade Brittany. Holding a flaming torch in one hand and a sword in the other, she spread terror along the coast of Normandy.

...FASCINATING FACT...

Grace O'Malley was also known by the surname Granuaile, which means 'bald'. It is believed that Grace got the name after she cut her hair short to look like the male sailors at sea.

Chinese pirates

- **China** was also renowned for its pirates. Their ships and methods were, however, very different from the Atlantic and Mediterranean pirates.

- **The steady decline** of central authority in China at the end of the 13th century resulted in the increase in piracy in the region.

- **O-po-tae**, Ching Shih, Cheng I, Pinyin Zheng Zhilong, Cui Apu, Huang P'ei-mei and Honcho Lo were amongst the leading Chinese pirates.

- **Pinyin Zheng Zhilong** first joined a band of pirates in Nassau, who attacked Dutch and Chinese merchant vessels. He went on to become a famous pirate leader in China during the period between the Ming and Ching dynasties.

- **Ching Shih and Cheng I** were perhaps the most famous Chinese pirates. This married couple enjoyed a long reign of terror in the South China Sea.

- **Ching Shih** was regarded as the pirate queen of the South China Sea. She married Cheng I in 1801

- **Cheng I** had a huge fleet of 400 ships and over 50,000 men working for him. The fleet was known as the 'Red Flag Fleet'.

- **After Cheng I died**, Ching Shih took charge of his fleet and put Chang Poa, Cheng I's adopted son and right-hand man, in charge. She later married Poa.

- **Ching Shih** established a strict code of laws for her crews, with severe punishments for offenders. It is thought that her code stated that deserters would have their ears cut off.

- **In 1810,** when she was captured, Ching Shih asked for mercy. Upon being pardoned, Ching Shih left piracy. She ran a gambling house in Guangzhou, China, until her death in 1844.

▼ *Chinese pirates sailed in flat-bottomed junks that carried about 30 large guns.*

Pirate ships

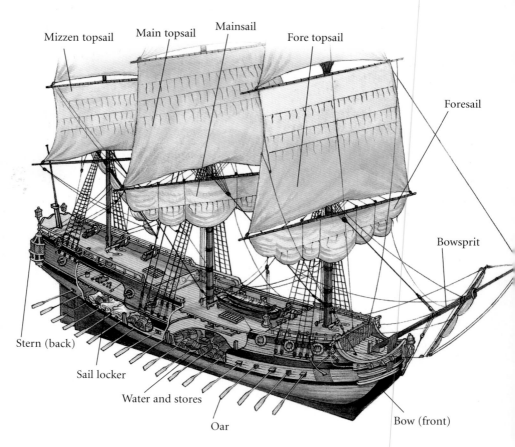

Mizzen topsail
Main topsail
Mainsail
Fore topsail
Foresail
Bowsprit
Stern (back)
Sail locker
Water and stores
Oar
Bow (front)

▲ *Pirates of the Mediterranean commonly used galleys,*
which had narrow hulls, square sails and a row of oars.

- **The right ship** was of utmost importance to pirates, since their livelihood depended on it. Pirates sailed in all kinds of ships and boats.

- **Brigantines**, sloops, schooners, junks, galleys and caravels were the most commonly used pirate vessels. These were lightweight, fast and could be manoeuvred easily on water. They could carry many weapons and large amounts of stolen goods.

- **In ancient Greece**, some pirates used triremes as they could smash holes in enemy ships. Galleys were used as they were fast and easy to steer. They were also lightweight and had shallow hulls.

- **Chinese pirates** used junks. Most Chinese merchants also sailed in junks, and hence from a distance, it was difficult to differentiate between merchant and pirate junks. Chinese pirates used this to their advantage.

- **The schooner** was a favourite among pirates of the Caribbean and the Atlantic. It had a large sail stretched over one mast and a small, narrow hull.

- **Schooners** were also sturdy and spacious, with enough room for weapons, cargo and about 75 crew members.

- **Sloops** were also preferred by many pirates. They were almost as sleek as schooners, and easy to move in both shallow and deep waters.

- **These ships** were flexible and allowed for a number of sail combinations. The bigger sloops could hold as many as 14 cannons.

- **The brigantine** was another popular pirate vessel. The square-sailed brigantines were big and heavy. They were most preferred for prolonged battles.

- **Pirate ships** were often carved with intricate and decorative patterns. Ancient Greek and Roman pirates were known to paint eyes on their vessels. They believed that the eyes of their deities would protect them from danger.

445

Pirate ship care

- **Pirates** spent most of their lives at sea. Long and continuous periods at sea and the ravages of battle took its toll on their ships.

- **Pirates** recognized the importance of safeguarding their vessels, and were known for their high standards of ship maintenance. In fact, much of their time was dedicated to cleaning and repairing their ships.

- **There was usually** at least one carpenter on board a pirate ship, to repair any part of the vessel that may have been damaged during battle or rough sailing.

- **Pirate crews** also had a boatswain, who supervised the maintenance of the vessel. The boatswain had to inspect the ship, its sails and rigging every day.

- **The master gunner** was in charge of maintaining the ship's ammunition and armoury. His responsibilities included sifting gunpowder to ensure it was always dry, and making sure that the cannon balls were kept rust-free and that all weapons were working.

- **The mate** assisted the boatswain, gunner and carpenter. His job was to fit the vessel with pulleys, sails, ropes and the like. While at sea, the mate had to hoist the anchor and check the tackle everyday.

- **In port**, the mate was responsible for getting the ship's cables and ropes repaired. He also managed the sails, yards and the ship's mooring.

- **Pirates** often made stopovers on land to service their ships. The process of bringing their vessels to shore was known as careening and it involved the cleaning of weeds and barnacles from the bottom of the ship.

- **When on land**, pirates employed the method of caulking for ship repair. This involved plugging the gaps between the vessel's planks with tar to ensure that it was watertight.

● **Besides general ship maintenance** and repair, pirates also renovated their vessels from time to time. Most pirate vessels were stolen, and they preferred to redesign and customize them to suit their own requirements.

▼ *Most pirates disliked careening, as it was a tedious task. Barnacles and seaweed had to be scraped off from the ship's hull, and any holes in the vessel had to be sealed before sailing.*

A pirate's life

- **Pirates at sea** faced many challenges. Sailing for long periods of time led to boredom. With very limited scope for activity, they struggled to fill their time.

- **Life aboard a pirate ship** was not full of continuous excitement. Activities like battles and raids were not frequent.

- **The lack of activity** on a pirate ship sometimes led to quarrels between crew members. Pirates played cards and other games to keep themselves occupied.

- **Everyone on board** a pirate ship did their share of work. Daily chores were divided among the crew members.

- **Each crew member** had specific duties. The captain, who was in charge of the crew, had to display good leadership and navigational skills.

- **Pirates** were usually very disciplined when at sea. Most pirate ships had a code of conduct that was strictly followed. According to this, lights had to be switched off by eight o' clock at night, and nobody was allowed to smoke or gamble after that.

- **Sleeping arrangements** were cramped, with a majority of the crew having quarters belowdeck. The pirate captain had a separate cabin on the quarterdeck, near the stern of the ship.

◄ *Very often the cook on board a pirate ship was a disabled person who was given shelter in exchange for his services.*

▲ *Most members of a pirate crew slept in hammocks below deck.*

● **Pirate ships** had large stocks of long-lasting food and drink. Fresh water was needed as seawater was too salty to drink. Other drinks were rum and beer. Limes were essential, since the vitamin C they contained prevented the disease scurvy.

● **The most common pirate food** was a dry, hard biscuit, known as 'hardtack', which lasted a long time. The meat of Caribbean Sea turtles was a favourite food, while wealthier pirates even carried hens for meat and eggs. On deserted islands, pirates hunted wild animals.

● **Pirates** made the most of their time on land. They were notorious for drinking late into the night in taverns, sword-fighting duels, and gambling.

... FASCINATING FACT ...
According to a popular story, pirates at sea sometimes became so hungry that they ate their leather satchels! This belief stems from a recipe that was written by a member of Sir Henry Morgan's crew: "…slice the leather into pieces then soak, beat and rub between stones to tenderise. Scrape off the hair and roast or grill. Cut into smaller pieces and serve with water…"

449

Pirate victims

- **Pirates** were greatly feared and disliked, because they would usually attack any vessel that they could capture.

- **In the early days**, pirates targeted trading routes in ancient Greece and Rome, raiding vessels for grains and olive oil. Large corn ships that transported Egyptian wheat to Italy were also targeted.

- **In the 1800s**, pirates in China were known to write letters demanding money to the residents of coastal towns. If the money was not paid, the pirates threatened to capture and enslave the residents.

- **The rise of exploration** and trade led to a great increase in pirate raids and attacks. Pirates plundered as much as they could, attacking at will and killing their victims.

- **With the discovery** of the Caribbean Islands and the Americas, some European countries were able to acquire vast amounts of wealth.

- **The Spanish** were the first to occupy these rich lands. After the conquest of the Incas and the capture of their riches, large treasure fleets frequently sailed back to Spain.

- **Spanish galleons**, usually loaded with valuable cargo, were favourite targets. The number of pirate attacks on galleons increased so much that these vessels had to sail in fleets to protect each other.

- **Slave ships** were one of the few vessels that pirates avoided attacking. Slave ships were large and carried many people. So pirates preferred not to waste their gunfire and effort on these ships.

- **Pirates** also plundered colonies and towns, throwing people out of their houses, holding them hostage and threatening their lives.

- **Viking pirates** were said to target wealthy monasteries along the French coast and in the British Isles.

▶ *Pirates also looted towns and cities, burning houses and kidnapping local residents for ransom.*

Pirate weapons

- **Pirates** carried a wide range of weapons, both at sea and on land. Pirate ships also had a well-stocked armoury of weapons and ammunition ready for attacks on ships.

- **Pirates mainly** used cannon shots to fire warnings to the enemy or damage a ship's mast.

- **They used a variety** of shots for their cannons. Some common ones included the bar and chain shots. The bar shot, which resembled a dumbbell, was useful for destroying ship sails. The chain shot comprised a chain attached to two cannon balls, and could attack sails and other parts of a ship with power and speed.

- **The grapeshot** was another type of cannonball that was very commonly used by the pirates. These were, in fact, little iron balls wrapped in canvas and fired at the enemy.

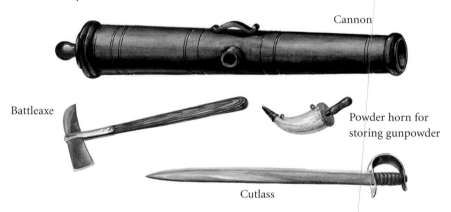

Cannon

Battleaxe

Powder horn for storing gunpowder

Cutlass

▲ *Pirates used an array of weapons, from cutlasses and cannons to swords and daggers.*

- **Swivel guns** were similar to cannons. These guns were named after the swivels, or rotating axles, they were mounted upon. Pirates would swing the swivel guns and shoot to clear the entire deck of an enemy ship in a single sweep.

- **Besides cannons**, hand-held guns too were part of the pirate armoury. Pirates commonly carried blunderbusses, muskets and pistols.

- **The blunderbuss** was a heavy gun used for short-range shooting. Its funnel-shaped barrel allowed for the simultaneous firing of multiple bullets in different directions.

- **The musket**, an early form of the modern rifle, was also popular with pirates. Muskets had single shots and extremely long barrels, and were useful for firing from a distance. They were not as effective for close range shooting.

- **The weapon** that is most closely associated with pirates is the cutlass. This is believed to have originated from the long knives that the buccaneers used for butchering meat. The short sword and wide blade of the cutlass made it suitable for hand-to-hand combat on cramped ship decks.

- **Pirates** also used crowsfeet, which were sharp spikes that injured anyone who stepped on them. Knowing that sailors usually remained barefoot on slippery decks, pirates often threw crowsfeet onto the decks of enemy ships.

> ...FASCINATING FACT...
> Stinkpots were among the most unusual weapons used by pirates. These pots, filled with chemicals, let out a foul smell when set on fire! Pirates threw these pots on to the decks of enemy ships, with the intention of catching the enemy off-guard with the bad odour!

Battle tactics

- **Pirate crews** had many different methods for attacking the enemy. Most pirates preferred to surprise their victims by suddenly boarding the enemy ship.

- **Pirates** used psychological warfare to frighten their victims before boarding the enemy ship. They were quick to use their weapons if the victims resisted.

- **Cannonballs** were shot only to destroy the enemy vessel's sails and rigging. Pirates considered ships as treasure, and did not like to sink them. Their sole intention was to scare the enemies, thus weakening them in battle.

- **Pirates** also scared enemies away with the size of their ship and crew. Most pirates managed to overpower their victims because their ships were larger and more powerful.

- **The selection** of a suitable ship was the first major step in a pirate attack. Pirates usually chose ships that were smaller and slower than their own ships.

- **Pirates** usually avoided frequently used sea routes, as merchant ships were often protected by navies in these areas.

- **Small fishing boats** and ships that veered off the route were easy targets. Such vessels were not only easier to overpower, but also provided the pirate crew with food.

- **Pirates** often used cries for help or false flags to trick the enemy. Flying false flags was especially common, as this took the enemy by surprise.

- **Once the enemy** was close, pirates raised a red banner to indicate that they were about to attack. This flag or signal was known as the 'No Quarter'.

- **After taking over the ship**, pirates were known to perform a ceremony called 'strike the colours'. This involved pulling down the flag of the enemy vessel, thus symbolizing its surrender.

◄ *Pirates climbing aboard a target ship. It is believed that pirates either simply jumped onto their target ship or used ropes with grappling hooks to climb aboard. Sometimes they threw a plank across the two ships, allowing them to walk on to their conquest.*

Pirate treasure

- **Pirates** have always been associated with treasure chests filled with gold coins and sparkling jewels. Pirate 'treasure' could, however, have meant something entirely different.

- **Pirates** rarely captured merchant ships laden with precious jewellery and gold and silver coins. Normally their haul of treasure consisted of grains, barrels of rum or wine, spices, weapons, medicines, food items, iron and the like.

▶ *Pirates are believed to have buried their treasures on deserted islands.*

- **They often looted** clothes from the ships they captured. Ships were considered to be the prize catch, and the victims were often taken aboard the pirate ship as slaves.

- **Spanish coins** were seen as especially valuable. They included silver coins, known as 'pieces of eight', and gold coins, or doubloons. It is believed that one doubloon was double the value of a sailor's total monthly wage.

- **Doubloons**, or *escudos*, were inscribed on one side with two columns representing the Pillars of Hercules, which became symbols of money. It is believed that the modern-day dollar sign originated from these pillars.

- **Attacking ships** were dangerous, and pirates were careful in their selection of a target. They chose only vessels that were likely to contain enough 'treasure'.

- **Pirates** also preferred certain regions to others. The Spanish Main, including the South American coast between the mouth of the Orinoco river and the Isthmus of Panama, was particularly favoured by pirates, since it was prosperous and several ships passed this way.

- **According to the pirate's** code of conduct, pirate booty was to be divided equally among the members of a crew. Most crew members received a share, but the captain and others higher up the hierarchy were usually given a larger portion.

- **A share was also reserved** to cover the expenses of ship maintenance and repair.

- **Many tales of pirate** treasure have been told, especially buried or sunken treasures. In 1984, hoards of silver and gold were discovered aboard the *Whydah*, the only pirate shipwreck to be found. The ship had sunk off the coast of Cape Cod in northeastern United States.

Pirate torture

- **Pirate attacks** led to many people being captured. These victims were taken aboard the pirate ships as hostages or prisoners.

- **The treatment** that pirates meted out to their prisoners was very cruel. Those who did not follow orders were given harsh punishments. Pirate prisoners were either killed or enslaved. Those who survived often became pirates themselves.

- **Slaves** were often tied to the pirate ship with gang chains and ankle fetters to keep them from escaping.

- **Flogging** was the most common form of punishment. It involved whipping a prisoner on his bare flesh with the cat o' nine tails – a whip made of nine frayed bits of cord entwined with sharp steel barbs. The number of lashings depended on the seriousness of the crime.

- **Sometimes**, when the crime was serious but did not warrant a death sentence, pirates often resorted to Moses' Law. The term refers to 39 lashes meted out with the cat o' nine tails. This name came from the biblical reference which stated that 40 lashes of a whip would kill a man, so 39 lashes would be just short of a death sentence.

- **Marooning** was reserved for those who murdered or stole. When people were marooned, they were left alone on deserted islands with barely enough to eat and drink and were sometimes given a pistol for self-defence.

- **Pirates** not only tortured prisoners, but also punished other pirates who disobeyed the code of conduct, which stated punishments for specific crimes.

- **If a pirate** stole from another crew member, he was either killed or marooned, after his ears and nose were cut off.

- **Keel hauling** was another form of torture. In this, the victim was stripped, tied to a rope and thrown overboard. He was then hauled back up from under the boat so his body scraped against the sharp barnacles on the boat's keel.

- **Pirates** were also thought to make their prisoners walk the plank. This involved tying a prisoner's hands and forcing them to walk off a plank of wood and into the ocean.

▲ *Although walking the plank is one of the most famous pieces of pirate lore, it was rarely used as a form of punishment.*

459

Punishing pirates

- **Piracy** has been looked upon as a crime since ancient times. In ancient Rome, there was a law against piracy, which was recorded in a document dated about 100BC.

- **By the time piracy** entered its golden age, it was considered to be a major crime. Pirates who were caught by the legal authorities were tried and punished severely.

- **To escape punishment**, some pirates would betray their fellow pirates by testifying against them and providing the authorities with valuable information. Then, the pirate received a pardon, once his fellow pirates were convicted.

- **The sentence** given to a pirate depended upon how dangerous he was thought to be. Infamous pirates were most often sentenced to a gruesome death.

- **Pirates** sentenced to execution were taken to the gallows to be hanged. The gallows were wooden, rectangular frames with a looped rope tied to them.

- **Fearless pirates** often made fun of their sentence with the phrase, 'dancing the hempen jig'. The phrase referred to the hanging as a death dance performed on a rope of hemp!

- **A pirate's execution** was usually carried out in public, and large crowds gathered to watch. The pirate was led in a procession to the gallows near the water, after which a chaplain, or priest, preached words of wisdom.

◀ *The bodies of executed pirates were cased inside gibbet cages and displayed to remind people about the consequences of piracy.*

◀ *Most pirates caught during the Golden Age of Piracy were held in the Newgate Prison in London before their execution.*

● **Just before the hanging**, pirates were allowed to speak to the public. Some expressed repentance and regret, while others were unrepentant and made jokes instead.

● **The dead bodies** of the most notorious pirates were usually covered in tar and placed inside a gibbet cage. This iron framework that held the body was then left hanging in the wind until the body decayed.

● **The bodies of less famous** pirates were often left hanging above the water until three tides washed over them.

> ···FASCINATING FACT···
> Shapur, the king of Persia (AD309–379), was renowned for his battles against the pirates of the Persian Gulf. It is believed that he actually pierced the shoulders of the pirates he captured, so that he could rope them together. It is for this reason that the king was also nicknamed Zulakaf, or 'Lord of the Shoulders'.

461

Pirate myths

▲ *R L Stevenson's* Treasure Island *is largely responsible for many of the myths surrounding pirates.*

- **The word 'pirate'** brings to mind images of an evil and drunken sailor sporting dirty clothes, a black eye-patch, a wooden leg and a hooked hand.

- **Many of the things** associated with pirates are merely myths. The popular image of the pirate derives from a combination of fact and legend.

- **A common myth** is that pirates kept pet parrots. The parrot, however, became a pirate icon only with the publication of *Treasure Island*, which included the character Long John Silver, who carried a parrot on his shoulder.

- **Most historians believe** that pirates probably never kept any pets. Some pirates, however, are said to have kept black cats for good luck!

- **Pirates were prone** to losing their limbs during battles, so hooked hands and peg legs may have been common. Such icons were popularized by fictional characters like Captain Hook and Long John Silver.

● **Long John Silver** in the book *Treasure Island* never sported a peg leg, but rather a crutch. Filmmakers have shown him and other pirates with peg legs, leading to this popular image.

● **The idea** that pirates dressed in gaudy and mismatched clothes is also probably correct. Pirates usually wore any clothing they stole from their victims, which often did not fit well. They were especially fond of wearing silver-buckled waistcoats and draping sashes across the shoulder.

● **Buried treasure** is perhaps the most exaggerated pirate lore. The discovery of Captain Kidd's treasure proved that there was some truth to this myth, but most pirates used up their treasure by drinking and gambling.

● **Making victims** walk the plank is another popular misconception. There are no actual records of any pirate prisoner being made to walk the plank.

● **Pirates are often depicted** as wearing metal earrings. They are said to have pierced their ears because they thought this would improve their eyesight!

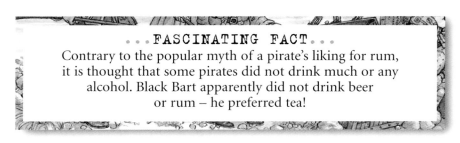

...FASCINATING FACT...
Contrary to the popular myth of a pirate's liking for rum, it is thought that some pirates did not drink much or any alcohol. Black Bart apparently did not drink beer or rum – he preferred tea!

463

Pirates in fiction

- **Through the ages**, pirates have fascinated and stirred the imaginations of many. The popular image of the pirate has been based mainly on fiction.

- **Our modern image** of pirates is largely drawn from literary, cinematic and theatrical works like *Long John Silver*, *Captain Hook*, *Treasure Island* and *Peter Pan*. It is through these that pirates have come to be known as they are.

- **After the Golden Age of Piracy**, pirates faded into history. But fiction soon took over and painted a glamorous picture of the pirate world, thus bringing these outlaws back into the limelight.

- **Pirates in literature** began in the 1680s with Alexander Exquemelin's book *The Buccaneers of America*. The author's firsthand experience with real buccaneers and buccaneer raids appealed to readers.

- **The success** of non-fiction books on pirates encouraged fiction writers to embrace the subject. The early 1800s saw works like *The Corsair*, a poem by Lord Byron, and *The Pirate*, a book by Sir Walter Scott.

- **By the end of the 19th century** many children's writers had started to use pirates as subjects. Heroic swashbucklers who fought fearlessly against evil pirates became a favourite theme.

> ...**FASCINATING FACT**...
> *Pirates of the Caribbean*, a popular Disneyland attraction, was opened to the public in 1967. The ride, which Walt Disney helped to design, offers visitors an amazing pirate experience, complete with cannon blasts! The ride also inspired the making of the 2003 blockbuster film *Pirates of the Caribbean: The Curse of the Black Pearl*.

- **R L Stevenson (1850–94)**, the Scottish novelist, created the most enduring image of the pirate. In his book *Treasure Island*, he portrayed pirates as crude men with eye patches and pet parrots.

- **In 1920**, *Treasure Island* was filmed as a silent film. It spawned the production of classic pirate movies like *Captain Blood* (1935), *The Sea Hawk* (1940) and *The Black Swan* (1942).

- **Fictional pirate stories** soon became very popular. In the 1950s, about nine such films were released within two years.

- **Cinematic adaptations** distorted the real face of pirates even more. The 1951 production *Anne of the Indies*, which recounted the life of Ann Bonny, made an incorrect reference to Blackbeard as Ann Bonny's former captain.

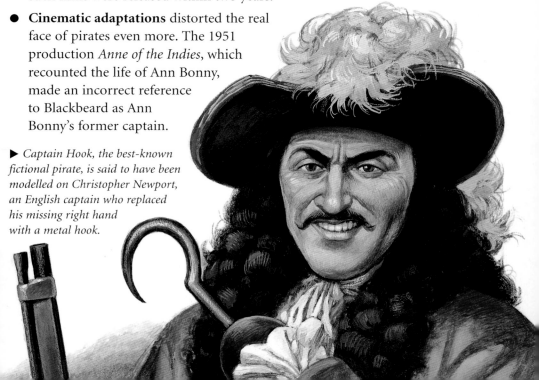

▶ *Captain Hook, the best-known fictional pirate, is said to have been modelled on Christopher Newport, an English captain who replaced his missing right hand with a metal hook.*

Greenhouse effect

- **Rapid industrial development** and population growth are taking their toll on the oceans. Some of the factors that are affecting marine life and the environment include chemical pollution, global warming, oil spills and overfishing.

- **Global warming** is one of the factors that can have an alarming effect on oceans and, thus, life on Earth. The increase in temperature of the Earth's atmosphere and the oceans is called global warming. Some scientists believe that it is the direct result of the greenhouse effect.

- **The Sun's heat** is absorbed by the Earth's atmosphere and radiated back into space. Certain gases in the Earth's atmosphere trap a part of this reflected heat, thus keeping the Earth warm. This process is termed 'natural greenhouse effect'.

- **The greenhouse effect** is similar to what happens in a greenhouse filled with plants. The surrounding glass allows sunlight in but blocks the heat from going out, thus keeping the temperature warm even when it becomes cold outside.

- **The greenhouse gases** in the atmosphere include water vapour, carbon dioxide, methane, nitrous oxide, ozone and chlorofluorocarbons (CFCs). The amount of greenhouse gases in the atmosphere determines the amount of trapped heat.

- **Water vapour** is the most important greenhouse gas. It is responsible for over 60 percent of the greenhouse effect. Carbon dioxide is the other significant contributor. Chlorofluorocarbons can trap more heat than any other greenhouse gas, but very little of these exist in the atmosphere.

- **Greenhouse gases** in normal quantities are essential, since they provide insulation to the Earth and help sustain life. Industrialization has increased the level of greenhouse gases in the atmosphere, thus trapping more heat than is required. This is called the 'enhanced greenhouse effect'.

▼ *While a large part of the Sun's heat is reflected back by the Earth's surface, some of it is trapped by the greenhouse gases in the atmosphere as shown in the diagram.*

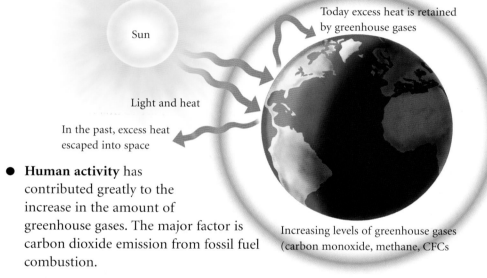

Sun

Today excess heat is retained by greenhouse gases

Light and heat

In the past, excess heat escaped into space

Increasing levels of greenhouse gases (carbon monoxide, methane, CFCs

- **Human activity** has contributed greatly to the increase in the amount of greenhouse gases. The major factor is carbon dioxide emission from fossil fuel combustion.

- **Deforestation** contributes heavily to the increased levels of carbon dioxide in the atmosphere. Trees that have been cut down release carbon dioxide as they decay.

- **Global warming** can cause significant changes in the climatic conditions across the world, thus affecting life on the planet. An increase in temperatures would lead to faster rates of evaporation, the melting of glaciers and polar ice caps, and a rise in sea levels. It would also have an adverse effect on agriculture.

467

Oceans in danger

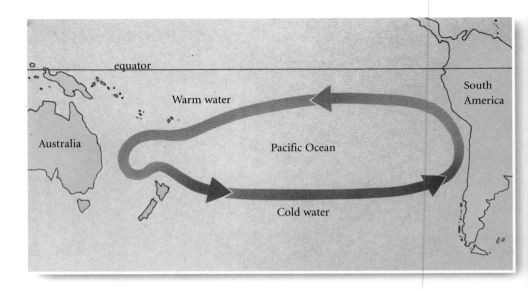

▲ *High atmospheric pressure develops over the Pacific Ocean that causes trade winds to blow from east to west carrying warm surface waters towards the west. This is called the El Niño effect and usually occurs during December.*

- **Oceans,** which occupy about seven tenths of the Earth's surface, absorb much of the solar heat and are therefore the most affected by global warming.

- **Scientists** believe that the enhanced greenhouse effect could cause more water to be formed due to the melting of glaciers and ice caps than is possible naturally.

- **Global warming** caused by greenhouse gases has increased the Earth's surface temperature by about 0.6 degrees centigrade over the last century.

- **Higher surface temperatures** can melt mountain glaciers and parts of polar ice caps, causing the sea level to go up by a metre within a century or two.

- **This could** have a dangerous effect on the coastlines and the people living in these regions. Many marine species could become extinct if global warming is not checked.

- **El Niño**, a sudden surge of warm waters off the west coast of South America, is a significant climatic phenomenon some scientists attribute to global warming.

- **Oceans** play an important part in controlling the weather. Hence, an increase in their surface temperature will also affect weather patterns. Prolonged drought or increased flooding can wreak havoc on land masses.

- **Global warming** is also responsible for the melting of sea ice and ice caps in the Polar regions. According to recent studies, glaciers along the coast of Greenland are becoming thinner by about one metre every year. The melting of glaciers and sea ice can also increase sea levels, thus reducing coastlines and beaches.

- **Oceans** are considered to be biological pumps for carbon dioxide. They are full of microscopic phytoplanktons, which remove almost half of the natural carbon dioxide formed. Any change in their habitat may lead to further damage, thus directly increasing the amount of carbon dioxide in the atmosphere.

- **Sensing the dangers**, many nations have finally swung into action to save the environment. The Kyoto Protocol, adopted in December 1997, requires the 127 countries that have signed it to take effective measures in order to reduce the amount of greenhouse gases in the atmosphere by 2012.

Sinking lands

- **The sea level** has already increased rapidly in the last 100 years due to global warming, with many coastal and low-lying areas threatened by flooding.

- **The major reason** for the rise in the level of the sea is the melting of the Arctic and Antarctic ice packs. The thickness of these packs has reduced in the last century, adding to the volume of water in the oceans.

- **Scientists** believe that the level of the oceans will rise more dramatically over the next 100 years, with temperatures expected to rise by almost four degrees centigrade.

- **Many major cities** of the world, such as New York, Los Angeles, Rio de Janeiro, London and Singapore, lie in coastal areas or near river mouths.

- **The constant melting** of mountain glaciers and ice packs could threaten these cities with flooding.

- **Scientists** believe that even a 50 cm rise in the sea level will affect millions of people in Bangladesh, India and Vietnam.

- **The population** of small island-states, such as the Seychelles, the Maldives and Tuvalu, will be seriously affected by a rise in the sea level since these countries are only a few meters above it.

- **Tuvalu** is a group of nine coral atolls that lie in the Pacific Ocean, just five metres above sea level. It is predicted that if the present situation continues, then these atolls will be completely submerged within 50 years.

- **Many ecologically sensitive zones**, such as the Everglades in Florida, United States, will become submerged.

- **The rising temperatures** are also destroying shallow-water marine life. Global warming is said to be responsible for the destruction of coral reefs in Belize. Even the Great Barrier Reef off the coast of Australia is now in grave danger.

▲ *The rising sea levels may cause coral reefs, such as the Great Barrier Reef, to become submerged.*

Crowding the coasts

▲ *Littering of beaches is one of the most common problems today. Tourists who visit coastal regions do not give much thought to the consequences of leaving behind debris such as plastic items.*

- **Coastal regions** are important for many reasons. The land along coasts is usually very fertile and therefore good for farming. The beaches also attract many tourists to coastal areas.

- **Since ancient times**, humans have made coastal areas their homes. Almost half of the world's population lives close to the coasts.

- **Most coastal regions** have, as a result, become overcrowded. This has led to pollution, damaged ecosystems and eroded coastlines.

- **People have built houses** and factories that discharge sewage and industrial waste into the seas. These damage the shores and pollute the oceans.

- **Industrial waste** contaminates bathing beaches and poisons shellfish beds. It also destroys natural habitats and has adverse affects on human health.

- **The development of ports**, roads, coastal construction, and mining of sand for construction material are destroying coastal habitats like coral reefs.

- **The shore** has also been damaged by attempts to control the movement of sediment such as sand and shingle. This prevents erosion in some places but leads to deposition of sediments in other areas.

- **Jetties and breakwaters** are built to protect harbour entrances and maintain a constant depth of water. These structures block the natural drift of sediment.

- **Artificial beaches** are built to reclaim land from the sea, thus damaging the coast beyond repair. Offshore dredging of sand to build beaches adds to the problem.

- **To attract tourists**, hotels and apartments are often built close to the water. This makes such areas vulnerable to pollution and disturbs the natural marine habitats and marine life.

Ocean pollution

- **People** have exploited oceans for their vast resources since ancient times. Excessive human activity in coastal areas has increased pollution and often caused irreparable damage to ocean life.

- **The discharge** of industrial waste and human sewage into the sea is the commonest form of pollution. This affects marine creatures and makes the sea unfit for bathing.

- **The pollution** that enters oceans can be categorized as coming from 'point sources' and 'non-point sources'. Sewer pipes and industrial waste pipes are point sources, as the discharge is from a single, identifiable point.

- **Non-point sources** of pollution are more difficult to tackle. These include water or sewage from farms containing fertilizers with a high chemical content.

- **Some chemicals** found in pesticides, however are biodegradable, and their effects are minimal and short-lived. Some remain dangerous for a long time.

- **Petroleum** and oil products are major pollutants that enter the water through spills from ships, and leakages from pipelines, tankers and storage tanks.

- **Power plants** are also a major source of pollution. The water discharged from power plants causes thermal pollution. The water is usually hot and so it alters the temperature of the sea water, affecting marine life adversely.

- **The numbers** of animals like dolphins, beluga whales, manatees, polar bears and other marine mammals have been diminished by industrial pollution and farm wastes.

- **Many beaches** have become tourist attractions. Plastic litter left on tourist beaches is a great hazard to marine life, proving fatal to some creatures.

- **Metals such as copper**, mercury, selenium and lead enter the oceans from industrial waste and automobile emissions. These can cause long-term health problems in both animals and humans.

▼ *Certain paints used to protect the hulls of ships and boats from barnacles contain poisonous chemicals and are fatal to marine creatures when discharged.*

Oil spills

▲ *Although oil tanker accidents, such as this, are considered to be most detrimental to marine life, they account for barely five percent of the total oil that flows into the oceans. The main oil pollutants are oil refineries and ships that wash their tanks at sea.*

- **Oil spills** are the worst form of ocean pollution. The effects of oil spills are long term and extremely damaging.

- **These are usually caused** when large ocean tankers have accidents while transporting their liquid cargo.

- **Oil does not mix** with water and so, during an oil spill, the oil spreads very fast, forming a thin, film-like layer on the surface. This layer is known as an 'oil slick'.

- **Oil also gets** into the oceans from pipelines and leaky, underground storage tanks. Heavier components of crude oil, such as polynuclear aromatic hydrocarbons, cause the most damage.

- **Oil slicks** are very harmful to marine life, as well as birds and mammals living near the oceans. Oil damages the water-repellent properties in the fur of mammals like sea otters and the wings of birds.

- **Coral reefs**, mangroves and estuaries are very sensitive to oil spills.

- **The effects of oil spills** are not always immediate and the harm caused may be long-term. Oil spills often cause diseases of the liver and reproductive and growth problems in marine creatures.

- **The oil tanker** *Exxon Valdez* ran aground in 1989, dumping more than 38 million litres of oil into Prince William Sound, off the coast of Alaska. The damage caused was the worst in history.

- **The environmental damage** caused by the *Exxon Valdez* prompted the United States Congress to pass safety laws for oil tankers and barges. Oil companies were also made responsible for spill cleanup.

- **Another huge oil spill** was caused in 1978, by the American supertanker *Amoco Cadiz*, which ran aground off the coast of Brittany, France. The spill resulted in one of the largest ever losses of marine life.

Bleaching the reefs

- **The impact** of global warming on the oceans is most marked in the bleaching of coral reefs.

- **Reefs** are very delicate and sensitive structures, formed by coral polyps. Although polyps feed on passing plankton, their main source of food is the unicellular algae, called 'zooxanthellae', which live within their tissues.

- **The algae feed** on the nitrogen waste produced by the corals. Like all plants, zooxanthellae also produce food using sunlight. It is this that forms the main food of corals.

- **Zooxanthellae** also provide the reefs with their magnificent colouring, which attracts many other marine creatures, thus forming an ecosystem.

- **Reefs** lose colour and die when these zooxanthellae are damaged. This is known as 'bleaching'.

- **Global warming** is the main cause of bleaching. A rise in the temperature of the oceans interferes with the photosynthetic process, eventually poisoning the zooxanthellae. Corals, in turn, are forced to expel the dead zooxanthellae, along with some of their own tissue.

- **Once the algae are expelled**, the corals lose their colour and main source of food. Unless the algae are able to grow again, the corals will gradually starve to death.

> ...FASCINATING FACT...
> Bleaching is dangerous because it affects not only the coral reefs, but also a large number of marine creatures that depend on it for food.

▲ *Like hard corals, non-reef building corals, or soft corals, are also susceptible to bleaching. Soft corals, however, are able to withstand short-term bleaching much more than hard corals.*

- **Widespread bleaching** took place at reefs around Okinawa, Easter Island, and in the Caribbean Sea in 1979 and 1980. The Great Barrier Reef has also undergone bleaching in the last 20 years.

- **Some of the coral reefs** that have been permanently damaged are in the warm waters of the Indian Ocean, including those off the coasts of the Maldives, Sri Lanka, Kenya and Tanzania.

- **Bleached coral reefs** take years to recuperate. Sometimes they get bleached again before they can fully recover from the first attack.

Endangered species

▲ *The sea otter is a protected species. This marine mammal was hunted in large numbers by humans because of its fur, which is the thickest in the animal kingdom.*

- **Endangered species** are animals and plants that are facing extinction. These species will die out if nothing is done to keep them alive.

- **The main reasons** for a species becoming endangered are the destruction of their habitat by people, pollution and commercial exploitation by way of hunting and trade in animal parts such as elephant tusks.

- **Around 34,000 plant species** and 5200 animal species are close to extinction.

- **The current rate** of extinction is thought to be around 20,000 species every year. Studies suggest that this is the first age of mass extinction since the dinosaurs disappeared, nearly 65 million years ago.

- **When their habitats are destroyed**, many animals are not able to adapt quickly enough to the changed surroundings, which eventually leads to their extinction.

- **For marine life**, pollution and hunting are the major causes of extinction and endangerment. Excessive hunting has greatly reduced the numbers of sea turtles. Sea turtle eggs are a favourite food of both humans and animals.

- **Between the 1800s and the early 1900s**, whales were killed in large numbers for their meat and blubber. This led to the endangerment of many whale species.

- **Higher water temperatures**, along with pollution, have endangered several fish species. Oil spills kill many birds, fish and marine mammals.

- **Changes in biodiversity** can also lead to extinction. Biodiversity is where particular species thrive and depend on each other.

- **The kelp forest** in the North Pacific used to be one of the richest biodiversity zones. When humans killed sea otters in large numbers, the population of sea urchins, the main food of sea otters, increased. The sea urchins then ate much more of the kelp, leading to the collapse of the entire ecosystem.

Whaling and fishing

- **Whaling** is the commercial hunting of whales for oil, meat, whalebone and other products. Whaling activity is believed to have begun in western Europe around the 900s.

- **In the 1100s**, whales were hunted off the coasts of Spain and Germany until their numbers were drastically depleted. Whaling in North America began with its colonization and was on an all-time high by the 1700s.

- **In the early 19th century**, whales were usually killed by harpoons and other weapons. Whaling became easier with the arrival of large boats, called 'factory ships', which were equipped with machinery to process slaughtered whales.

- **Sperm whales** were killed mainly for the type of oil that they produced, known as spermaceti. This was used as lubricants and in medicines.

- **The International Whaling Commission** was established in 1946, when whale populations began falling alarmingly. It regulated the hunting of whales, eventually leading to an increase in their numbers.

- **Fishing** is one of the biggest commercial activities carried out in the oceans. Fish are caught in large numbers to meet ever-growing demands. They are valuable protein sources.

- **Mackerel**, herring and tuna are among the most caught and eaten fish around the world. Sharks are considered a delicacy in some parts of the world. Shellfish such as shrimps and lobsters are also popular.

...FASCINATING FACT...
Sport fishing, also called 'angling', is one of the most popular recreational activities in the world. Anglers use fishing rods and lines to catch game fish like marlin and swordfish.

▲ *Fishing trawlers are not only responsible for decreasing numbers of fish, but they also damage coral reefs. The heavy chains used to weigh down the nets often crush the reefs and kill enormous amounts of other marine creatures in the process.*

● **Overfishing** has led to the endangerment of many fish species such as cod, mackerel and tuna.

● **The increasing world demand** for fish has led to the development of fish farms, where fish are grown and harvested for food.

● **Fish farming** provides about a fifth of all fish eaten – salmon, shrimp and carp are the most harvested. China leads the world in fish farming.

483

Saving ocean life

▲ *These fish are proof of the horrors of chemical pollution. Thousands of dead marine creatures are washed ashore every year.*

- **Many marine species** have already become extinct, while several more are endangered.

- **Destruction of habitats**, pollution and overfishing are the main reasons for this. Efforts are being undertaken around the world to save marine creatures.

- **Some ocean regions** are being specially protected. Fishing and other activities that disturb marine life in these areas are prohibited.

- **These regions** have been established as safe havens for endangered species and the protection of commercial fish stocks.

- **Only one percent** of the world's oceans, however, are protected. Many organizations, like the World Wildlife Fund, are trying to increase the coverage of protected areas.

- **Some habitats** are protected by the prohibition of destructive fishing gear. This ensures the development of the ecosystem, thus allowing fish species to grow to their normal size and produce more offspring.

- **The Great Barrier Reef** is one of the largest protected marine ecosystems. Commercial fishing and bleaching have destroyed vast stretches of these reefs.

- **Drilling for minerals**, oil or gas continues to pose a major threat to sensitive habitats. Efforts are being made to persuade companies to use methods that do not harm sea life.

- **Eco-tourism**, which brings people who are concerned about the environment to areas of natural beauty, is helping to fund conservation projects.

- **The population** of endangered marine species is being increased by many projects. Turtles, sharks and dolphins, for example, are being bred artificially under controlled conditions and then let out into the open seas.

Cleaning the oceans

- **People** are directly responsible for the dangers facing the oceans today. Our increasing demands have resulted in endangered marine animals, damaged ecosystems, melting ice caps and polluted seas.

- **The value** of the oceans' resources is now being recognized. Efforts are being made across the world to control the deterioration. Some nations are spending large amounts of money to protect the oceans.

- **The biggest problem** facing the oceans is global warming. Reducing the emission of greenhouse gases could stop global warming. Cleaner energy sources will control the release of carbon dioxide into the atmosphere.

- **The Kyoto Protocol**, a treaty aimed at reducing the release of greenhouse gases has been agreed upon by many nations. However, some of the largest polluting nations, such as the United States, have yet to sign it.

- **The harm caused** by synthetic chemicals and fertilizers that run off to the oceans, is being reversed by the use of eco-friendly chemicals. These chemicals are bio-degradable, which means that they decompose in a harmless way.

- **New devices** are being developed to absorb oil spills, which are one of the biggest threats to marine life. Heavier oil products often settle to the bottom, killing fragile, bottom-dwelling marine creatures.

- **Oil spills** are cleaned using booms, skimmers and chemical dispersants. On shore, low- or high-pressure water hoses and vacuum trucks are also used.

- **Floating barriers,** called 'booms', are placed around oil spills or their sources to prevent the oil from spreading further. Skimmers are boats with plastic ropes that skim over the surface, absorbing the oil after the booms have been set up.

- **Chemical dispersants** break down oil into its chemical constituents, thus making it less harmful to the marine environment.

- **To save coastlines**, many nations are imposing strict building regulations. Construction activity and tourism have damaged many coastal ecosystems.

▲ *Sorbents, or large sponges, are used in the final stages of a clean-up. These materials can absorb oil effectively, especially from beaches.*

487

Index

501

506

Acknowledgements

All artworks are from Miles Kelly Artwork Bank

The Publishers would like to thank the following picture sources whose
photographs appear in this book:
Page 49 Stephen Frink/CORBIS; Page 213 Tui De Roy/Minden Pictures/FLPA;
Page 214 Yva Momatiuk/John Eastcott/Minden Pictures/FLPA; Page 320
PhotoLibrary.com; Page 365 David Rubinger/CORBIS; Page 369 Warner
Bros/Pictorial Press; Page 417 20th Century Fox/Pictorial Press
Page 418 Walt Disney/Pictorial Press

All other photographs from:
Castrol, CMCD, Corbis, Corel, digitalSTOCK, digitalvision
Flat Earth, Hemera, ILN, John Foxx, PhotoAlto, PhotoDisc
PhotoEssentials, PhotoPro, Stockbyte